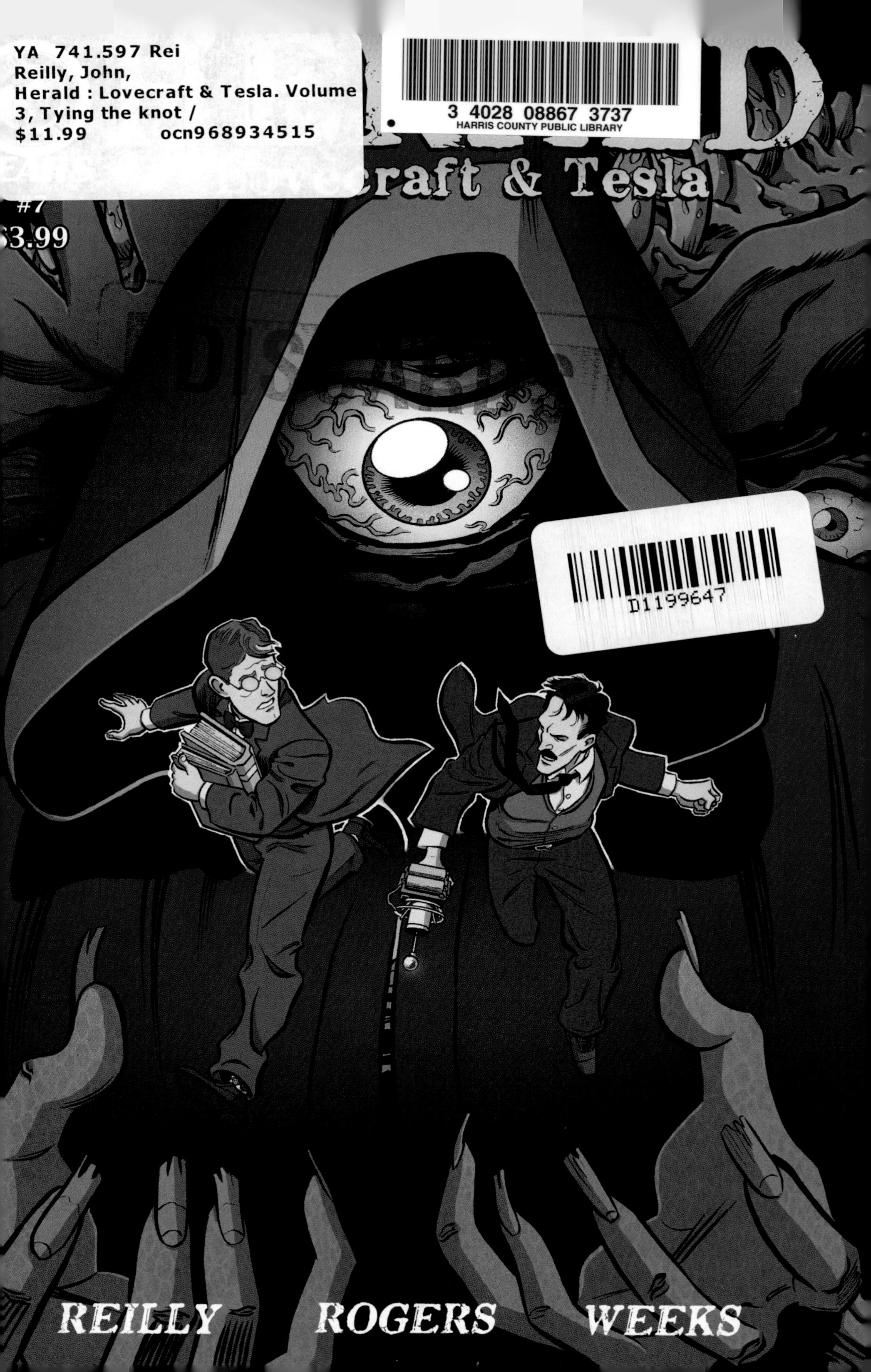
craft & Tesla
#7
3.99
REILLY
ROGERS
WEEKS

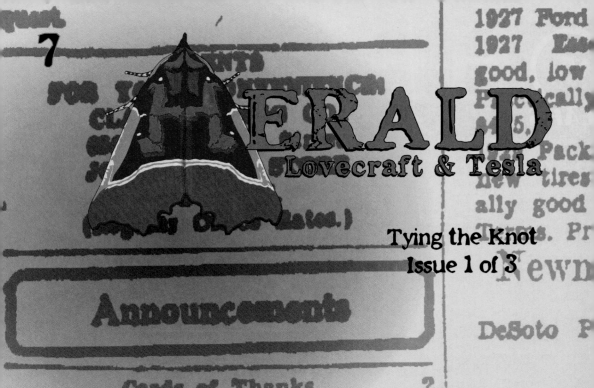

HERALD
Lovecraft & Tesla

Tying the Knot
Issue 1 of 3

Announcements

Cards of Thanks 2

"The most selfish and hateful life of all is that of two beings who unite in order to enjoy life."

-Leo Tolsto

Written by **John Reilly** Pencils by **Tom Rogers** Color, Letters by **Dexter Week**

Special Notices 6A

Action Lab Comics
Publisher - Bryan Seaton   President - Dave Dwonch
Editor-in-Chief - Shawn Gabborin   Publisher-Danger Zone - Jason Martin
Vice-President of Marketing - Jamal Igle   Social Media Director - Jim Dietz
Editor - Nicole D'Andria   Best Man - Chad Cicconi

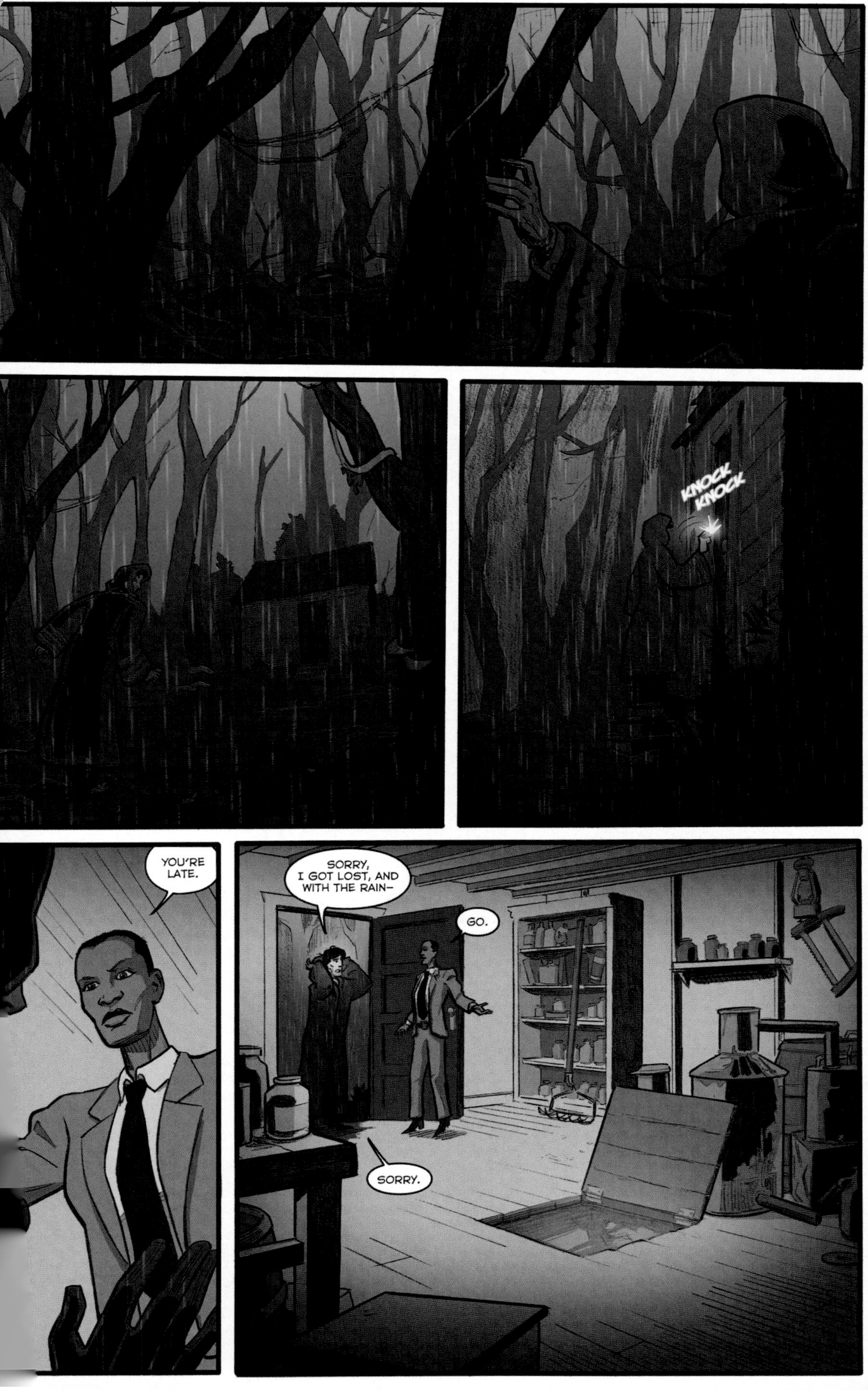
KNOCK KNOCK
YOU'RE LATE.
SORRY, I GOT LOST, AND WITH THE RAIN–
GO.
SORRY.

WERE YOU NERVOUS WHEN YOU DID IT?

I MEAN, WERE EITHER OF YOU NERVOUS?

I MEAN—

IS THAT WHAT YOU'RE WEARING?

OH, I THOUGHT—WHY, DON'T WE?

NO ONE WEARS ROBES ANYMORE.

OH, SORRY.

HEY, FANTASTIC! NEIL'S HERE. WE WERE STARTING TO WORRY THERE, CHAMP.

SORRY.

THANK YOU FOR COMING, EVERYBODY. ISN'T IT JUST A PERFECT NIGHT TO DEVOTE OURSELVES TO HIS DARK DESIGN?

YOU KNOW, I WAS SPEAKING WITH NEIL HERE JUST THE OTHER DAY—COME HERE, NEIL.

NEIL IS A GREAT GUY, HE REALLY IS. WOULD YOU LOOK AT THESE ROBES? HE'S SO ENTHUSIASTIC, I LOVE IT.

WE WERE TALKING ABOUT THE CEREMONY TONIGHT, AND I ASKED HIM IF HE HAD ANY RESERVATIONS... BECAUSE...YOU KNOW...

YOU NEVER KNOW HOW THESE TURN OUT AND YOU KNOW WHAT HE TOLD ME?

HE LOOKED ME STRAIGHT IN THE EYE—

—AND HE SAID "HEY, I NEVER EXⁱ ANYWAY, RIGHTⁱ

I MEⁱ DOESN'ⁱ JUST Bⁱ ALLⁱ

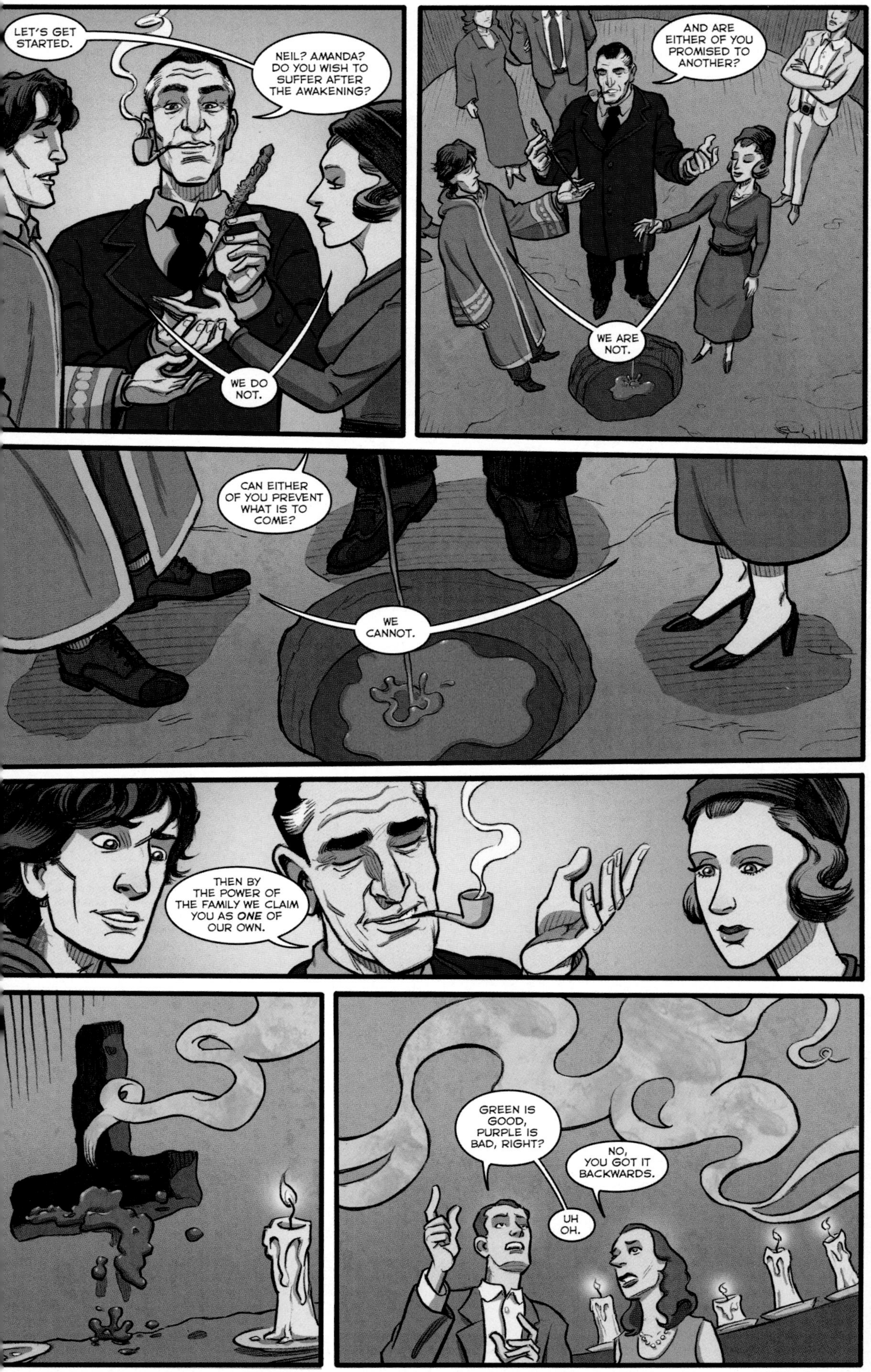
LET'S GET STARTED.
NEIL? AMANDA? DO YOU WISH TO SUFFER AFTER THE AWAKENING?
WE DO NOT.
AND ARE EITHER OF YOU PROMISED TO ANOTHER?
WE ARE NOT.
CAN EITHER OF YOU PREVENT WHAT IS TO COME?
WE CANNOT.
THEN BY THE POWER OF THE FAMILY WE CLAIM YOU AS *ONE* OF OUR OWN.
GREEN IS GOOD, PURPLE IS BAD, RIGHT?
NO, YOU GOT IT BACKWARDS.
UH OH.

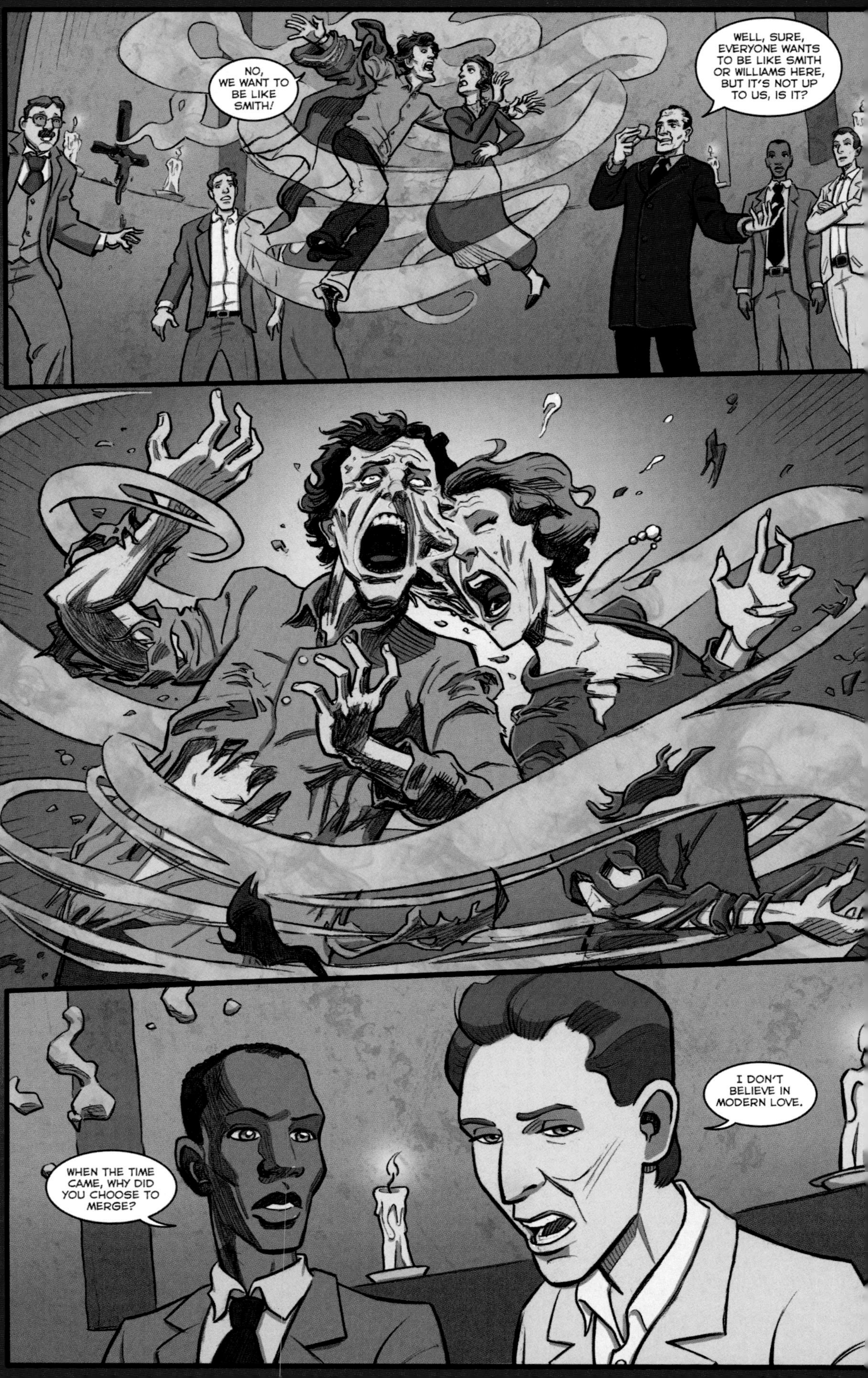
NO, WE WANT TO BE LIKE SMITH!
WELL, SURE, EVERYONE WANTS TO BE LIKE SMITH OR WILLIAMS HERE, BUT IT'S NOT UP TO US, IS IT?
WHEN THE TIME CAME, WHY DID YOU CHOOSE TO MERGE?
I DON'T BELIEVE IN MODERN LOVE.

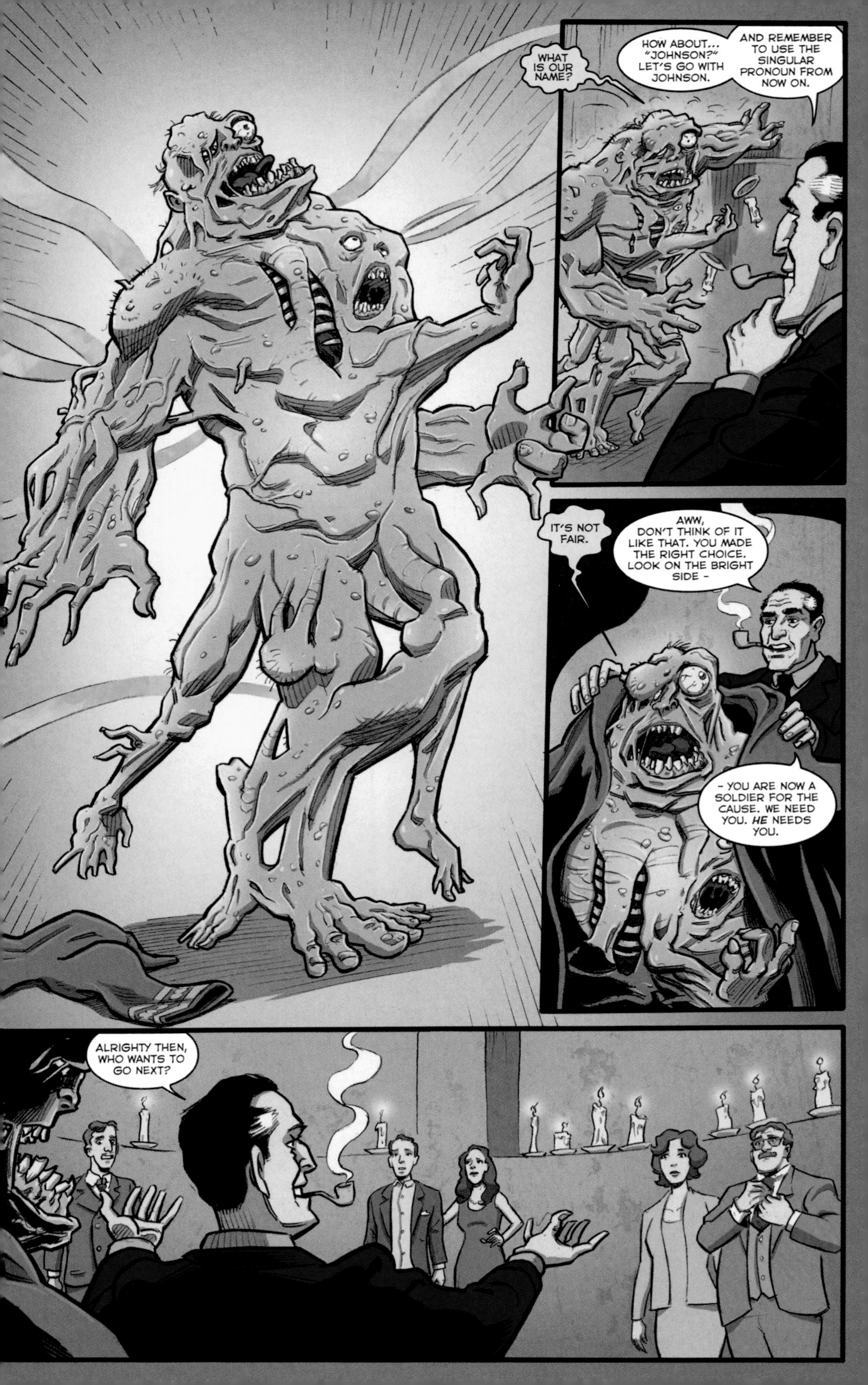

WHAT IS OUR NAME?
HOW ABOUT... "JOHNSON?" LET'S GO WITH JOHNSON.
AND REMEMBER TO USE THE SINGULAR PRONOUN FROM NOW ON.
IT'S NOT FAIR.
AWW, DON'T THINK OF IT LIKE THAT. YOU MADE THE RIGHT CHOICE. LOOK ON THE BRIGHT SIDE -
- YOU ARE NOW A SOLDIER FOR THE CAUSE. WE NEED YOU. *HE* NEEDS YOU.
ALRIGHTY THEN, WHO WANTS TO GO NEXT?

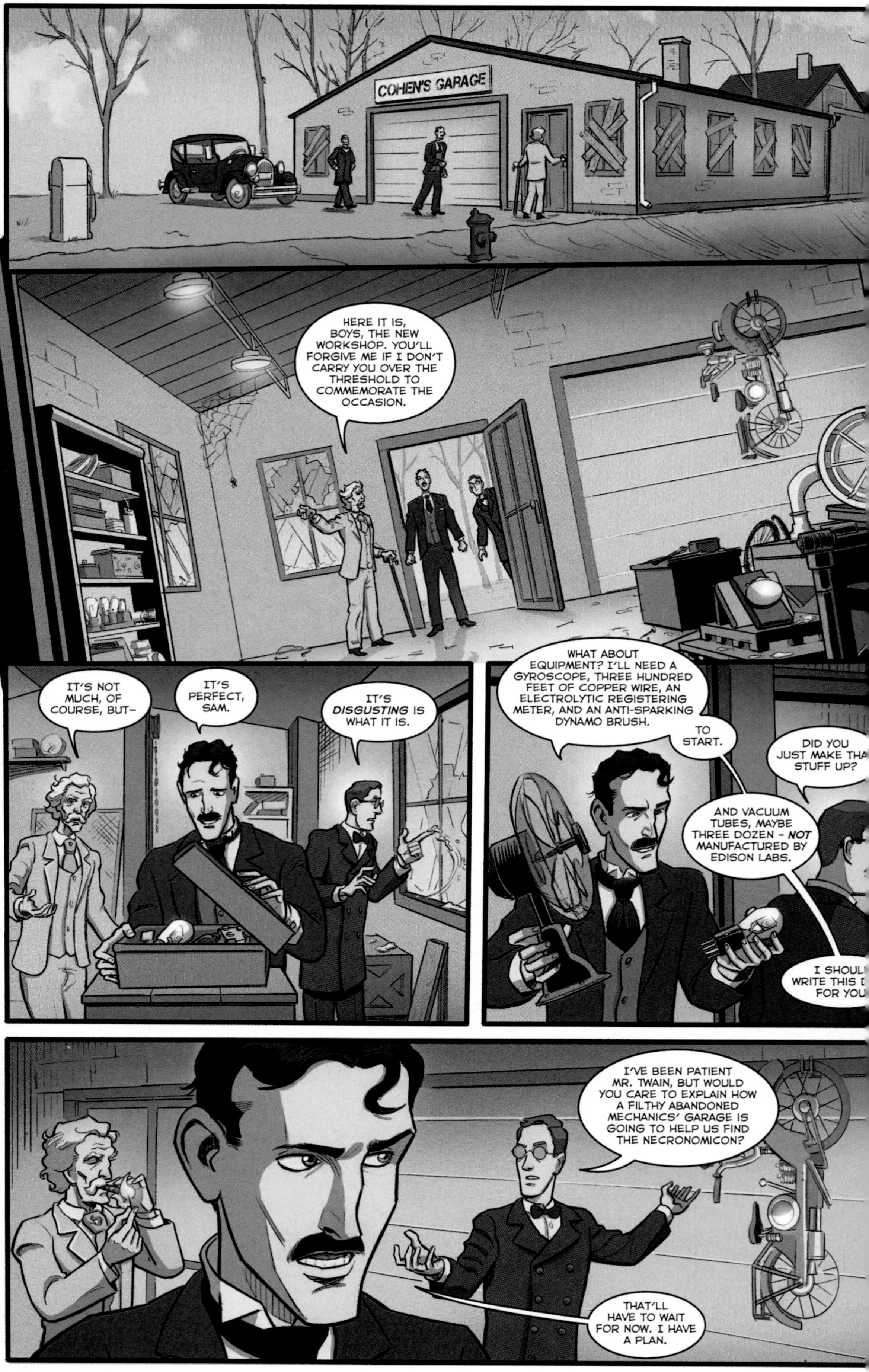
COHEN'S GARAGE
HERE IT IS, BOYS, THE NEW WORKSHOP. YOU'LL FORGIVE ME IF I DON'T CARRY YOU OVER THE THRESHOLD TO COMMEMORATE THE OCCASION.
IT'S NOT MUCH, OF COURSE, BUT–
IT'S PERFECT, SAM.
IT'S *DISGUSTING* IS WHAT IT IS.
WHAT ABOUT EQUIPMENT? I'LL NEED A GYROSCOPE, THREE HUNDRED FEET OF COPPER WIRE, AN ELECTROLYTIC REGISTERING METER, AND AN ANTI-SPARKING DYNAMO BRUSH.
TO START.
DID YOU JUST MAKE THA
STUFF UP?
AND VACUUM TUBES, MAYBE THREE DOZEN – *NOT* MANUFACTURED BY EDISON LABS.
I SHOUL
WRITE THIS D
FOR YOU
I'VE BEEN PATIENT MR. TWAIN, BUT WOULD YOU CARE TO EXPLAIN HOW A FILTHY ABANDONED MECHANICS' GARAGE IS GOING TO HELP US FIND THE NECRONOMICON?
THAT'LL HAVE TO WAIT FOR NOW. I HAVE A PLAN.

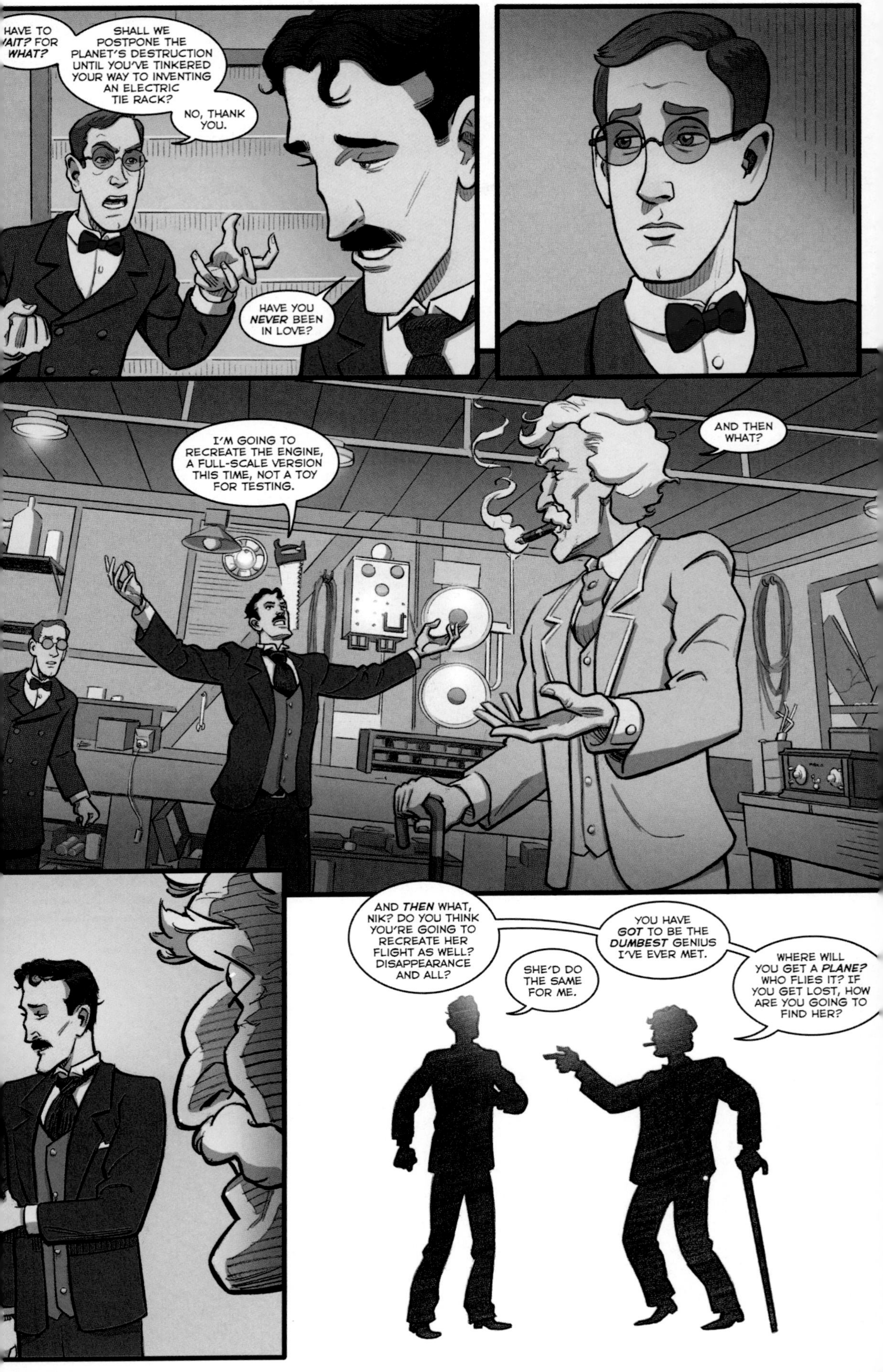

HAVE TO WAIT? FOR WHAT?
SHALL WE POSTPONE THE PLANET'S DESTRUCTION UNTIL YOU'VE TINKERED YOUR WAY TO INVENTING AN ELECTRIC TIE RACK?
NO, THANK YOU.
HAVE YOU NEVER BEEN IN LOVE?
I'M GOING TO RECREATE THE ENGINE, A FULL-SCALE VERSION THIS TIME, NOT A TOY FOR TESTING.
AND THEN WHAT?
AND THEN WHAT, NIK? DO YOU THINK YOU'RE GOING TO RECREATE HER FLIGHT AS WELL? DISAPPEARANCE AND ALL?
SHE'D DO THE SAME FOR ME.
YOU HAVE GOT TO BE THE DUMBEST GENIUS I'VE EVER MET.
WHERE WILL YOU GET A PLANE? WHO FLIES IT? IF YOU GET LOST, HOW ARE YOU GOING TO FIND HER?

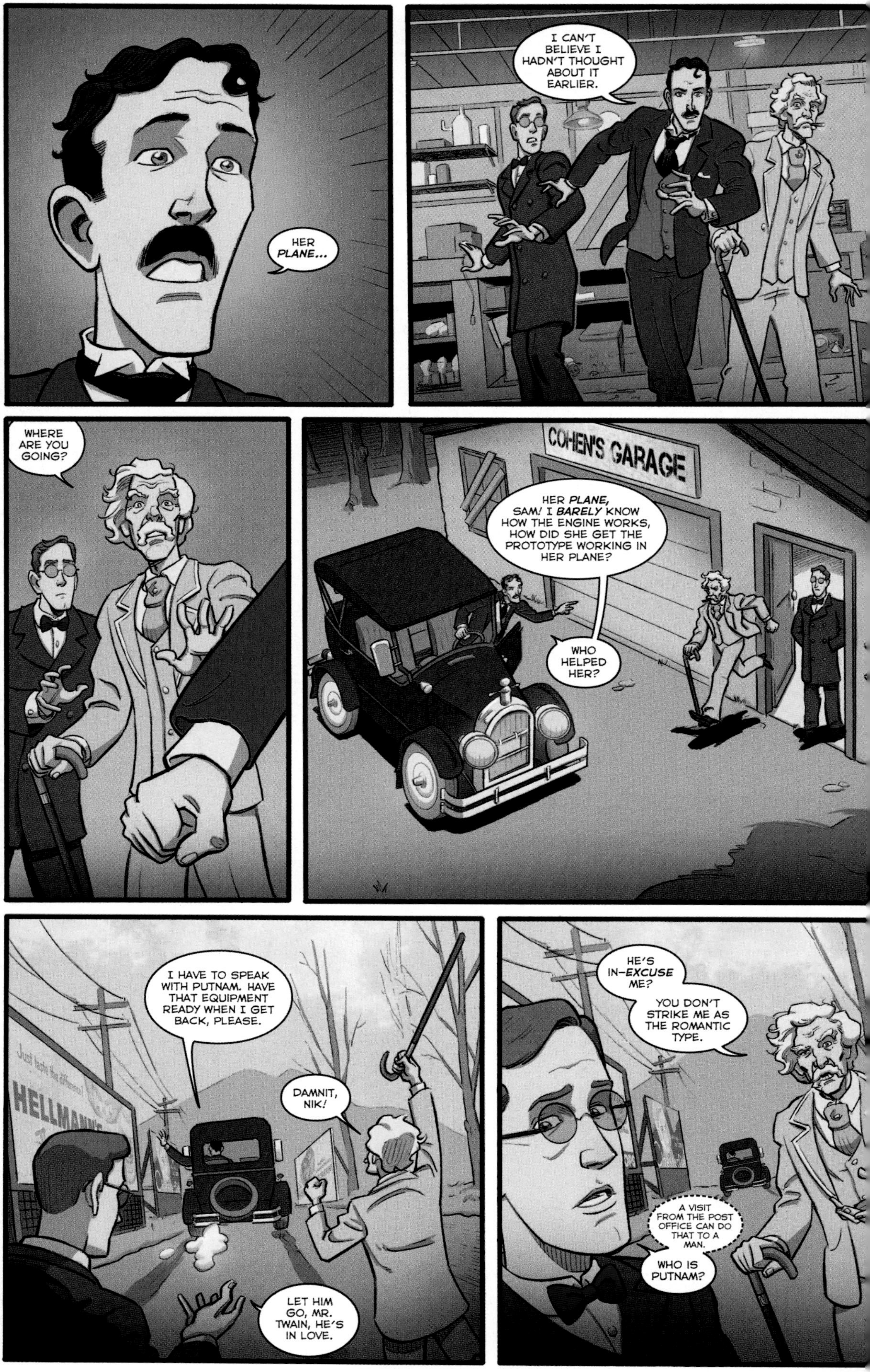
HER PLANE...
I CAN'T BELIEVE I HADN'T THOUGHT ABOUT IT EARLIER.
WHERE ARE YOU GOING?
COHEN'S GARAGE
HER PLANE, SAM! I BARELY KNOW HOW THE ENGINE WORKS, HOW DID SHE GET THE PROTOTYPE WORKING IN HER PLANE?
WHO HELPED HER?
Just taste the difference!
HELLMANN'S
I HAVE TO SPEAK WITH PUTNAM. HAVE THAT EQUIPMENT READY WHEN I GET BACK, PLEASE.
DAMNIT, NIK!
LET HIM GO, MR. TWAIN, HE'S IN LOVE.
HE'S IN—EXCUSE ME?
YOU DON'T STRIKE ME AS THE ROMANTIC TYPE.
A VISIT FROM THE POST OFFICE CAN DO THAT TO A MAN.
WHO IS PUTNAM?

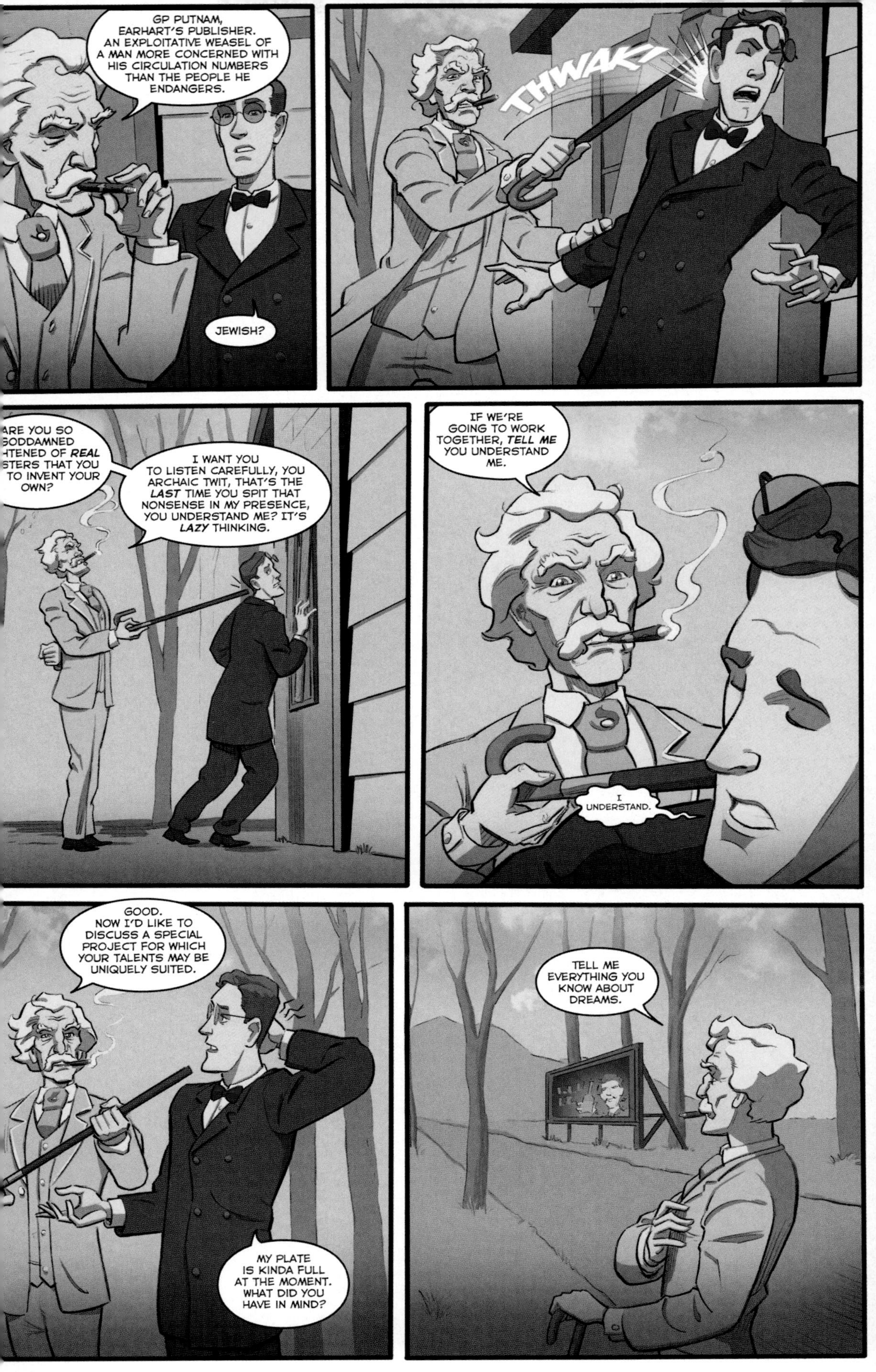
GP PUTNAM, EARHART'S PUBLISHER. AN EXPLOITATIVE WEASEL OF A MAN MORE CONCERNED WITH HIS CIRCULATION NUMBERS THAN THE PEOPLE HE ENDANGERS.
JEWISH?
THWAK!
ARE YOU SO GODDAMNED
HTENED OF REAL
STERS THAT YOU
TO INVENT YOUR OWN?
I WANT YOU TO LISTEN CAREFULLY, YOU ARCHAIC TWIT, THAT'S THE LAST TIME YOU SPIT THAT NONSENSE IN MY PRESENCE, YOU UNDERSTAND ME? IT'S LAZY THINKING.
IF WE'RE GOING TO WORK TOGETHER, TELL ME YOU UNDERSTAND ME.
I UNDERSTAND.
GOOD. NOW I'D LIKE TO DISCUSS A SPECIAL PROJECT FOR WHICH YOUR TALENTS MAY BE UNIQUELY SUITED.
MY PLATE IS KINDA FULL AT THE MOMENT. WHAT DID YOU HAVE IN MIND?
TELL ME EVERYTHING YOU KNOW ABOUT DREAMS.

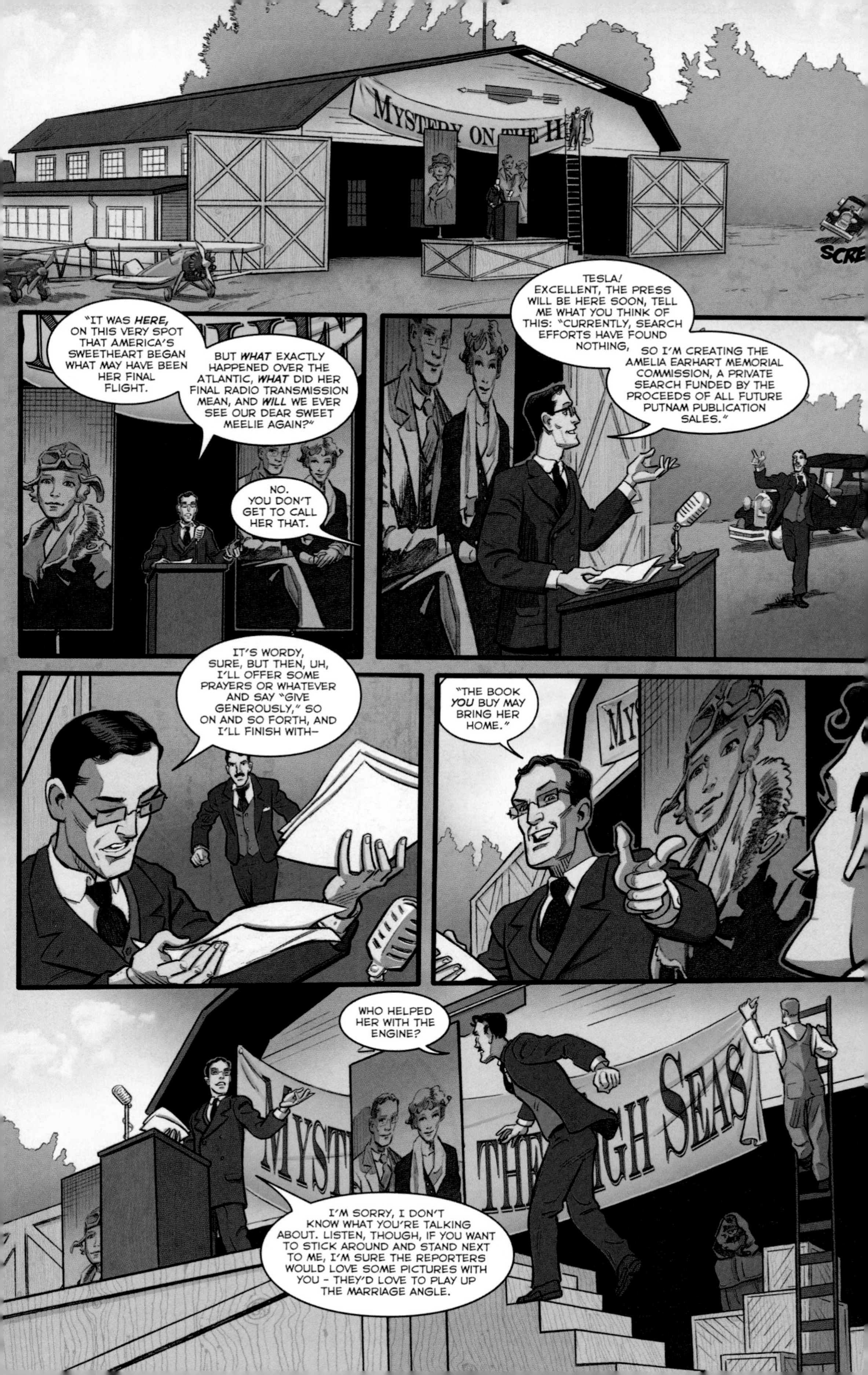
MYSTERY ON THE HI
SCRE
"IT WAS HERE, ON THIS VERY SPOT THAT AMERICA'S SWEETHEART BEGAN WHAT MAY HAVE BEEN HER FINAL FLIGHT.
BUT WHAT EXACTLY HAPPENED OVER THE ATLANTIC, WHAT DID HER FINAL RADIO TRANSMISSION MEAN, AND WILL WE EVER SEE OUR DEAR SWEET MEELIE AGAIN?"
NO. YOU DON'T GET TO CALL HER THAT.
TESLA! EXCELLENT, THE PRESS WILL BE HERE SOON, TELL ME WHAT YOU THINK OF THIS: "CURRENTLY, SEARCH EFFORTS HAVE FOUND NOTHING,
SO I'M CREATING THE AMELIA EARHART MEMORIAL COMMISSION, A PRIVATE SEARCH FUNDED BY THE PROCEEDS OF ALL FUTURE PUTNAM PUBLICATION SALES."
IT'S WORDY, SURE, BUT THEN, UH, I'LL OFFER SOME PRAYERS OR WHATEVER AND SAY "GIVE GENEROUSLY," SO ON AND SO FORTH, AND I'LL FINISH WITH–
"THE BOOK YOU BUY MAY BRING HER HOME."
WHO HELPED HER WITH THE ENGINE?
MYST THE IGH SEAS
I'M SORRY, I DON'T KNOW WHAT YOU'RE TALKING ABOUT. LISTEN, THOUGH, IF YOU WANT TO STICK AROUND AND STAND NEXT TO ME, I'M SURE THE REPORTERS WOULD LOVE SOME PICTURES WITH YOU - THEY'D LOVE TO PLAY UP THE MARRIAGE ANGLE.

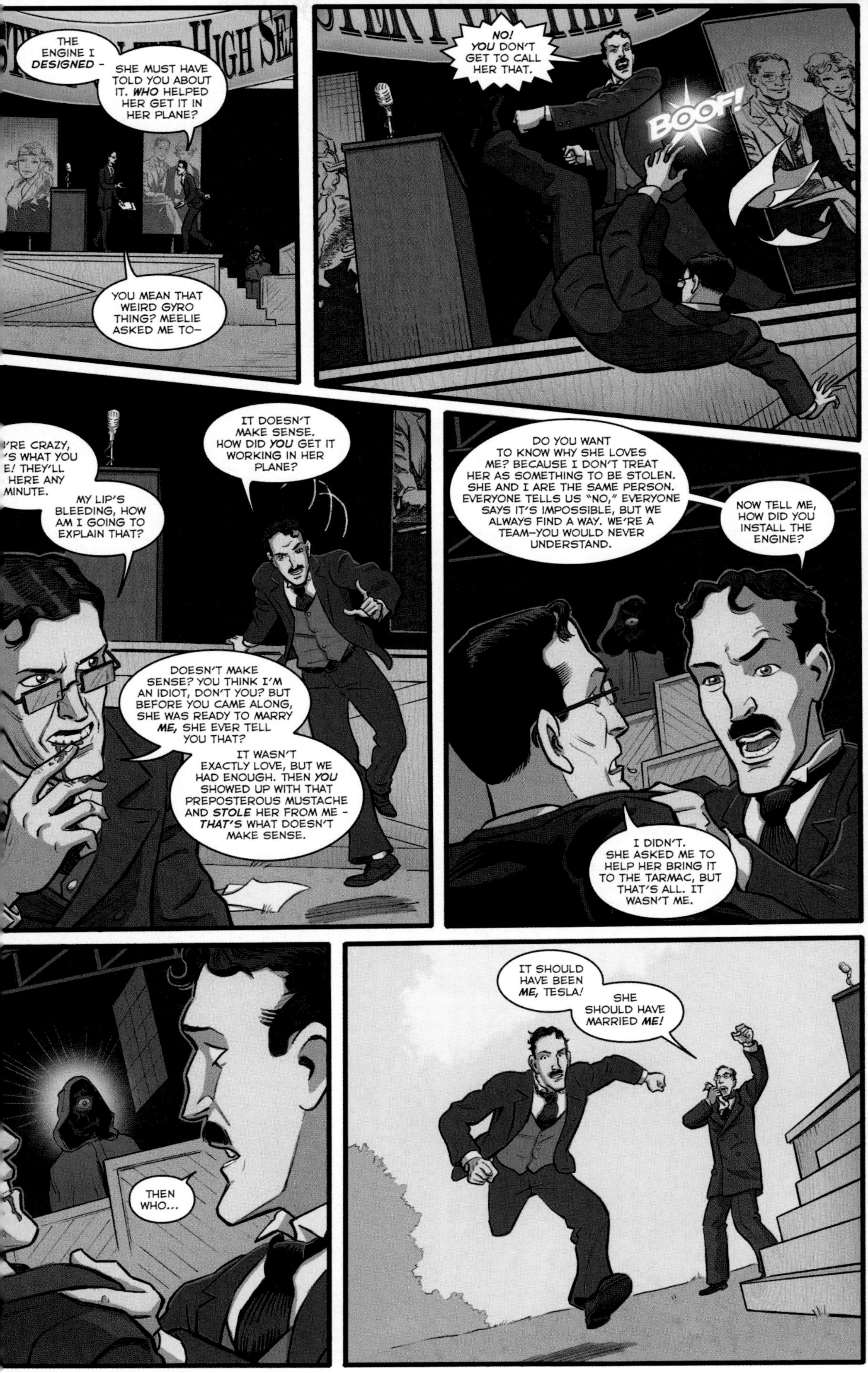
THE ENGINE I *DESIGNED* -
SHE MUST HAVE TOLD YOU ABOUT IT. *WHO* HELPED HER GET IT IN HER PLANE?
YOU MEAN THAT WEIRD GYRO THING? MEELIE ASKED ME TO–
NO! *YOU* DON'T GET TO CALL HER THAT.
BOOF!
'RE CRAZY, 'S WHAT YOU E! THEY'LL HERE ANY MINUTE.
MY LIP'S BLEEDING, HOW AM I GOING TO EXPLAIN THAT?
IT DOESN'T MAKE SENSE. HOW DID *YOU* GET IT WORKING IN HER PLANE?
DOESN'T MAKE SENSE? YOU THINK I'M AN IDIOT, DON'T YOU? BUT BEFORE YOU CAME ALONG, SHE WAS READY TO MARRY *ME*, SHE EVER TELL YOU THAT?
IT WASN'T EXACTLY LOVE, BUT WE HAD ENOUGH. THEN *YOU* SHOWED UP WITH THAT PREPOSTEROUS MUSTACHE AND *STOLE* HER FROM ME - *THAT'S* WHAT DOESN'T MAKE SENSE.
DO YOU WANT TO KNOW WHY SHE LOVES ME? BECAUSE I DON'T TREAT HER AS SOMETHING TO BE STOLEN. SHE AND I ARE THE SAME PERSON. EVERYONE TELLS US "NO," EVERYONE SAYS IT'S IMPOSSIBLE, BUT WE ALWAYS FIND A WAY. WE'RE A TEAM–YOU WOULD NEVER UNDERSTAND.
NOW TELL ME, HOW DID YOU INSTALL THE ENGINE?
I DIDN'T. SHE ASKED ME TO HELP HER BRING IT TO THE TARMAC, BUT THAT'S ALL. IT WASN'T ME.
THEN WHO...
IT SHOULD HAVE BEEN *ME*, TESLA!
SHE SHOULD HAVE MARRIED *ME!*

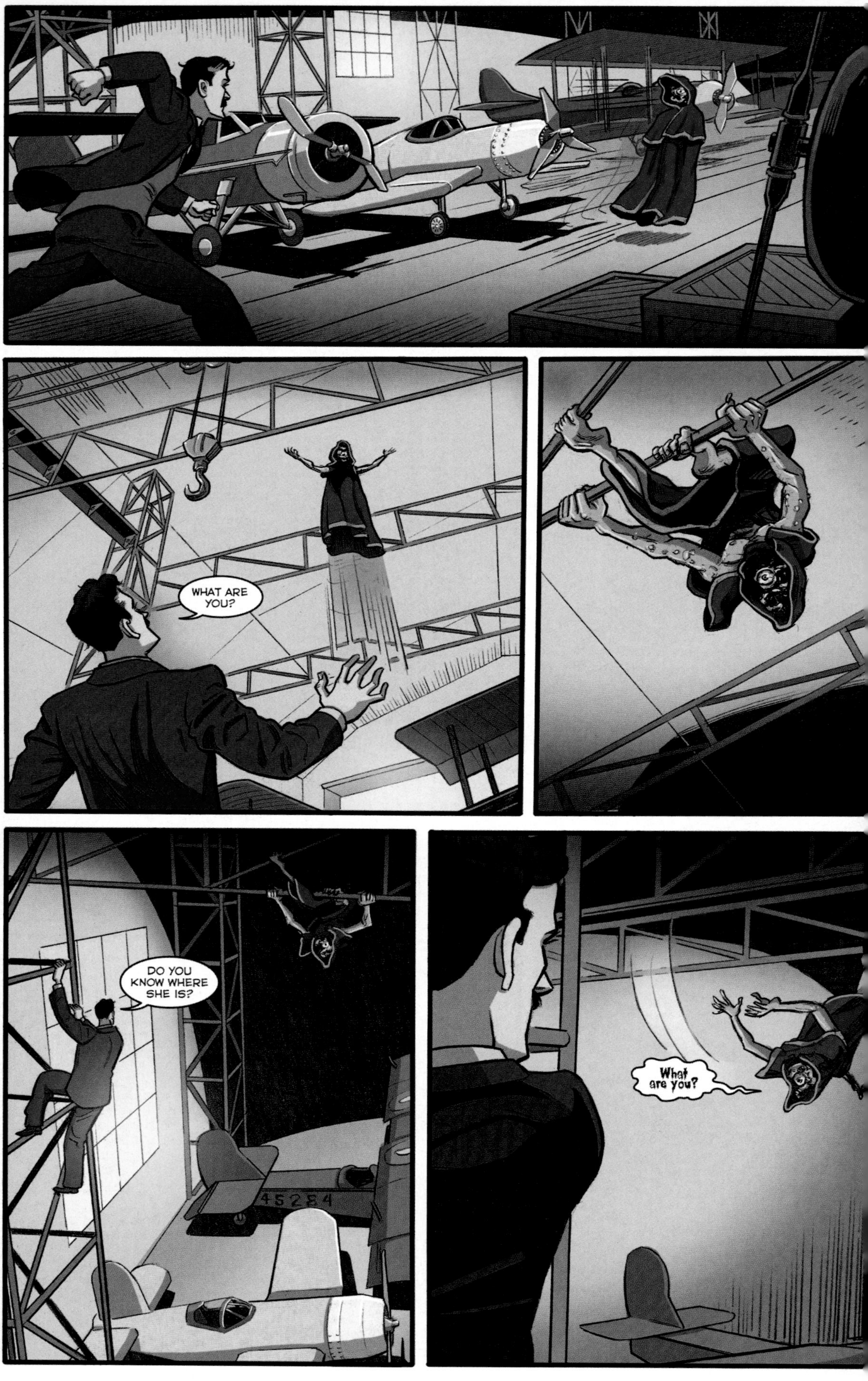
WHAT ARE YOU?
DO YOU KNOW WHERE SHE IS?
45284
What are you?

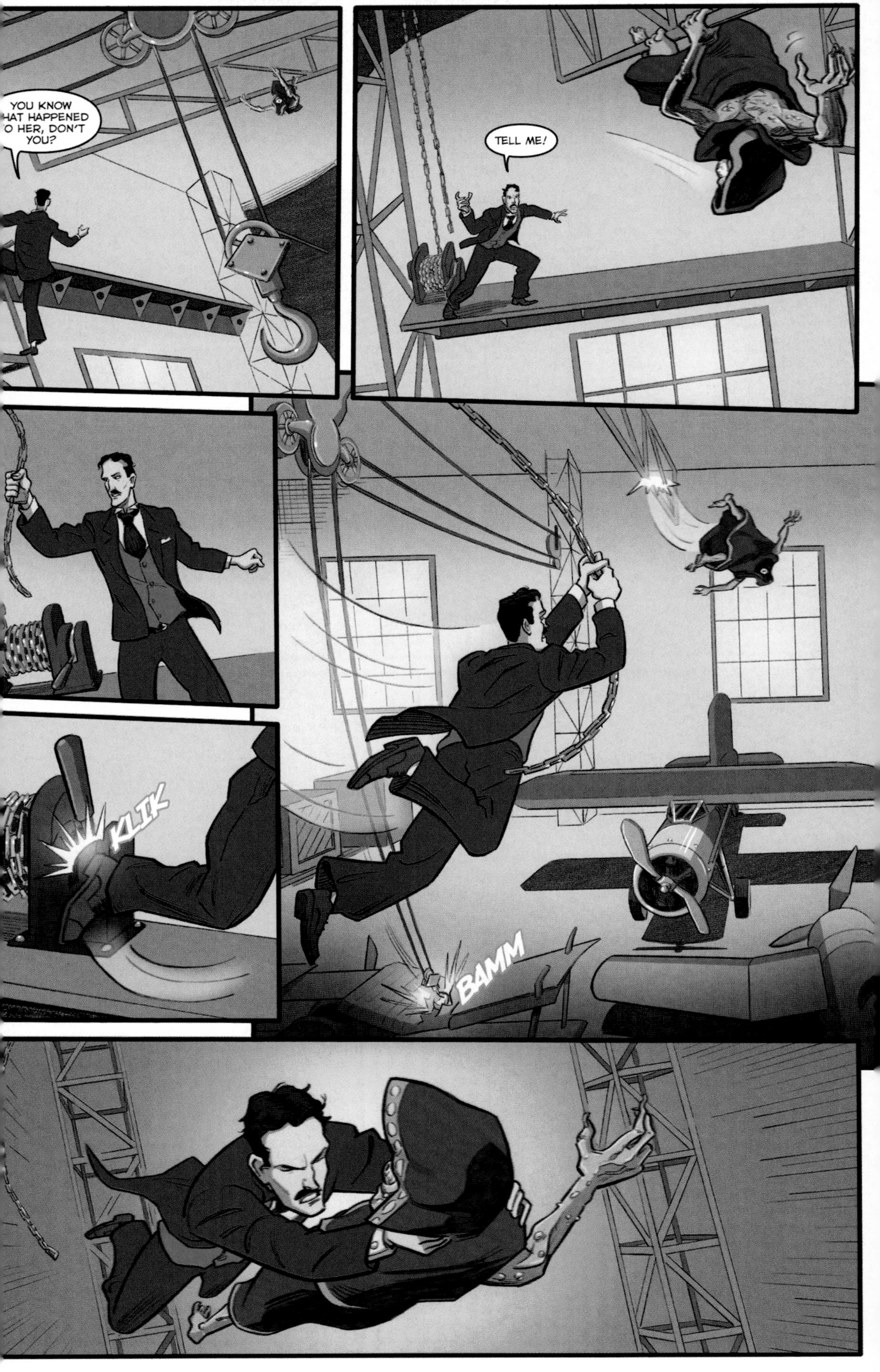
YOU KNOW
HAT HAPPENED
O HER, DON'T
YOU?
TELL ME!
KLIK
BAMM

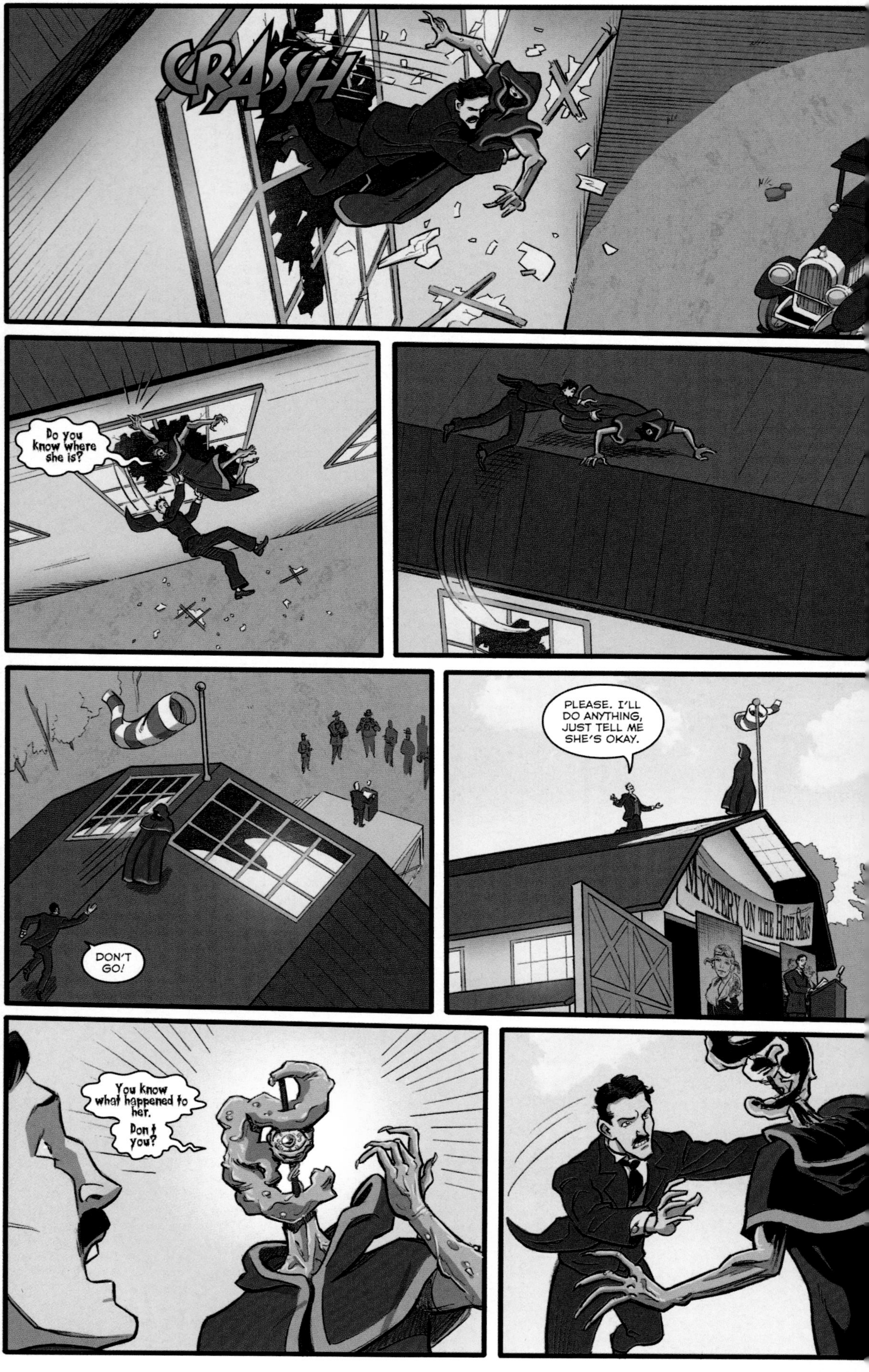
CRASH
Do you know where she is?
PLEASE. I'LL DO ANYTHING, JUST TELL ME SHE'S OKAY.
DON'T GO!
MYSTERY ON THE HIGH SEAS
You know what happened to her.
Don't you?

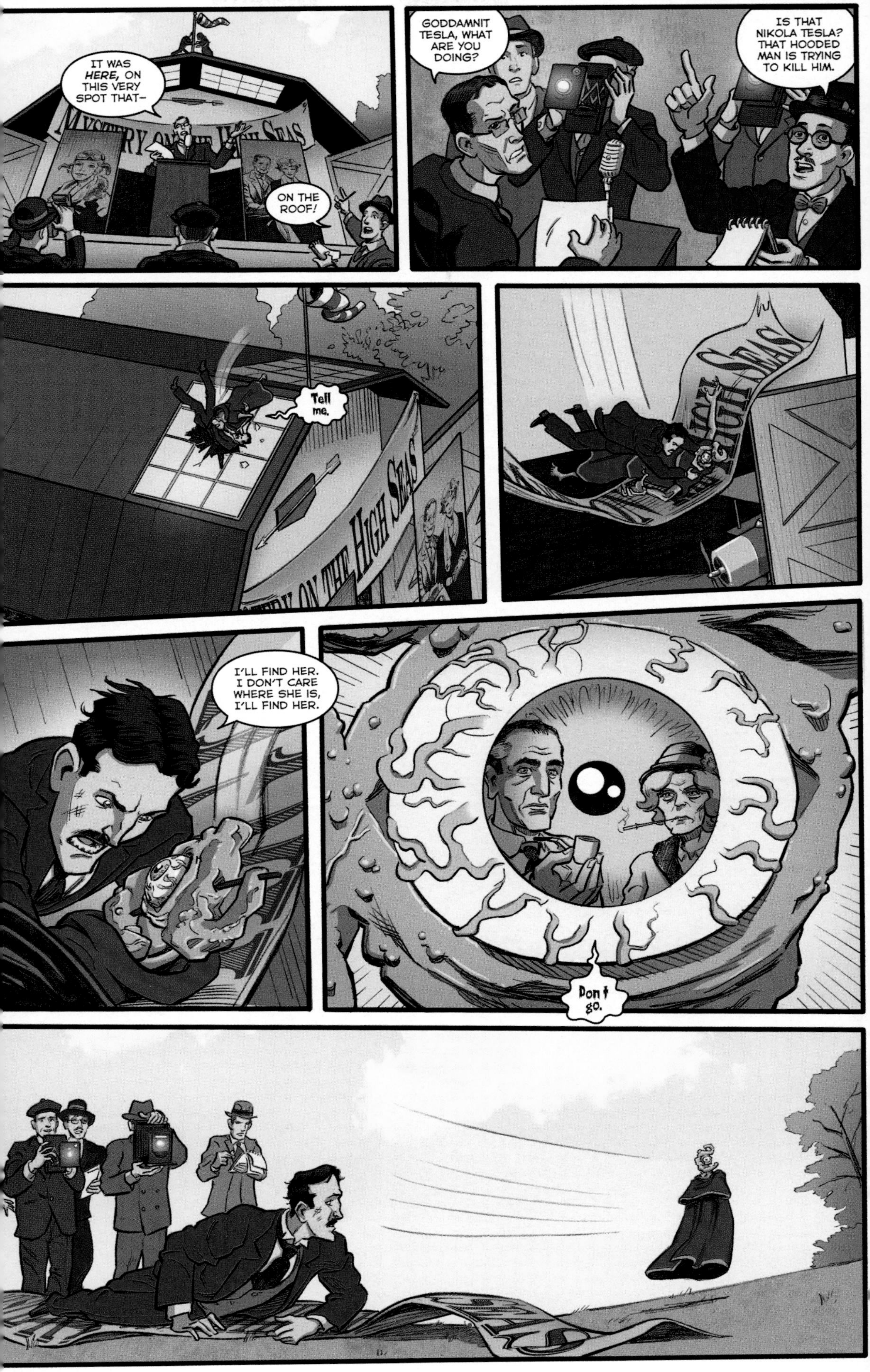
IT WAS HERE, ON THIS VERY SPOT THAT–
MYSTERY ON THE HIGH SEAS
ON THE ROOF!
GODDAMNIT TESLA, WHAT ARE YOU DOING?
IS THAT NIKOLA TESLA? THAT HOODED MAN IS TRYING TO KILL HIM.
Tell me.
MYSTERY ON THE HIGH SEAS
I'LL FIND HER. I DON'T CARE WHERE SHE IS, I'LL FIND HER.
Don't go.

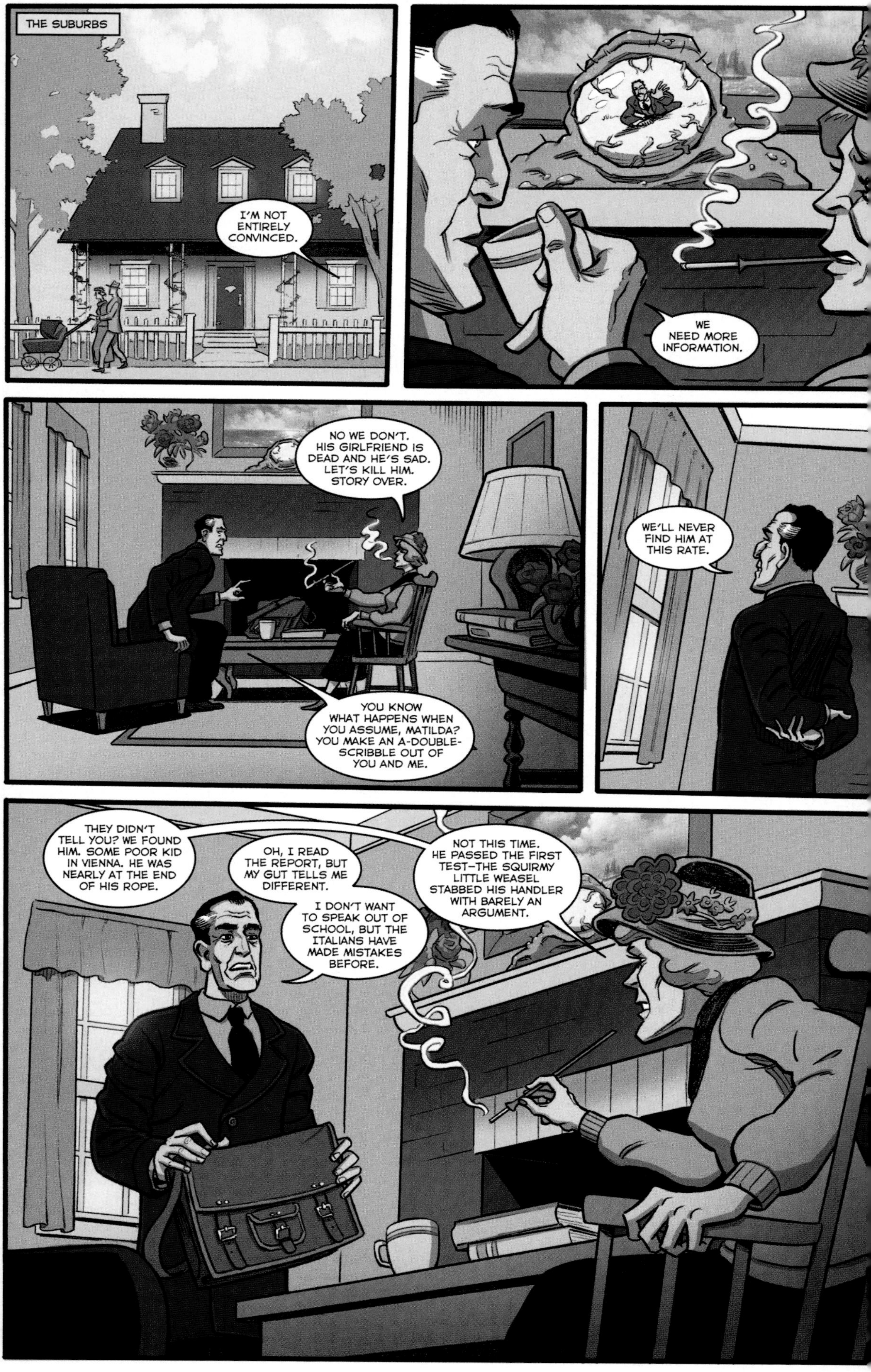

THE SUBURBS
I'M NOT ENTIRELY CONVINCED.
WE NEED MORE INFORMATION.
NO WE DON'T. HIS GIRLFRIEND IS DEAD AND HE'S SAD. LET'S KILL HIM. STORY OVER.
YOU KNOW WHAT HAPPENS WHEN YOU ASSUME, MATILDA? YOU MAKE AN A-DOUBLE-SCRIBBLE OUT OF YOU AND ME.
WE'LL NEVER FIND HIM AT THIS RATE.
THEY DIDN'T TELL YOU? WE FOUND HIM. SOME POOR KID IN VIENNA. HE WAS NEARLY AT THE END OF HIS ROPE.
OH, I READ THE REPORT, BUT MY GUT TELLS ME DIFFERENT.
I DON'T WANT TO SPEAK OUT OF SCHOOL, BUT THE ITALIANS HAVE MADE MISTAKES BEFORE.
NOT THIS TIME. HE PASSED THE FIRST TEST—THE SQUIRMY LITTLE WEASEL STABBED HIS HANDLER WITH BARELY AN ARGUMENT.

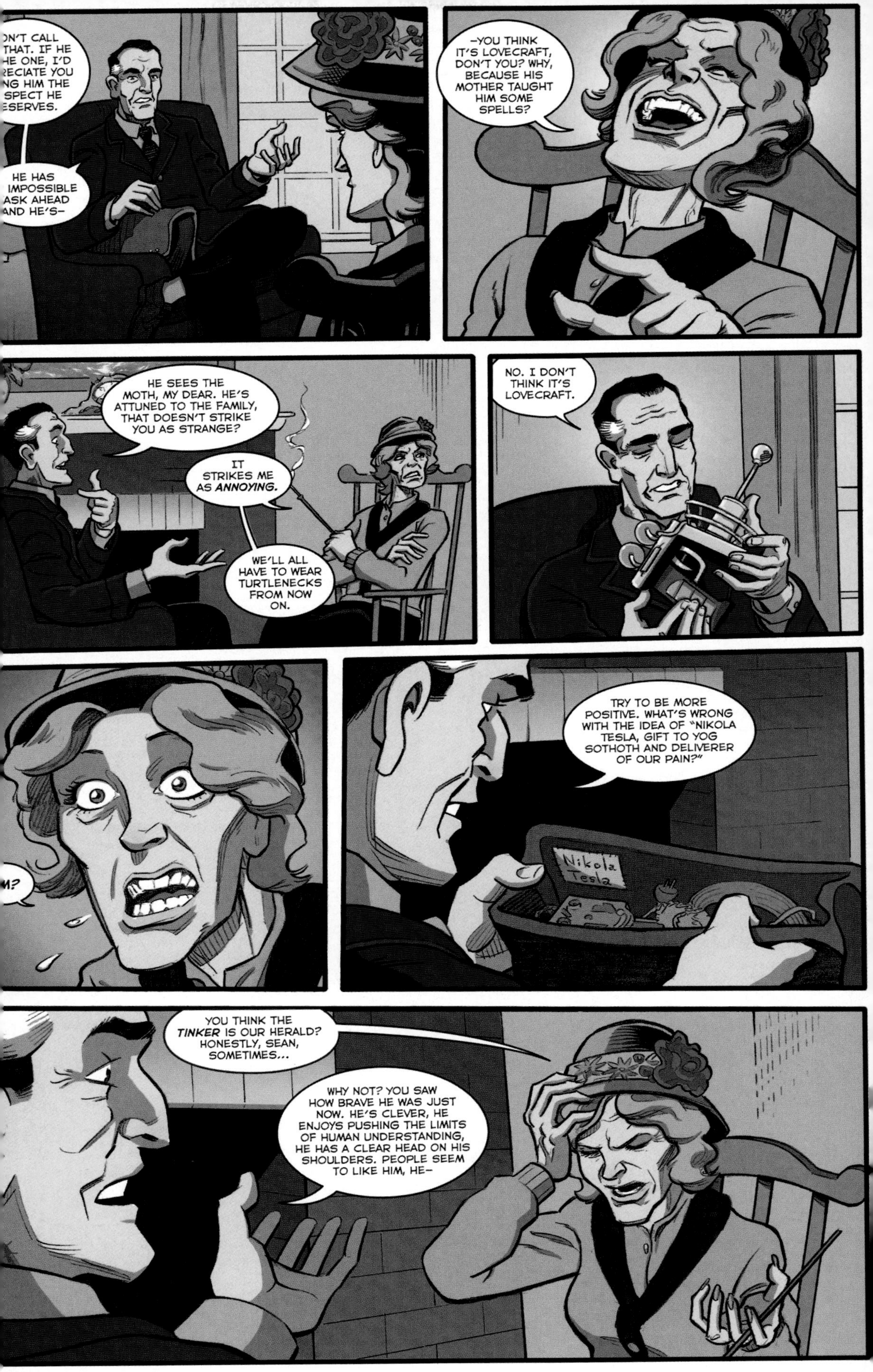

...N'T CALL ...THAT. IF HE ...HE ONE, I'D ...RECIATE YOU ...NG HIM THE ...SPECT HE ...ESERVES.
HE HAS ...IMPOSSIBLE ...ASK AHEAD ...AND HE'S–
–YOU THINK IT'S LOVECRAFT, DON'T YOU? WHY, BECAUSE HIS MOTHER TAUGHT HIM SOME SPELLS?
HE SEES THE MOTH, MY DEAR. HE'S ATTUNED TO THE FAMILY, THAT DOESN'T STRIKE YOU AS STRANGE?
IT STRIKES ME AS *ANNOYING.*
WE'LL ALL HAVE TO WEAR TURTLENECKS FROM NOW ON.
NO. I DON'T THINK IT'S LOVECRAFT.
...M?
TRY TO BE MORE POSITIVE. WHAT'S WRONG WITH THE IDEA OF "NIKOLA TESLA, GIFT TO YOG SOTHOTH AND DELIVERER OF OUR PAIN?"
Nikola Tesla
YOU THINK THE *TINKER* IS OUR HERALD? HONESTLY, SEAN, SOMETIMES...
WHY NOT? YOU SAW HOW BRAVE HE WAS JUST NOW. HE'S CLEVER, HE ENJOYS PUSHING THE LIMITS OF HUMAN UNDERSTANDING, HE HAS A CLEAR HEAD ON HIS SHOULDERS. PEOPLE SEEM TO LIKE HIM, HE–

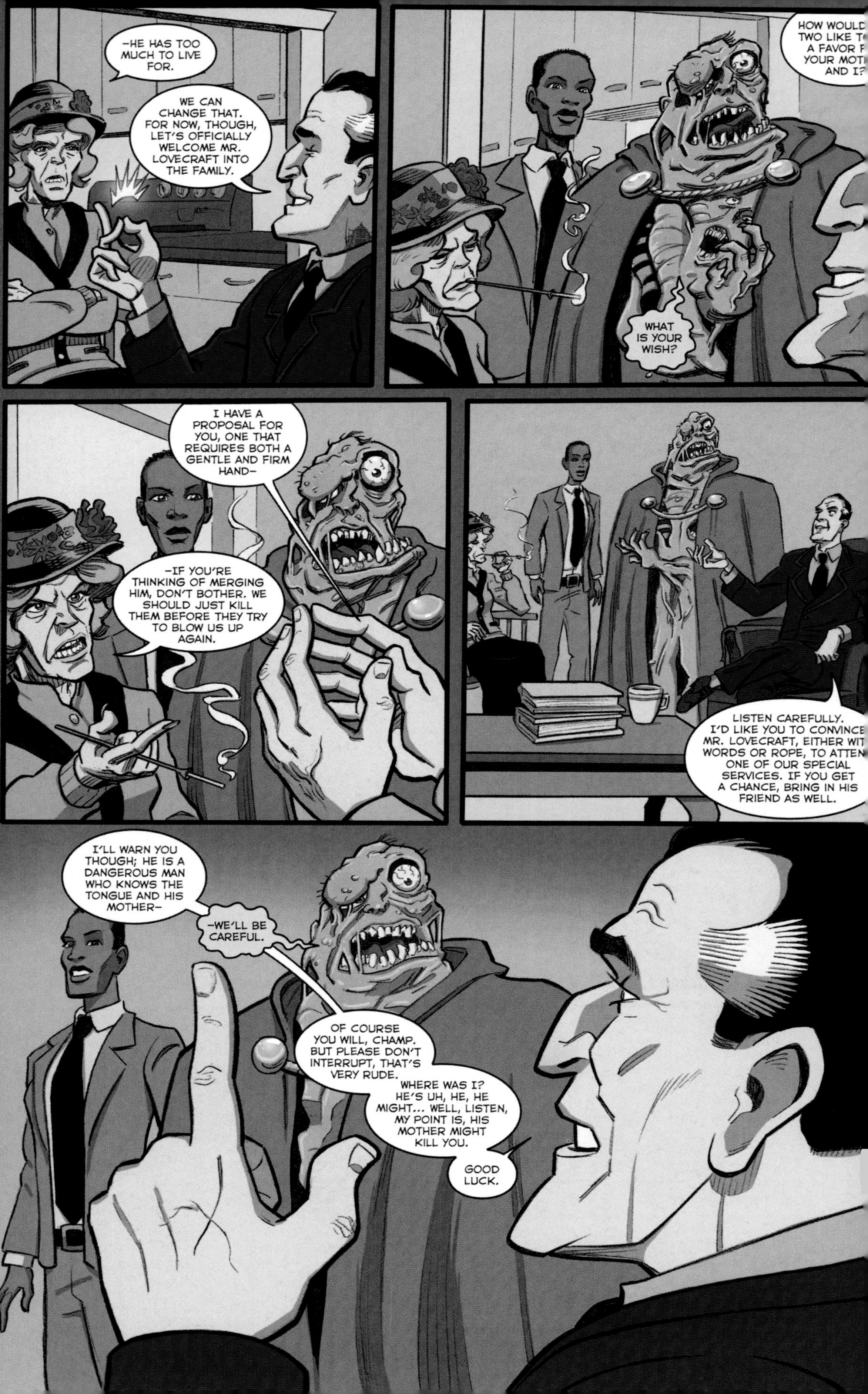
—HE HAS TOO MUCH TO LIVE FOR.
WE CAN CHANGE THAT. FOR NOW, THOUGH, LET'S OFFICIALLY WELCOME MR. LOVECRAFT INTO THE FAMILY.
HOW WOULD TWO LIKE T A FAVOR YOUR MOT AND I?
WHAT IS YOUR WISH?
I HAVE A PROPOSAL FOR YOU, ONE THAT REQUIRES BOTH A GENTLE AND FIRM HAND—
—IF YOU'RE THINKING OF MERGING HIM, DON'T BOTHER. WE SHOULD JUST KILL THEM BEFORE THEY TRY TO BLOW US UP AGAIN.
LISTEN CAREFULLY. I'D LIKE YOU TO CONVINCE MR. LOVECRAFT, EITHER WIT WORDS OR ROPE, TO ATTEN ONE OF OUR SPECIAL SERVICES. IF YOU GET A CHANCE, BRING IN HIS FRIEND AS WELL.
I'LL WARN YOU THOUGH; HE IS A DANGEROUS MAN WHO KNOWS THE TONGUE AND HIS MOTHER—
—WE'LL BE CAREFUL.
OF COURSE YOU WILL, CHAMP. BUT PLEASE DON'T INTERRUPT, THAT'S VERY RUDE.
WHERE WAS I? HE'S UH, HE, HE MIGHT... WELL, LISTEN, MY POINT IS, HIS MOTHER MIGHT KILL YOU.
GOOD LUCK.

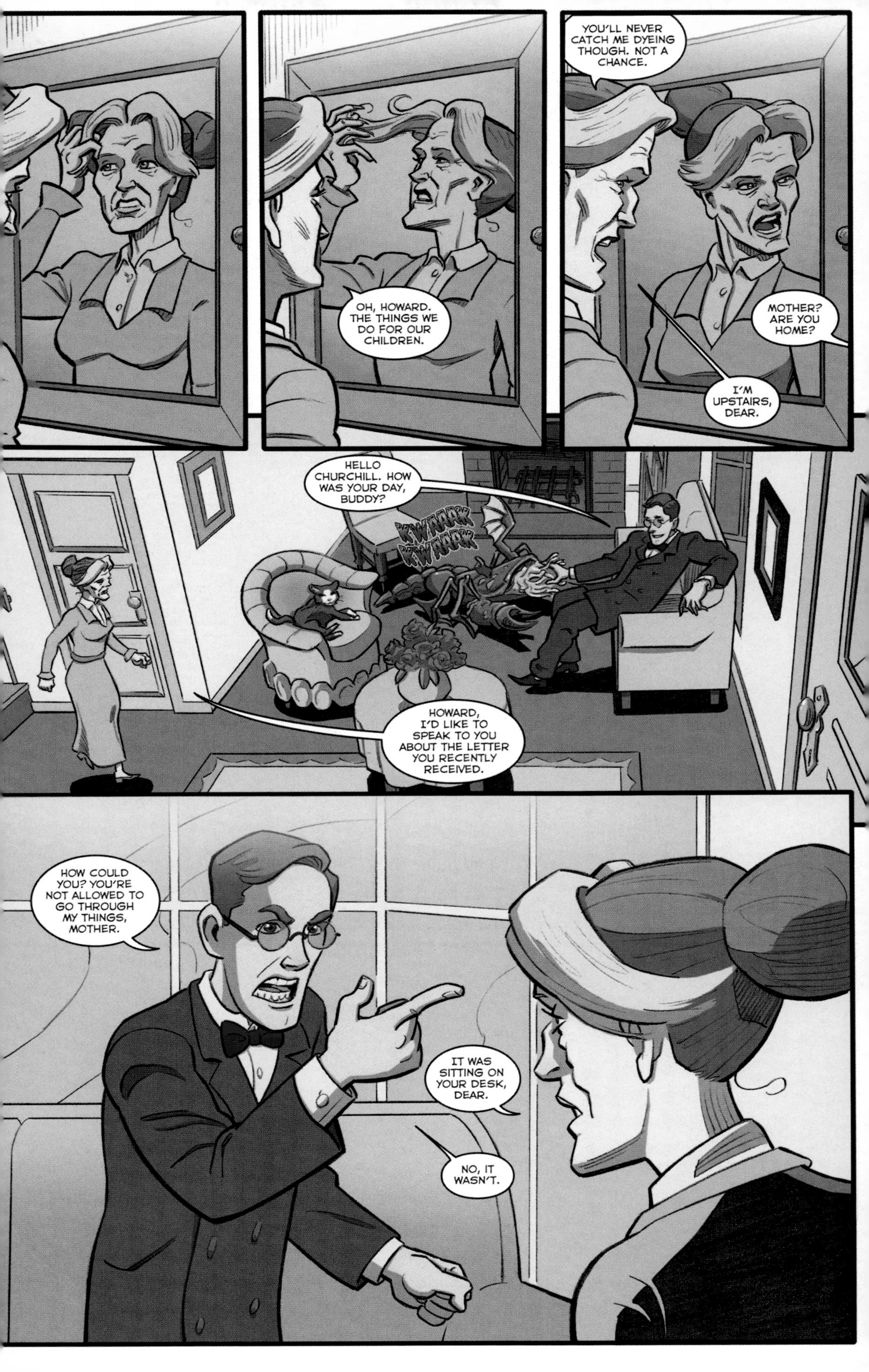
OH, HOWARD. THE THINGS WE DO FOR OUR CHILDREN.
YOU'LL NEVER CATCH ME DYEING THOUGH. NOT A CHANCE.
MOTHER? ARE YOU HOME?
I'M UPSTAIRS, DEAR.
HELLO CHURCHILL. HOW WAS YOUR DAY, BUDDY?
KWAAAK KWAAAK
HOWARD, I'D LIKE TO SPEAK TO YOU ABOUT THE LETTER YOU RECENTLY RECEIVED.
HOW COULD YOU? YOU'RE NOT ALLOWED TO GO THROUGH MY THINGS, MOTHER.
IT WAS SITTING ON YOUR DESK, DEAR.
NO, IT WASN'T.

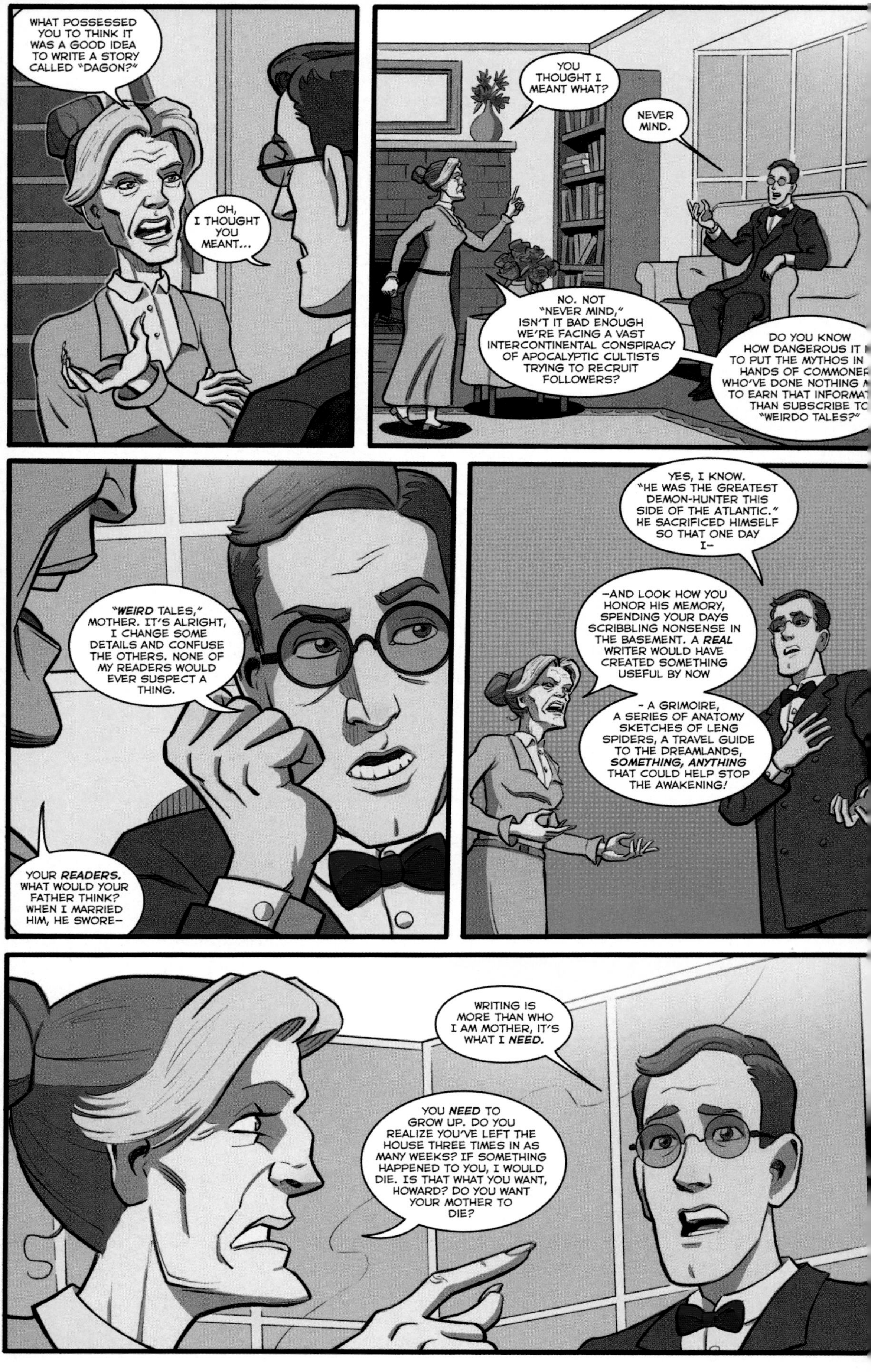
WHAT POSSESSED YOU TO THINK IT WAS A GOOD IDEA TO WRITE A STORY CALLED "DAGON?"
OH, I THOUGHT YOU MEANT...
YOU THOUGHT I MEANT WHAT?
NEVER MIND.
NO. NOT "NEVER MIND," ISN'T IT BAD ENOUGH WE'RE FACING A VAST INTERCONTINENTAL CONSPIRACY OF APOCALYPTIC CULTISTS TRYING TO RECRUIT FOLLOWERS?
DO YOU KNOW HOW DANGEROUS IT TO PUT THE MYTHOS IN HANDS OF COMMONER WHO'VE DONE NOTHING TO EARN THAT INFORMAT THAN SUBSCRIBE TO "WEIRDO TALES?"
"WEIRD TALES," MOTHER. IT'S ALRIGHT, I CHANGE SOME DETAILS AND CONFUSE THE OTHERS. NONE OF MY READERS WOULD EVER SUSPECT A THING.
YOUR READERS. WHAT WOULD YOUR FATHER THINK? WHEN I MARRIED HIM, HE SWORE-
YES, I KNOW. "HE WAS THE GREATEST DEMON-HUNTER THIS SIDE OF THE ATLANTIC." HE SACRIFICED HIMSELF SO THAT ONE DAY I-
-AND LOOK HOW YOU HONOR HIS MEMORY, SPENDING YOUR DAYS SCRIBBLING NONSENSE IN THE BASEMENT. A REAL WRITER WOULD HAVE CREATED SOMETHING USEFUL BY NOW
- A GRIMOIRE, A SERIES OF ANATOMY SKETCHES OF LENG SPIDERS, A TRAVEL GUIDE TO THE DREAMLANDS, SOMETHING, ANYTHING THAT COULD HELP STOP THE AWAKENING!
WRITING IS MORE THAN WHO I AM MOTHER, IT'S WHAT I NEED.
YOU NEED TO GROW UP. DO YOU REALIZE YOU'VE LEFT THE HOUSE THREE TIMES IN AS MANY WEEKS? IF SOMETHING HAPPENED TO YOU, I WOULD DIE. IS THAT WHAT YOU WANT, HOWARD? DO YOU WANT YOUR MOTHER TO DIE?

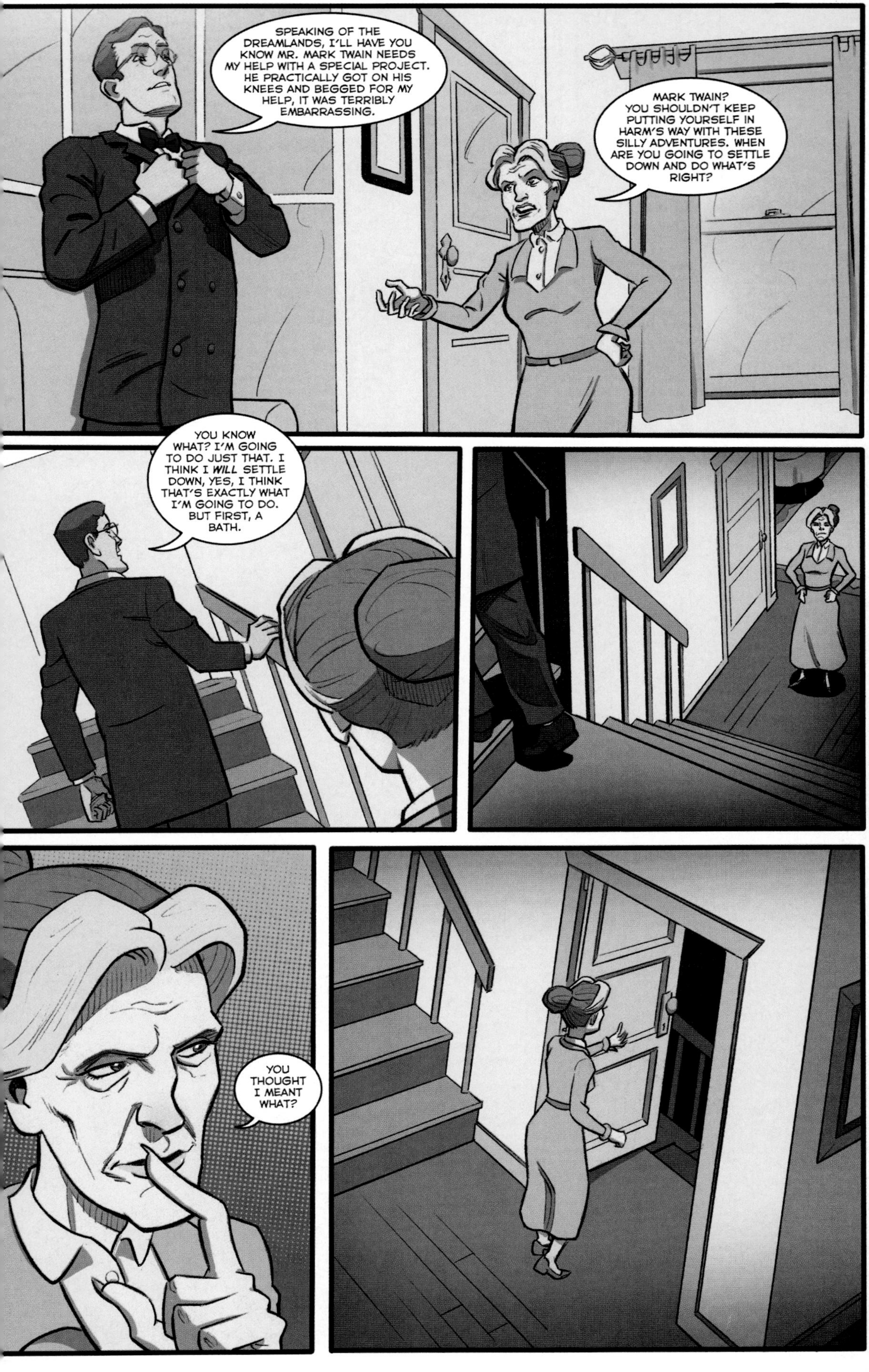
SPEAKING OF THE DREAMLANDS, I'LL HAVE YOU KNOW MR. MARK TWAIN NEEDS MY HELP WITH A SPECIAL PROJECT. HE PRACTICALLY GOT ON HIS KNEES AND BEGGED FOR MY HELP, IT WAS TERRIBLY EMBARRASSING.
MARK TWAIN? YOU SHOULDN'T KEEP PUTTING YOURSELF IN HARM'S WAY WITH THESE SILLY ADVENTURES. WHEN ARE YOU GOING TO SETTLE DOWN AND DO WHAT'S RIGHT?
YOU KNOW WHAT? I'M GOING TO DO JUST THAT. I THINK I *WILL* SETTLE DOWN, YES, I THINK THAT'S EXACTLY WHAT I'M GOING TO DO. BUT FIRST, A BATH.
YOU THOUGHT I MEANT WHAT?

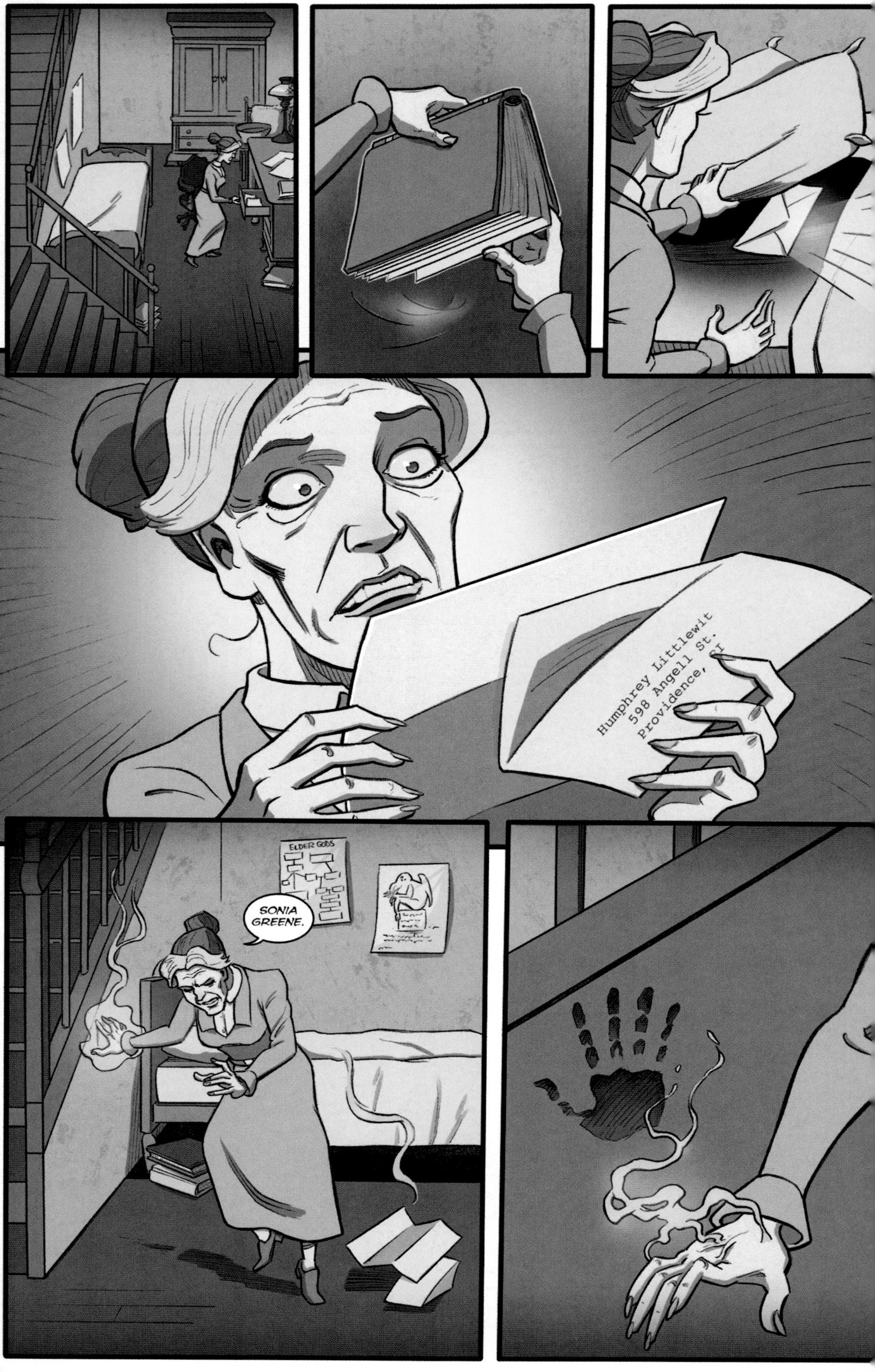
Humphrey Littlewit
598 Angell St.
Providence,
ELDER GODS
SONIA GREENE.

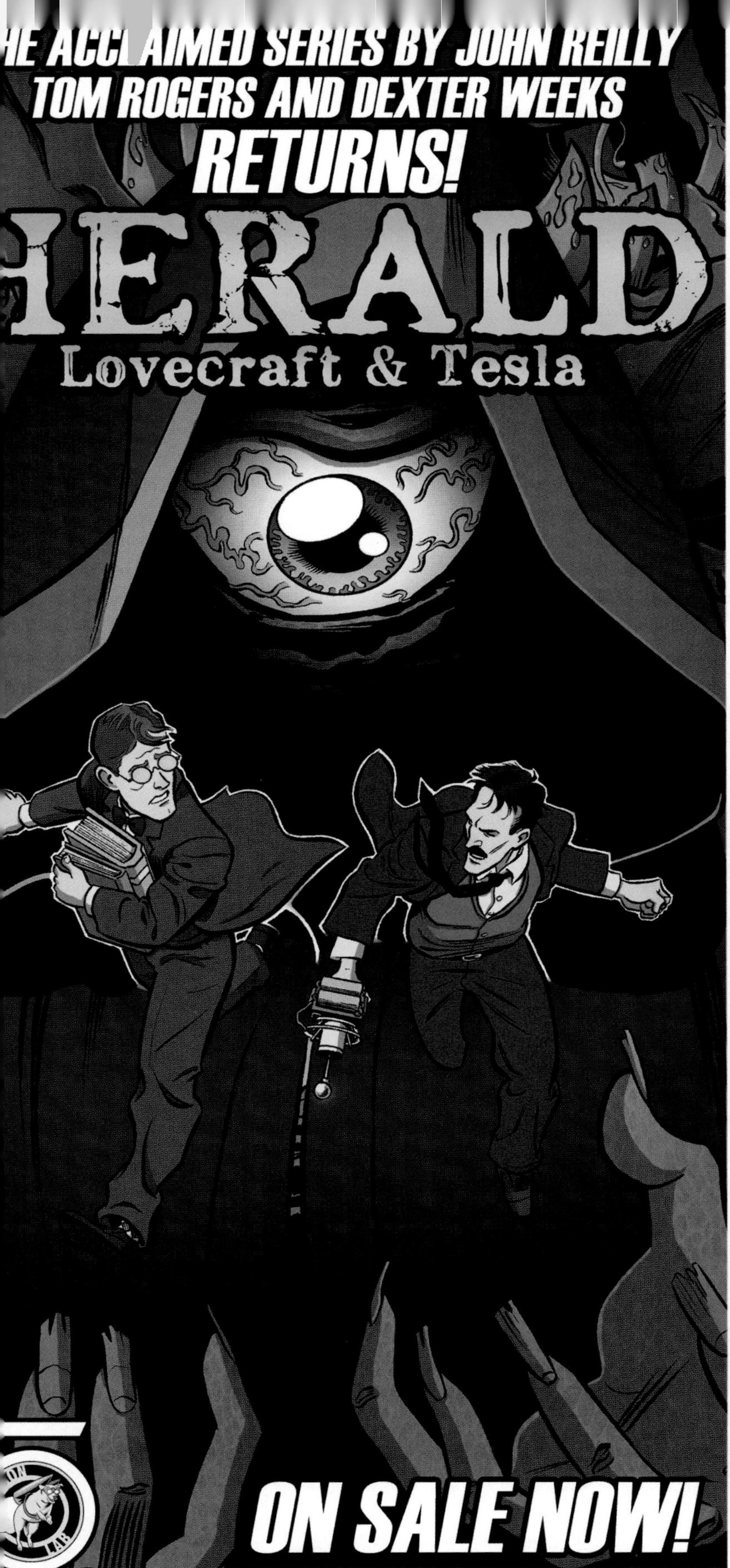

HE ACCLAIMED SERIES BY JOHN REILLY
TOM ROGERS AND DEXTER WEEKS
RETURNS!
HERALD
Lovecraft & Tesla
ON SALE NOW!

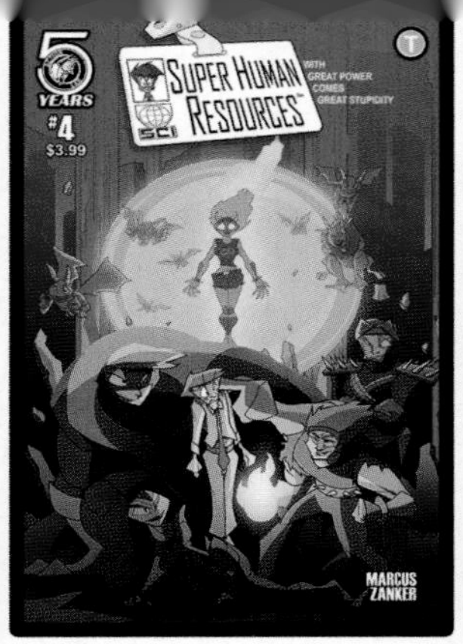

5 YEARS
#4
$3.99
SUPER HUMAN RESOURCES
MARCUS ZANKER

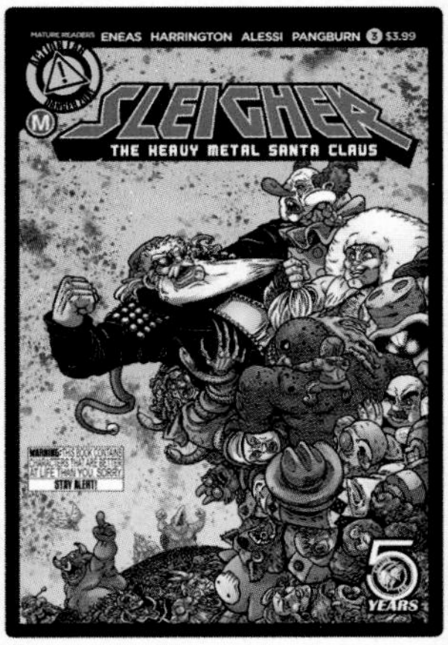

MATURE READERS ENEAS HARRINGTON ALESSI PANGBURN 3 $3.99
SLEIGHER
THE HEAVY METAL SANTA CLAUS
STAY ALERT!
5 YEARS

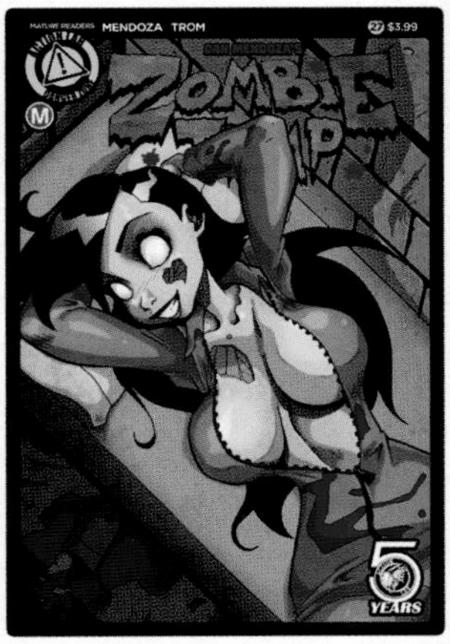

MATURE READERS MENDOZA TROM
27 $3.99
5 YEARS

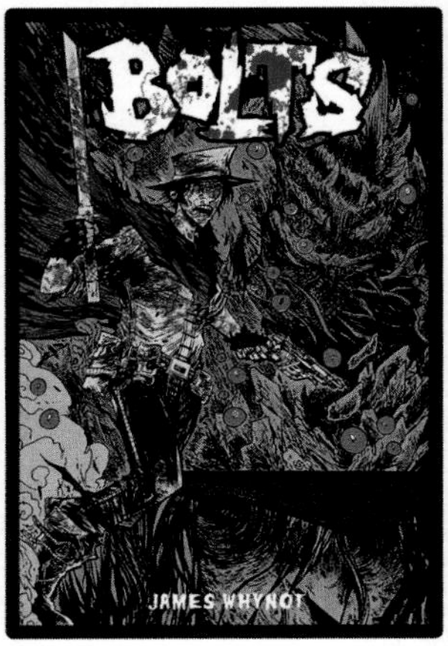

BOLTS
JAMES WHYNOT

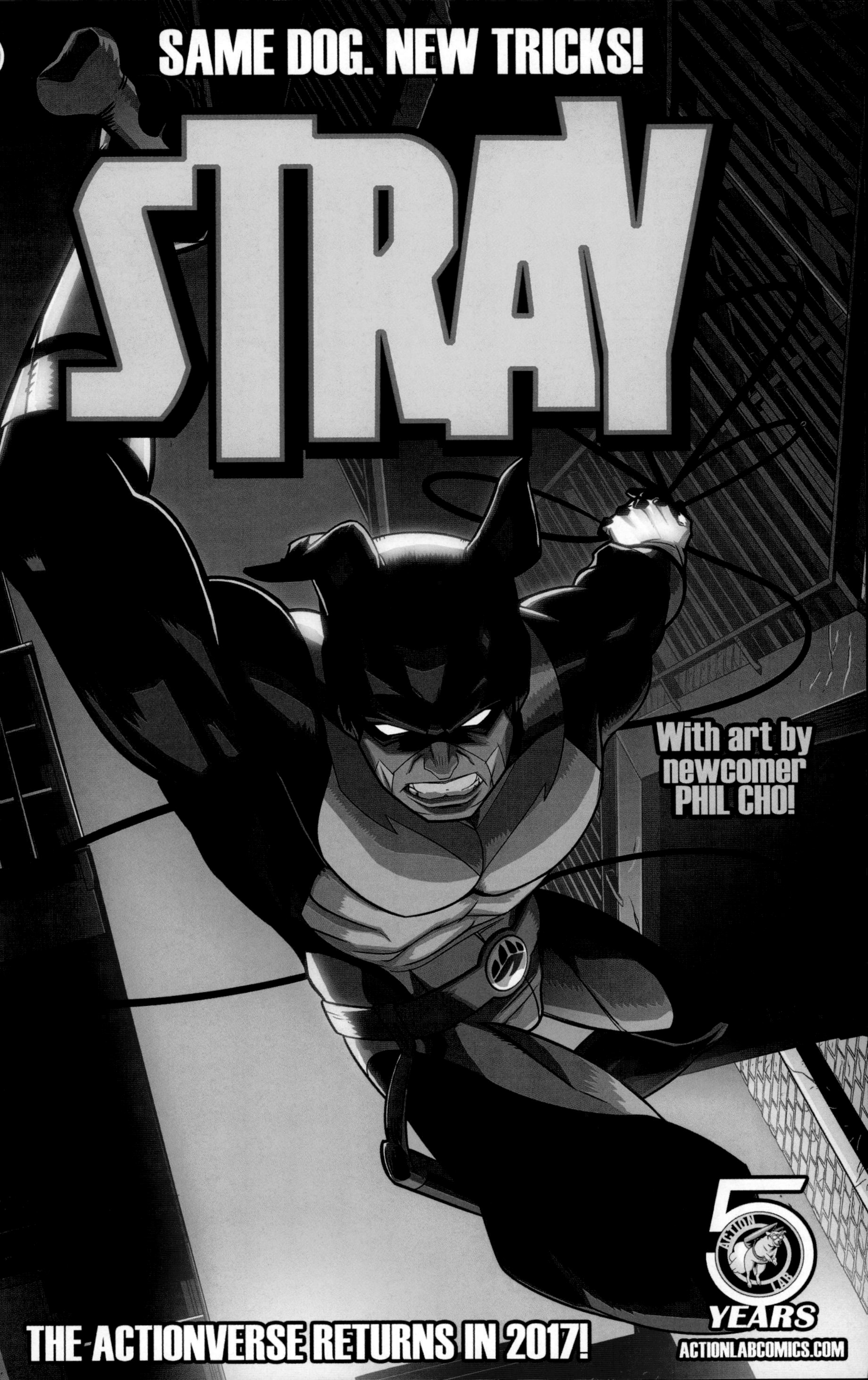
SAME DOG. NEW TRICKS!
STRAY
With art by newcomer PHIL CHO!
5 YEARS
ACTION LAB
THE ACTIONVERSE RETURNS IN 2017!
ACTIONLABCOMICS.COM

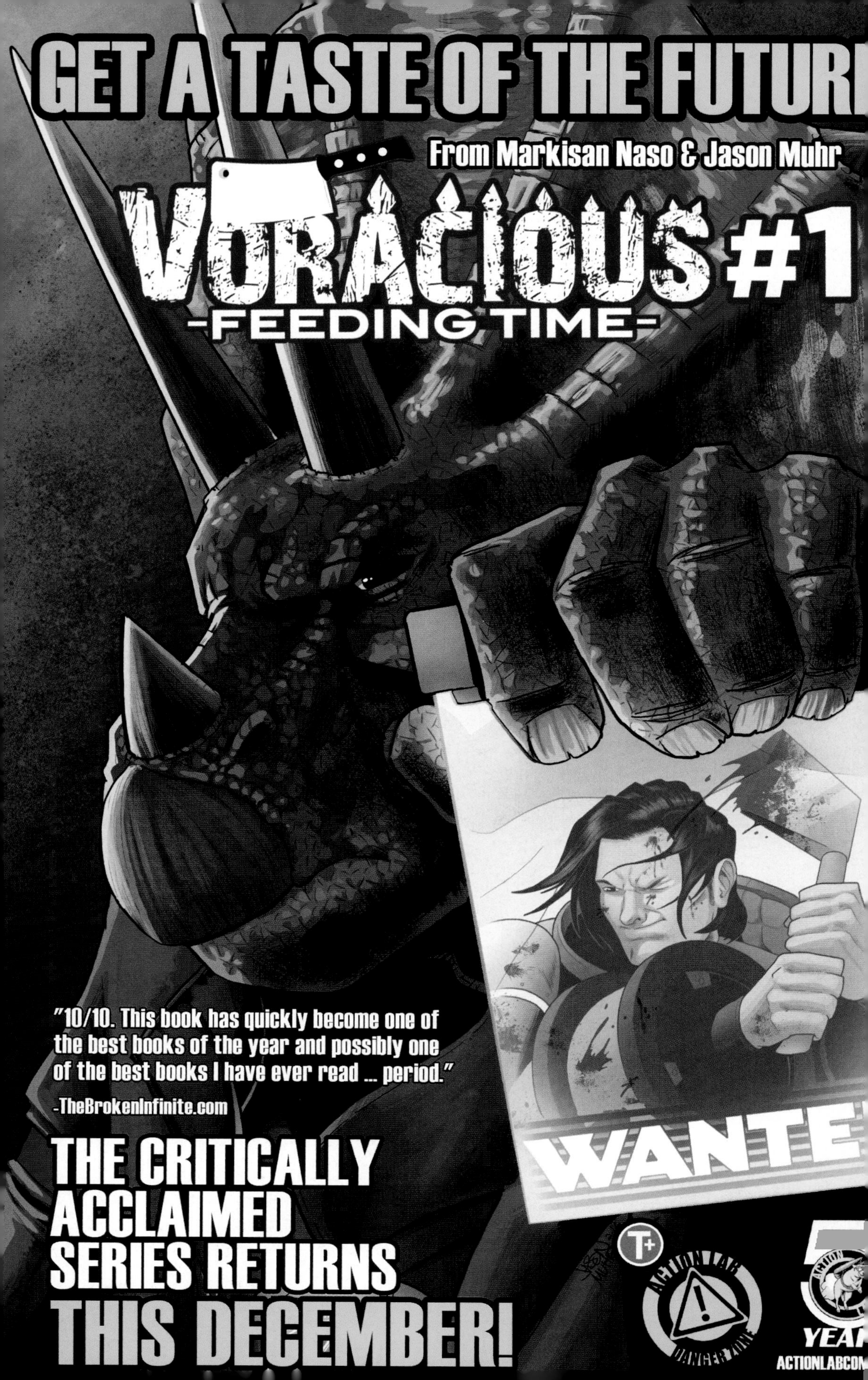
GET A TASTE OF THE FUTURE
From Markisan Naso & Jason Muhr
VORACIOUS #1
-FEEDING TIME-
WANTE
"10/10. This book has quickly become one of the best books of the year and possibly one of the best books I have ever read ... period."
-TheBrokenInfinite.com
THE CRITICALLY ACCLAIMED SERIES RETURNS
THIS DECEMBER!
T+
ACTION LAB
DANGER ZONE
YEA
ACTIONLABCOM

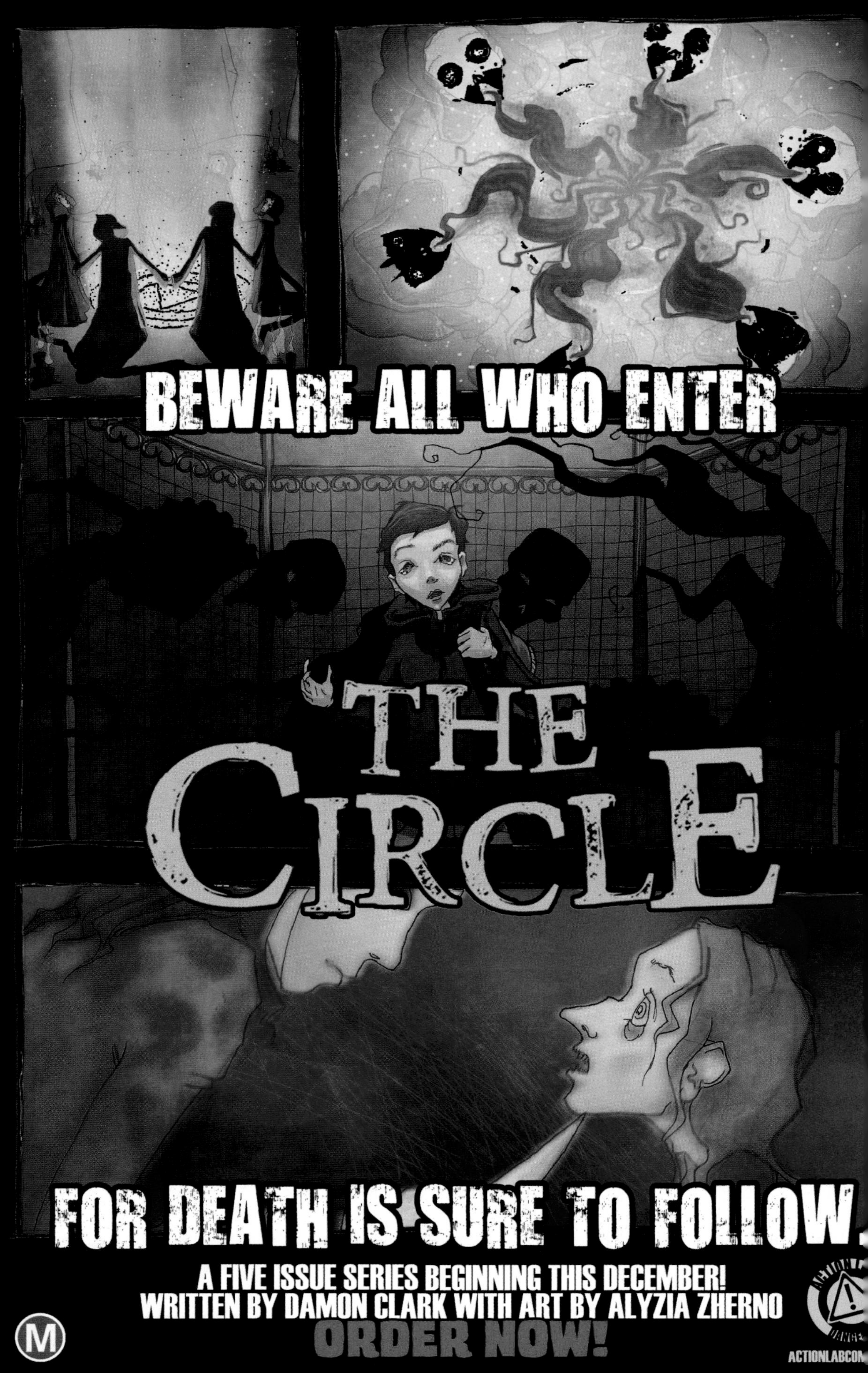

BEWARE ALL WHO ENTER

THE CIRCLE

FOR DEATH IS SURE TO FOLLOW.

A FIVE ISSUE SERIES BEGINNING THIS DECEMBER!
WRITTEN BY DAMON CLARK WITH ART BY ALYZIA ZHERNO
ORDER NOW!

ACTIONLABCOMICS

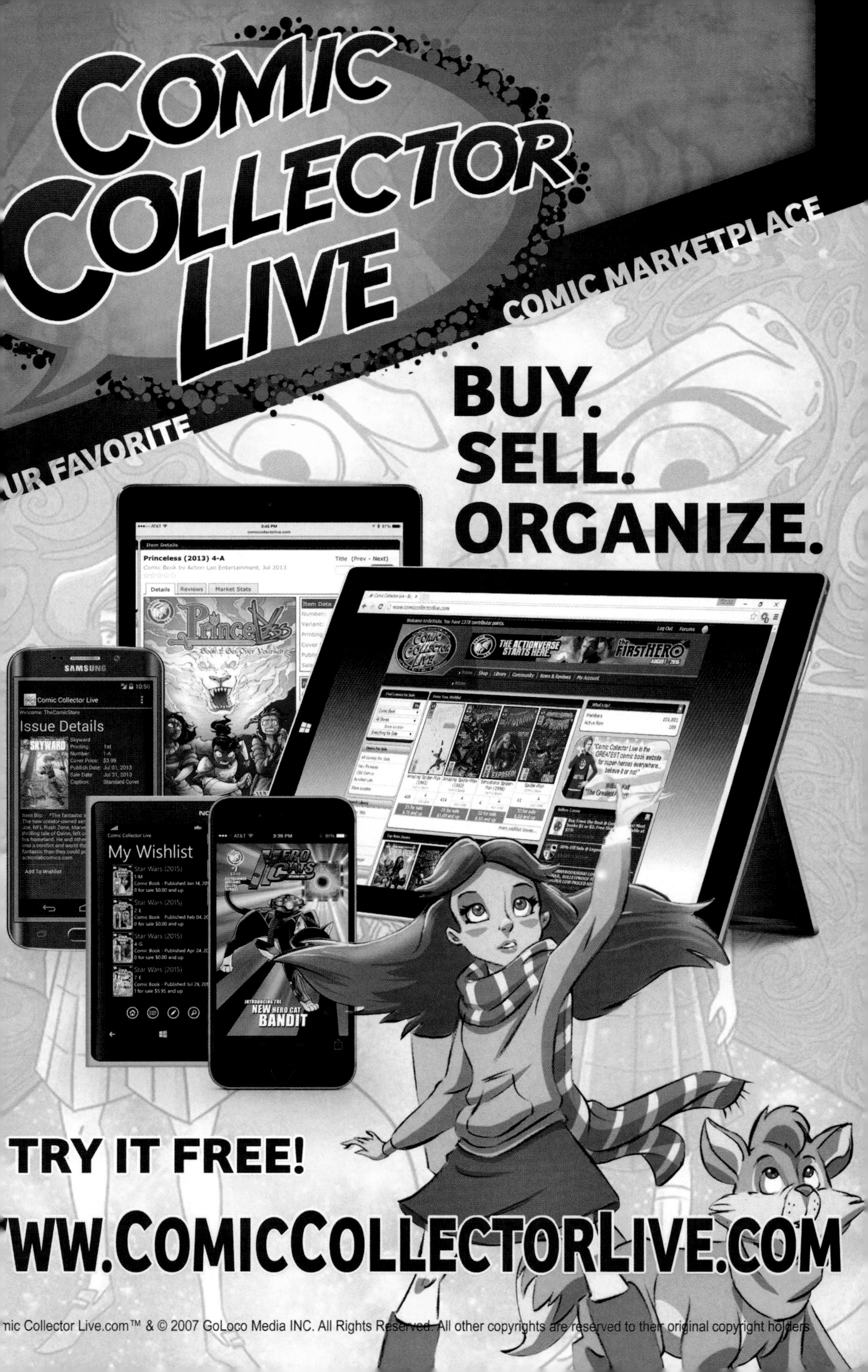

COMIC COLLECTOR LIVE
UR FAVORITE COMIC MARKETPLACE
BUY.
SELL.
ORGANIZE.
TRY IT FREE!
WW.COMICCOLLECTORLIVE.COM
mic Collector Live.com™ & © 2007 GoLoco Media INC. All Rights Reserved. All other copyrights are reserved to their original copyright holders

READ MORE NOW

Herald - Action Lab
www.actionlabcomics.com
00711
7 00465 77250 3

ACTIONLABCOMICS.COM

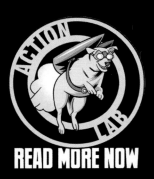

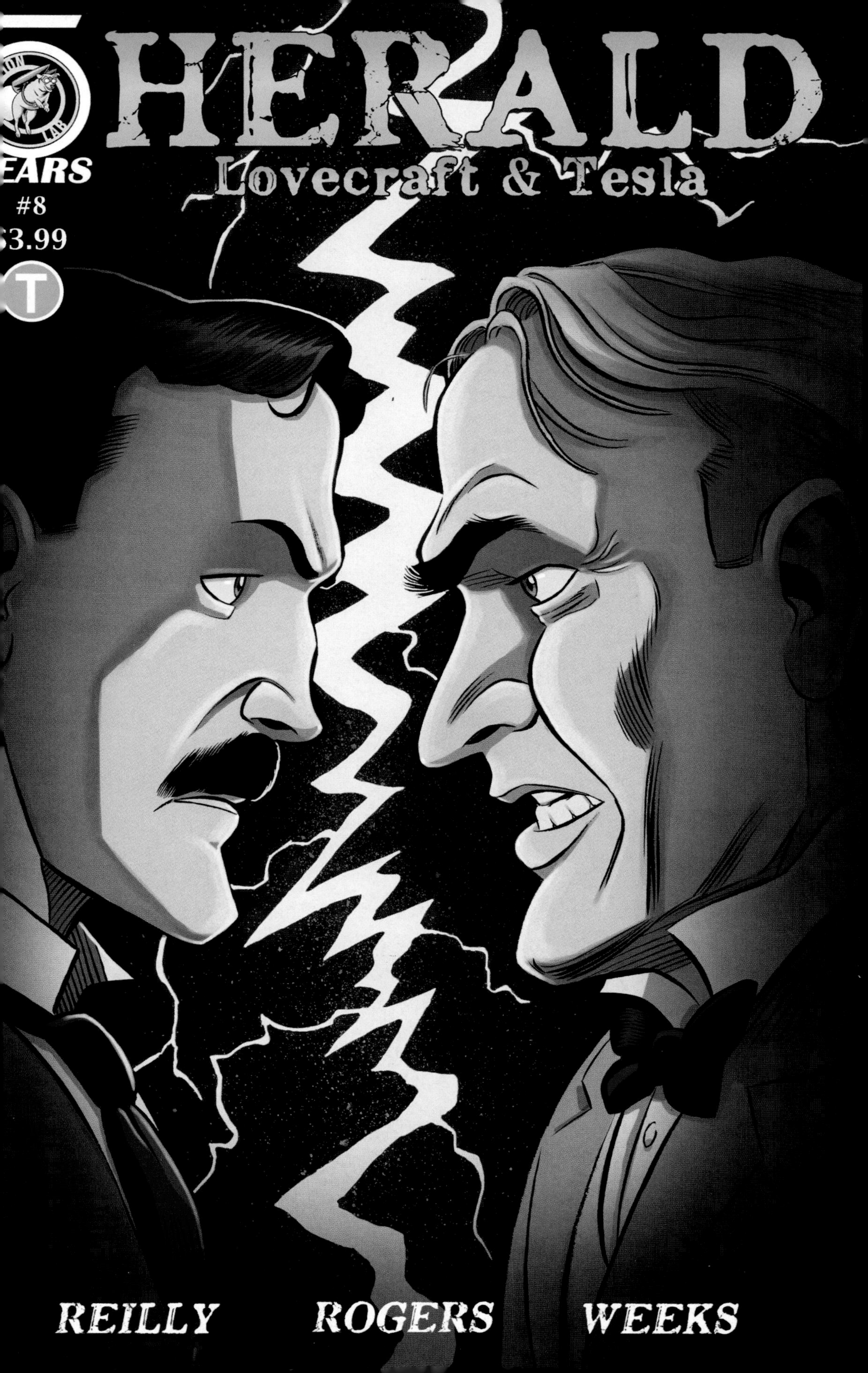

HERALD
Lovecraft & Tesla
#8
$3.99
REILLY ROGERS WEEKS

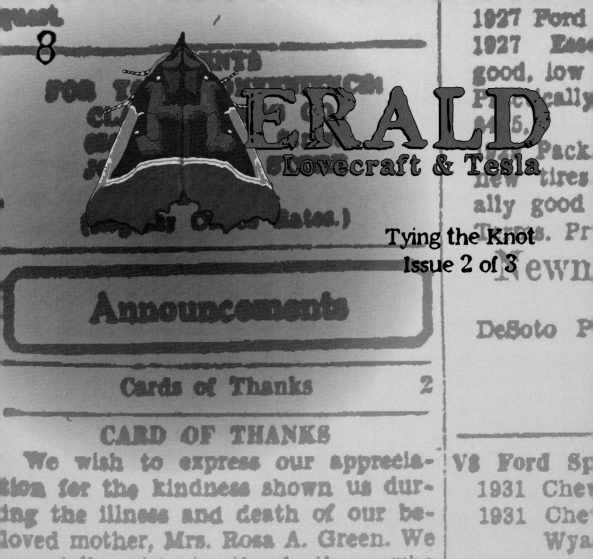

HERALD
Lovecraft & Tesla

Tying the Knot
Issue 2 of 3

Written by **John Reilly** Pencils by **Tom Rogers** Color, Letters by **Dexter Weeks**

Action Lab Comics
Publisher - Bryan Seaton President - Dave Dwonch
Editor-in-Chief - Shawn Gabborin Publisher-Danger Zone - Jason Martin
Vice-President of Marketing - Jamal Igle Social Media Director - Jim Dietz
Editor - Nicole D'Andria Best Man - Chad Cicconi

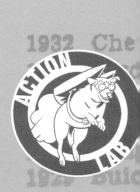

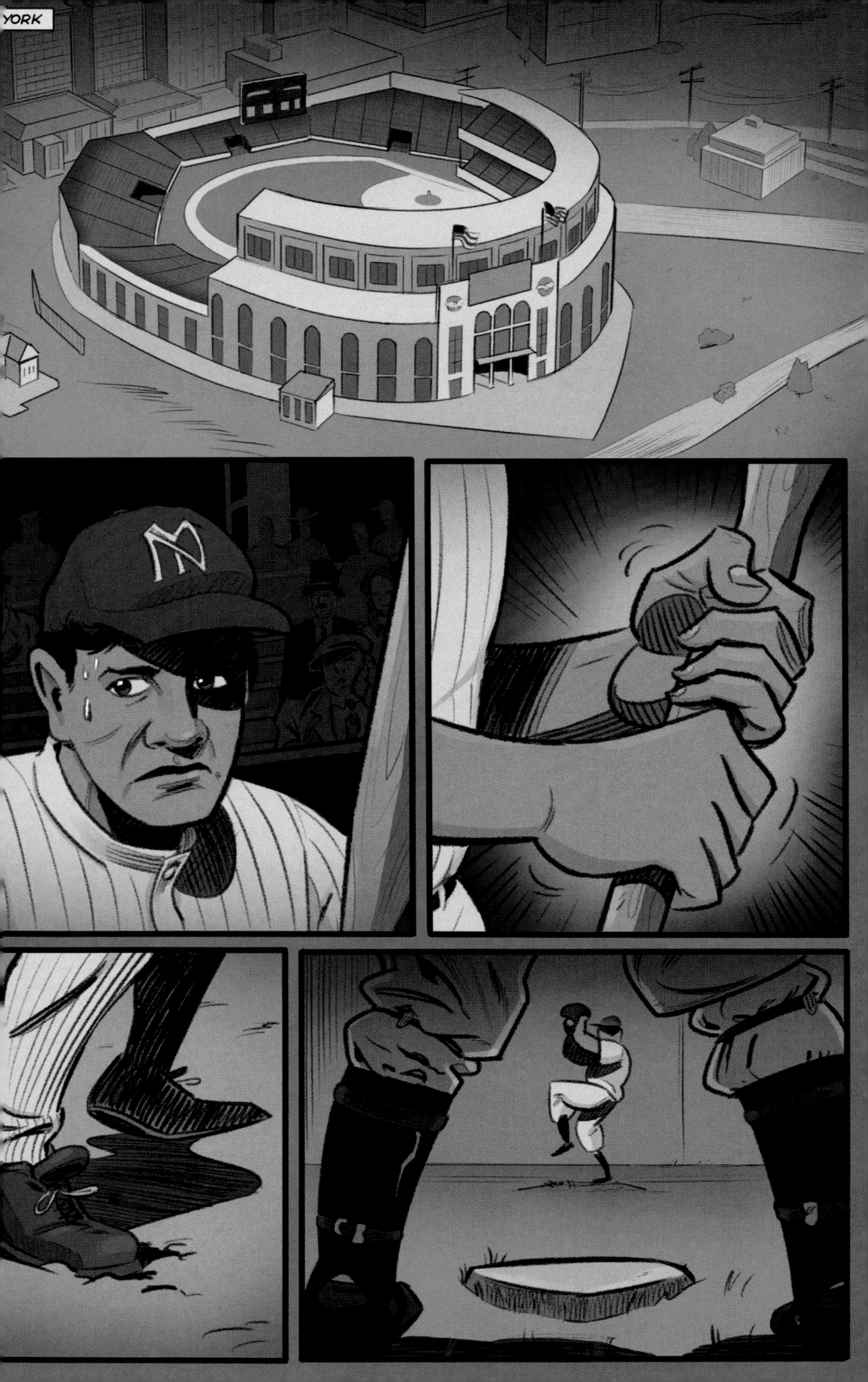
YORK

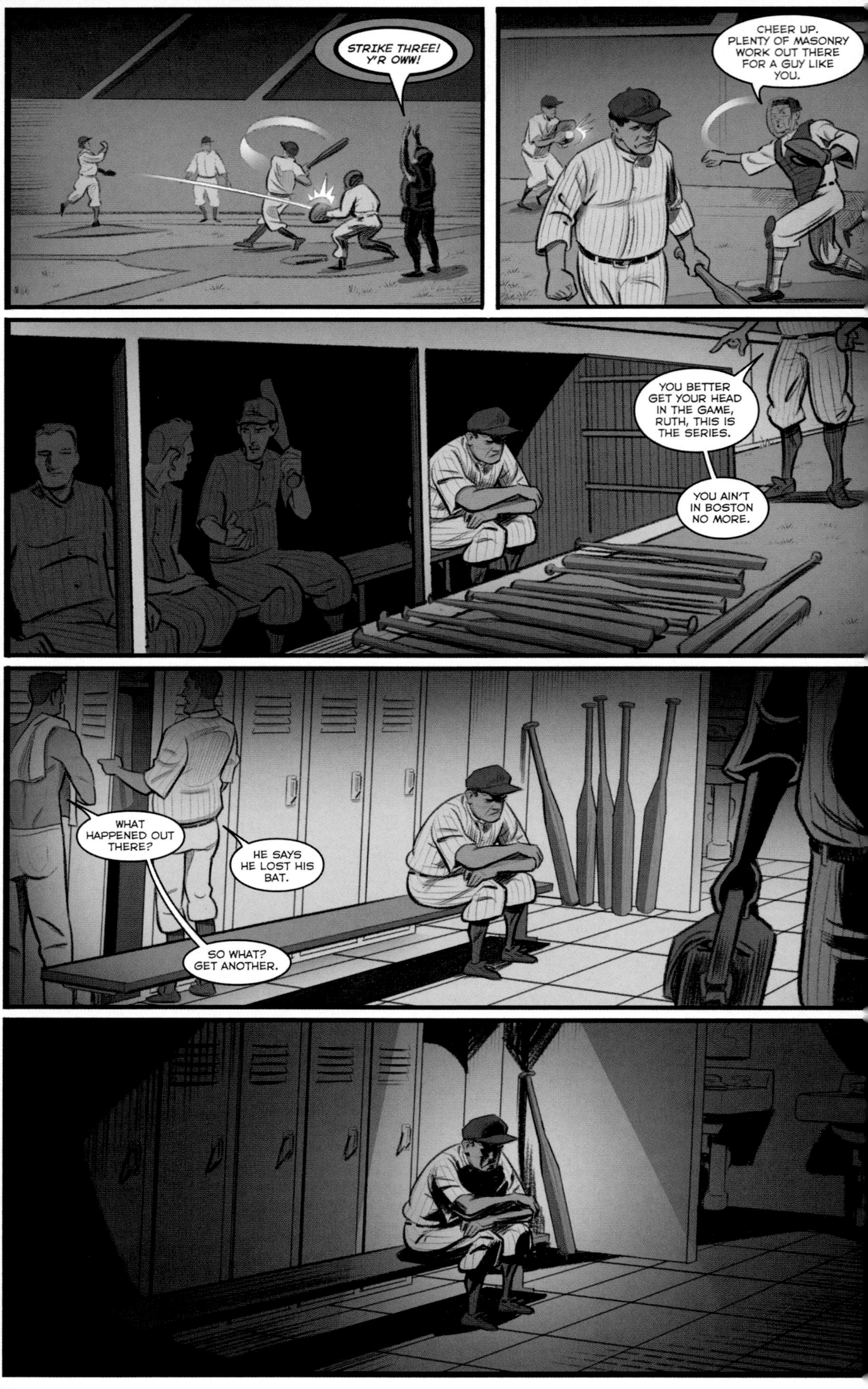
STRIKE THREE! Y'R OWW!
CHEER UP. PLENTY OF MASONRY WORK OUT THERE FOR A GUY LIKE YOU.
YOU BETTER GET YOUR HEAD IN THE GAME, RUTH, THIS IS THE SERIES.
YOU AIN'T IN BOSTON NO MORE.
WHAT HAPPENED OUT THERE?
HE SAYS HE LOST HIS BAT.
SO WHAT? GET ANOTHER.

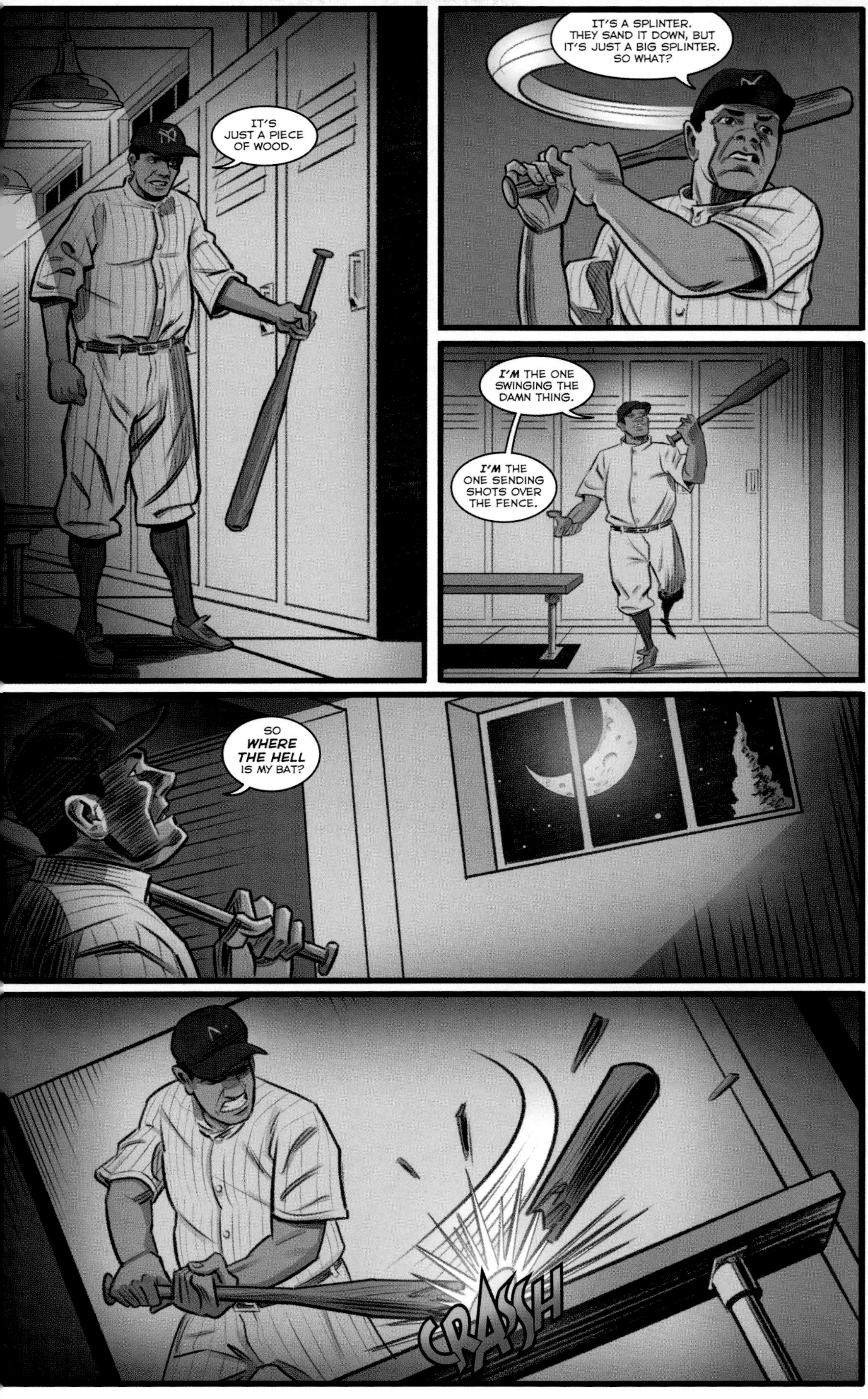
IT'S JUST A PIECE OF WOOD.
IT'S A SPLINTER. THEY SAND IT DOWN, BUT IT'S JUST A BIG SPLINTER. SO WHAT?
I'M THE ONE SWINGING THE DAMN THING.
I'M THE ONE SENDING SHOTS OVER THE FENCE.
SO WHERE THE HELL IS MY BAT?
CRASH

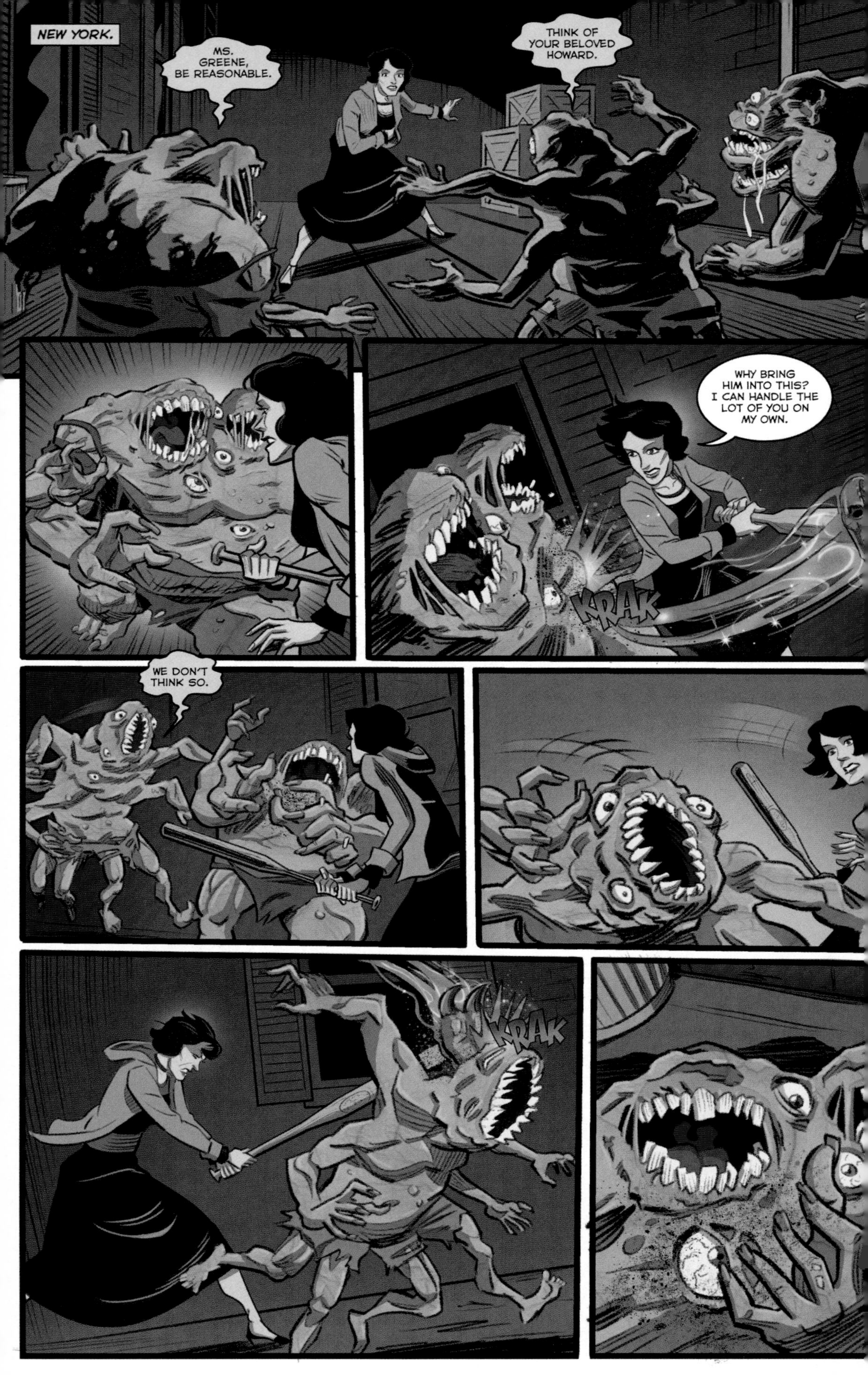
NEW YORK.
MS. GREENE, BE REASONABLE.
THINK OF YOUR BELOVED HOWARD.
WHY BRING HIM INTO THIS? I CAN HANDLE THE LOT OF YOU ON MY OWN.
KRAK
WE DON'T THINK SO.
KRAK

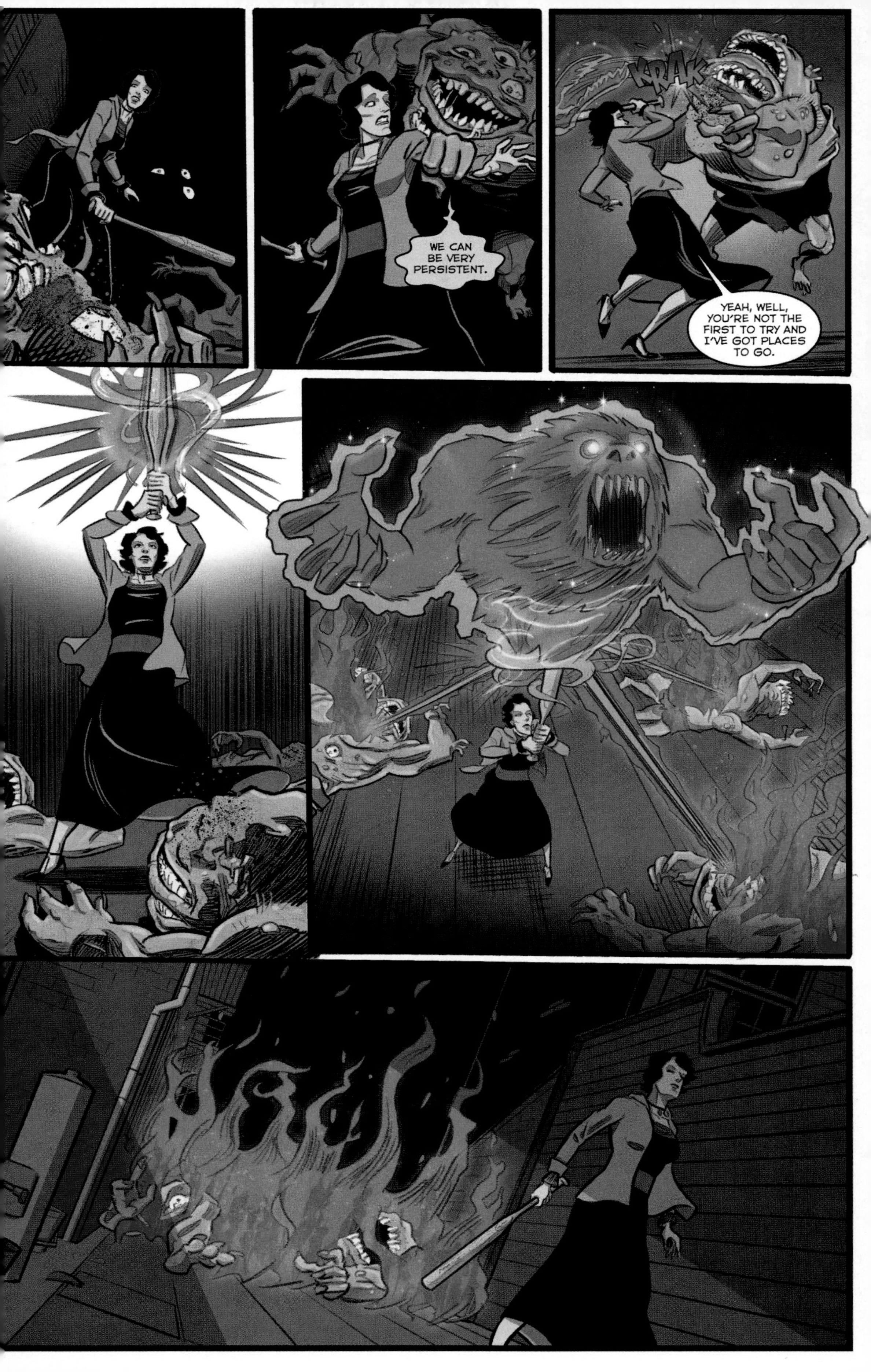
WE CAN BE VERY PERSISTENT.
KRAK
YEAH, WELL, YOU'RE NOT THE FIRST TO TRY AND I'VE GOT PLACES TO GO.

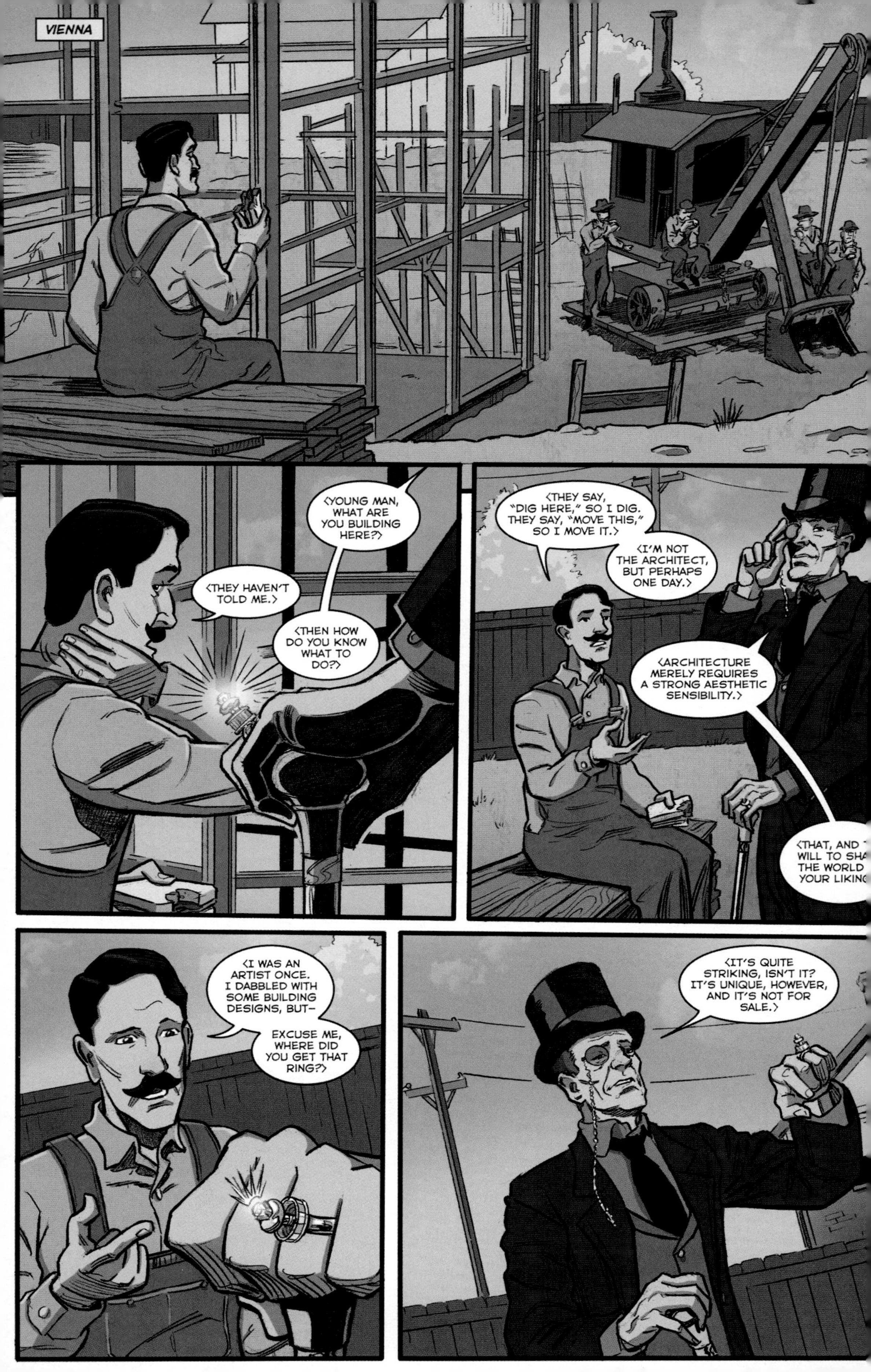
VIENNA
<YOUNG MAN, WHAT ARE YOU BUILDING HERE?>
<THEY HAVEN'T TOLD ME.>
<THEN HOW DO YOU KNOW WHAT TO DO?>
<THEY SAY, "DIG HERE," SO I DIG. THEY SAY, "MOVE THIS," SO I MOVE IT.>
<I'M NOT THE ARCHITECT, BUT PERHAPS ONE DAY.>
<ARCHITECTURE MERELY REQUIRES A STRONG AESTHETIC SENSIBILITY.>
<THAT, AND THE WILL TO SHA THE WORLD YOUR LIKING
<I WAS AN ARTIST ONCE. I DABBLED WITH SOME BUILDING DESIGNS, BUT–
EXCUSE ME, WHERE DID YOU GET THAT RING?>
<IT'S QUITE STRIKING, ISN'T IT? IT'S UNIQUE, HOWEVER, AND IT'S NOT FOR SALE.>

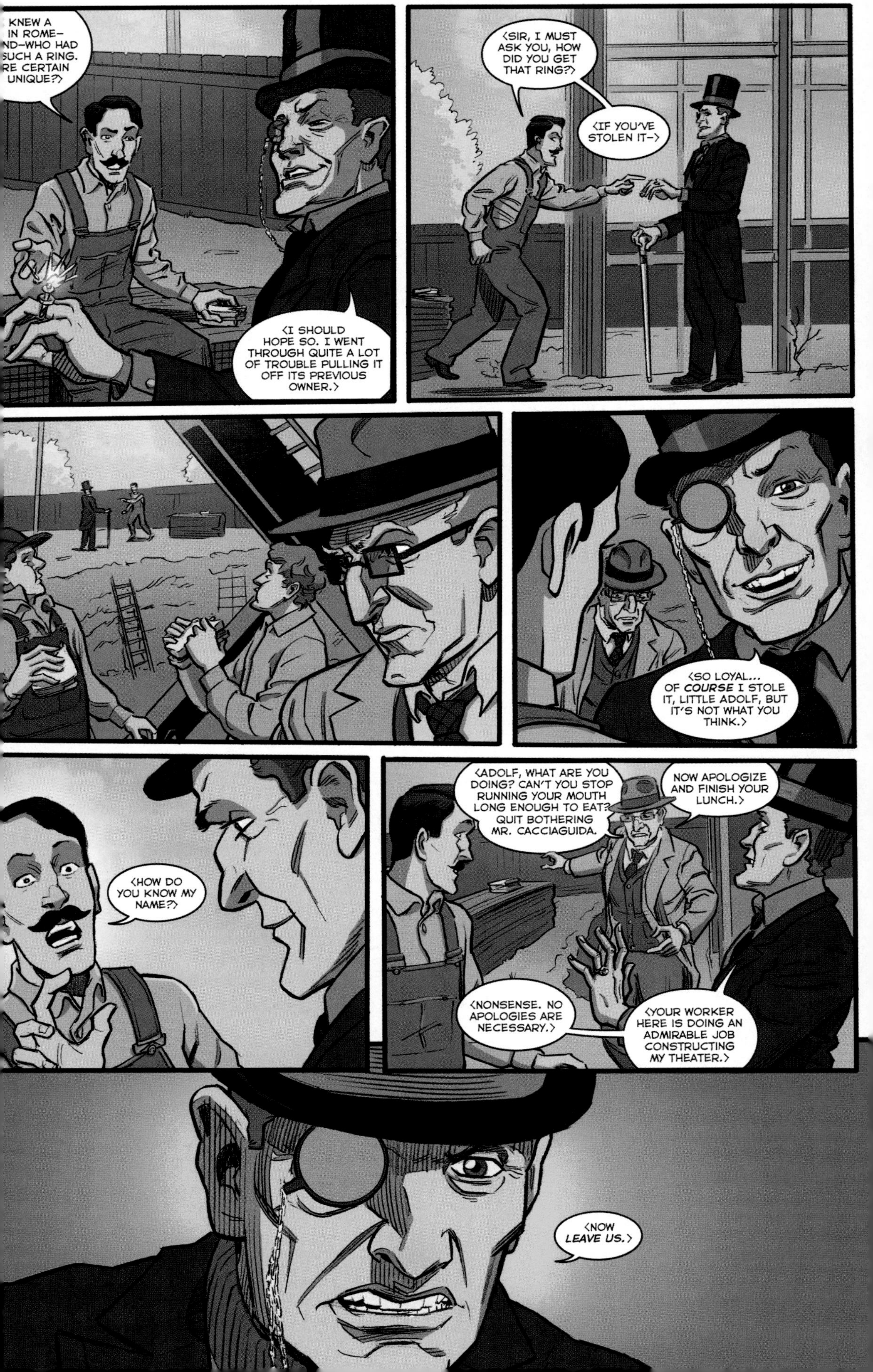

KNEW A IN ROME—ND—WHO HAD SUCH A RING. RE CERTAIN UNIQUE?>
<I SHOULD HOPE SO. I WENT THROUGH QUITE A LOT OF TROUBLE PULLING IT OFF ITS PREVIOUS OWNER.>
<SIR, I MUST ASK YOU, HOW DID YOU GET THAT RING?>
<IF YOU'VE STOLEN IT—>
<SO LOYAL... OF COURSE I STOLE IT, LITTLE ADOLF, BUT IT'S NOT WHAT YOU THINK.>
<HOW DO YOU KNOW MY NAME?>
<ADOLF, WHAT ARE YOU DOING? CAN'T YOU STOP RUNNING YOUR MOUTH LONG ENOUGH TO EAT? QUIT BOTHERING MR. CACCIAGUIDA.
NOW APOLOGIZE AND FINISH YOUR LUNCH.>
<NONSENSE. NO APOLOGIES ARE NECESSARY.
YOUR WORKER HERE IS DOING AN ADMIRABLE JOB CONSTRUCTING MY THEATER.>
<NOW LEAVE US.>

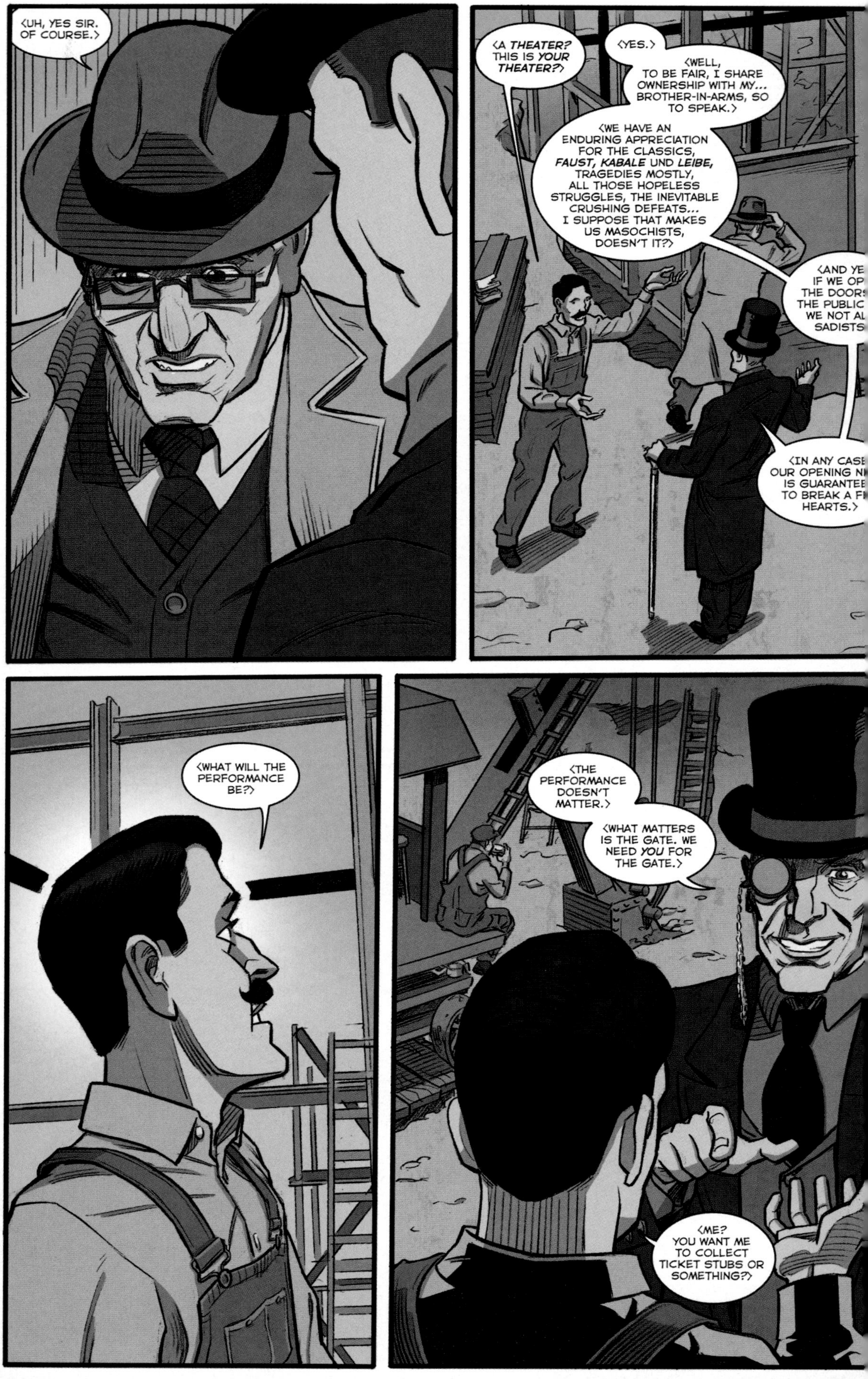

<UH, YES SIR. OF COURSE.>
<A *THEATER?* THIS IS *YOUR THEATER?*>
<YES.>
<WELL, TO BE FAIR, I SHARE OWNERSHIP WITH MY... BROTHER-IN-ARMS, SO TO SPEAK.>
<WE HAVE AN ENDURING APPRECIATION FOR THE CLASSICS, *FAUST, KABALE* UND *LEIBE,* TRAGEDIES MOSTLY, ALL THOSE HOPELESS STRUGGLES, THE INEVITABLE CRUSHING DEFEATS... I SUPPOSE THAT MAKES US MASOCHISTS, DOESN'T IT?>
<AND YE IF WE OP THE DOORS THE PUBLIC WE NOT AL SADISTS
<IN ANY CASE OUR OPENING N IS GUARANTEE TO BREAK A F HEARTS.>
<WHAT WILL THE PERFORMANCE BE?>
<THE PERFORMANCE DOESN'T MATTER.>
<WHAT MATTERS IS THE GATE. WE NEED *YOU* FOR THE GATE.>
<ME? YOU WANT ME TO COLLECT TICKET STUBS OR SOMETHING?>

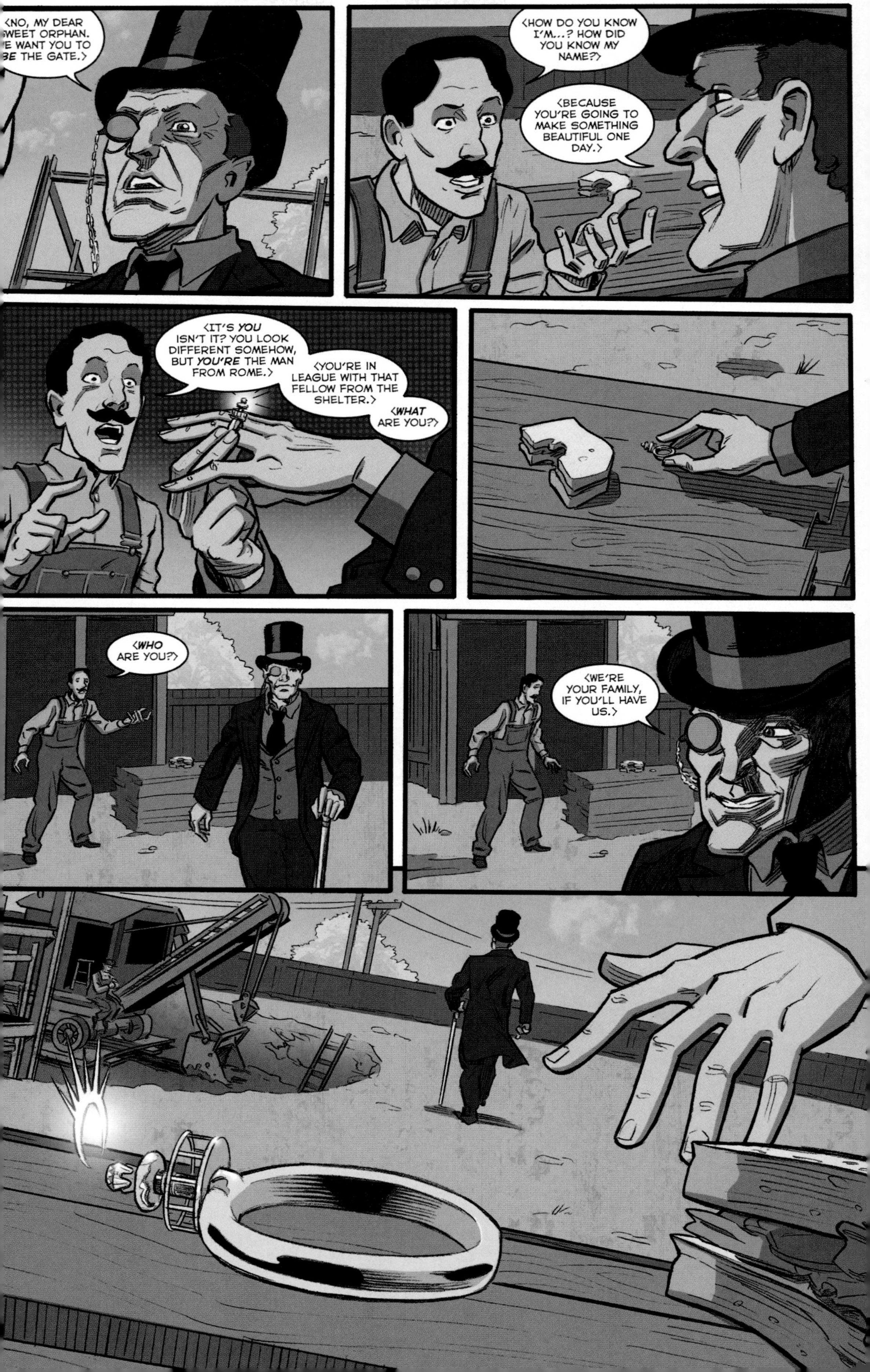

<NO, MY DEAR SWEET ORPHAN. WE WANT YOU TO BE THE GATE.>
<HOW DO YOU KNOW I'M...? HOW DID YOU KNOW MY NAME?>
<BECAUSE YOU'RE GOING TO MAKE SOMETHING BEAUTIFUL ONE DAY.>
<IT'S YOU ISN'T IT? YOU LOOK DIFFERENT SOMEHOW, BUT YOU'RE THE MAN FROM ROME.>
<YOU'RE IN LEAGUE WITH THAT FELLOW FROM THE SHELTER.>
<WHAT ARE YOU?>
<WHO ARE YOU?>
<WE'RE YOUR FAMILY, IF YOU'LL HAVE US.>

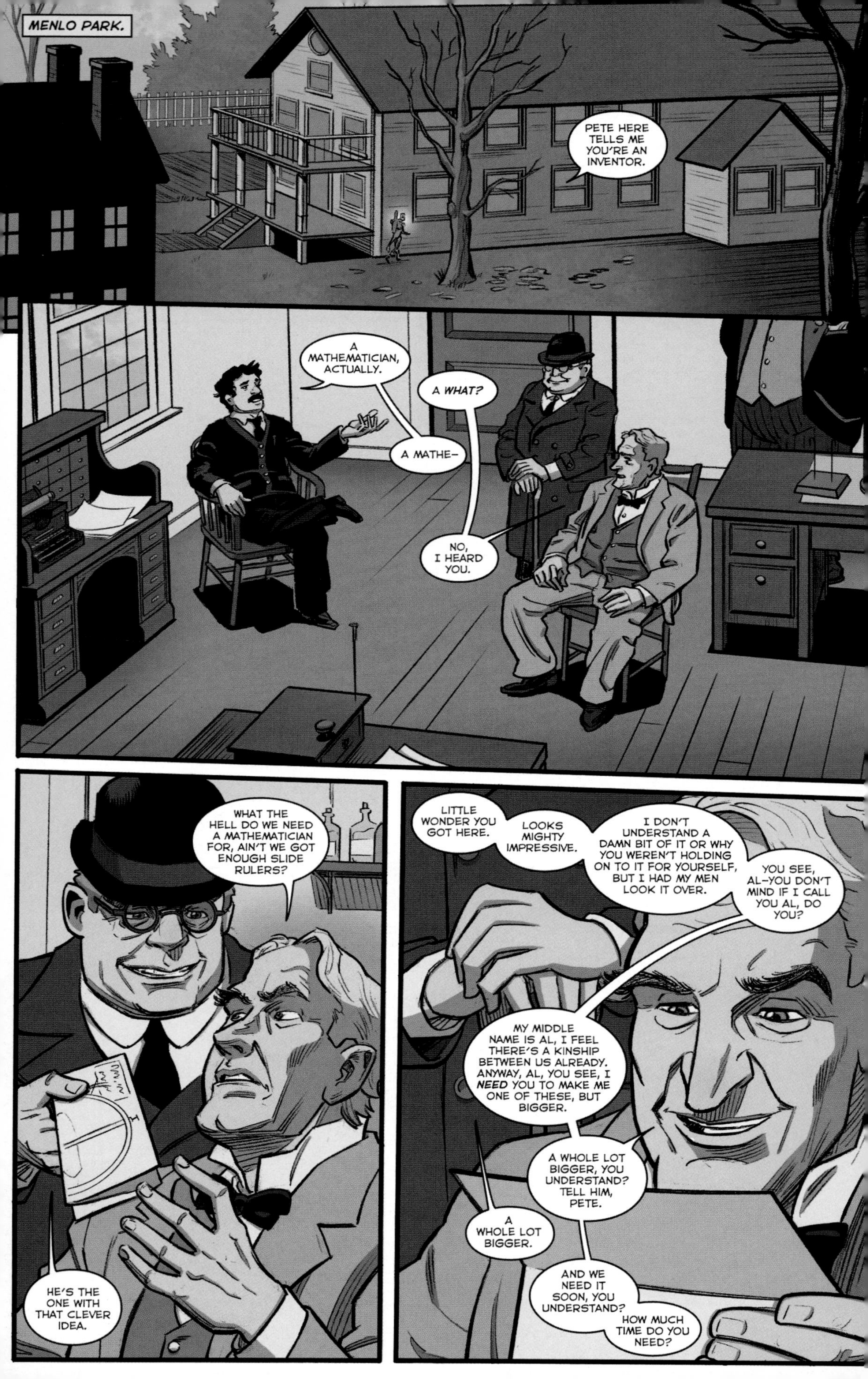
MENLO PARK.
PETE HERE TELLS ME YOU'RE AN INVENTOR.
A MATHEMATICIAN, ACTUALLY.
A WHAT?
A MATHE–
NO, I HEARD YOU.
WHAT THE HELL DO WE NEED A MATHEMATICIAN FOR, AIN'T WE GOT ENOUGH SLIDE RULERS?
HE'S THE ONE WITH THAT CLEVER IDEA.
LITTLE WONDER YOU GOT HERE.
LOOKS MIGHTY IMPRESSIVE.
I DON'T UNDERSTAND A DAMN BIT OF IT OR WHY YOU WEREN'T HOLDING ON TO IT FOR YOURSELF, BUT I HAD MY MEN LOOK IT OVER.
YOU SEE, AL–YOU DON'T MIND IF I CALL YOU AL, DO YOU?
MY MIDDLE NAME IS AL, I FEEL THERE'S A KINSHIP BETWEEN US ALREADY. ANYWAY, AL, YOU SEE, I NEED YOU TO MAKE ME ONE OF THESE, BUT BIGGER.
A WHOLE LOT BIGGER, YOU UNDERSTAND? TELL HIM, PETE.
A WHOLE LOT BIGGER.
AND WE NEED IT SOON, YOU UNDERSTAND?
HOW MUCH TIME DO YOU NEED?

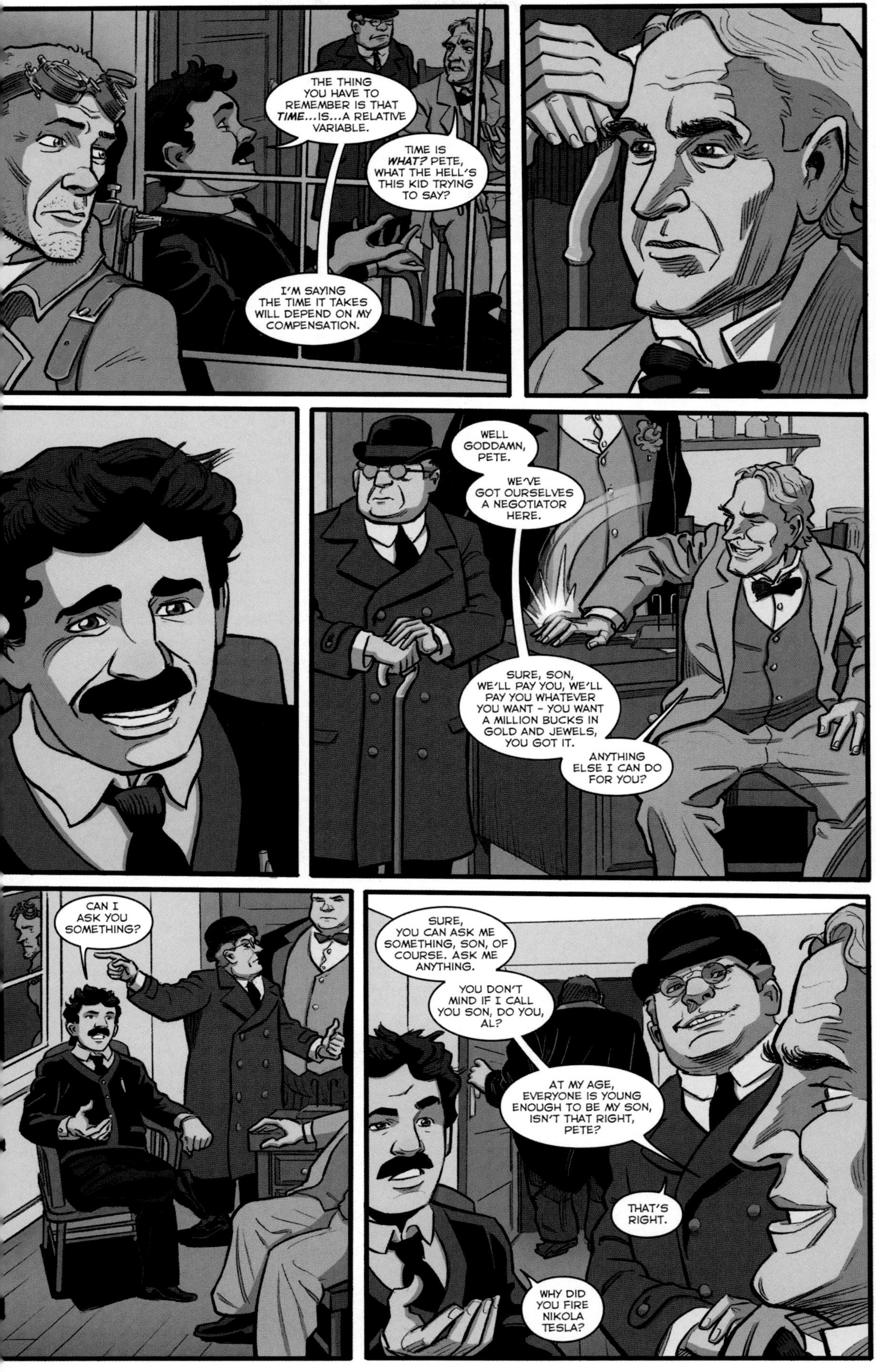
THE THING YOU HAVE TO REMEMBER IS THAT *TIME...*IS...A RELATIVE VARIABLE.
TIME IS *WHAT?* PETE, WHAT THE HELL'S THIS KID TRYING TO SAY?
I'M SAYING THE TIME IT TAKES WILL DEPEND ON MY COMPENSATION.
WELL GODDAMN, PETE.
WE'VE GOT OURSELVES A NEGOTIATOR HERE.
SURE, SON, WE'LL PAY YOU, WE'LL PAY YOU WHATEVER YOU WANT - YOU WANT A MILLION BUCKS IN GOLD AND JEWELS, YOU GOT IT.
ANYTHING ELSE I CAN DO FOR YOU?
CAN I ASK YOU SOMETHING?
SURE, YOU CAN ASK ME SOMETHING, SON, OF COURSE. ASK ME ANYTHING.
YOU DON'T MIND IF I CALL YOU SON, DO YOU, AL?
AT MY AGE, EVERYONE IS YOUNG ENOUGH TO BE MY SON, ISN'T THAT RIGHT, PETE?
THAT'S RIGHT.
WHY DID YOU FIRE NIKOLA TESLA?

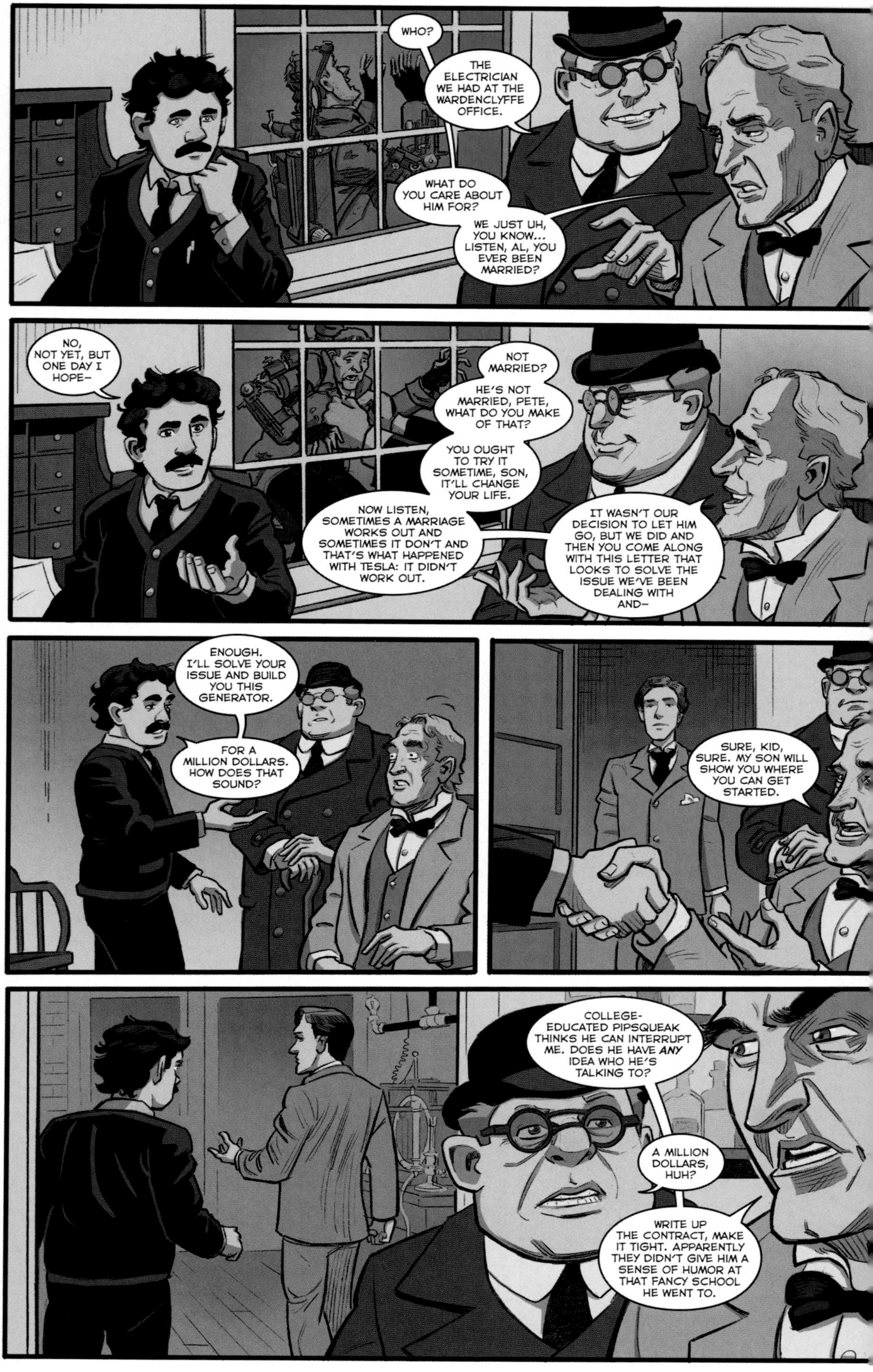
WHO?
THE ELECTRICIAN WE HAD AT THE WARDENCLYFFE OFFICE.
WHAT DO YOU CARE ABOUT HIM FOR?
WE JUST UH, YOU KNOW... LISTEN, AL, YOU EVER BEEN MARRIED?
NO, NOT YET, BUT ONE DAY I HOPE–
NOT MARRIED?
HE'S NOT MARRIED, PETE, WHAT DO YOU MAKE OF THAT?
YOU OUGHT TO TRY IT SOMETIME, SON, IT'LL CHANGE YOUR LIFE.
NOW LISTEN, SOMETIMES A MARRIAGE WORKS OUT AND SOMETIMES IT DON'T AND THAT'S WHAT HAPPENED WITH TESLA: IT DIDN'T WORK OUT.
IT WASN'T OUR DECISION TO LET HIM GO, BUT WE DID AND THEN YOU COME ALONG WITH THIS LETTER THAT LOOKS TO SOLVE THE ISSUE WE'VE BEEN DEALING WITH AND–
ENOUGH. I'LL SOLVE YOUR ISSUE AND BUILD YOU THIS GENERATOR.
FOR A MILLION DOLLARS. HOW DOES THAT SOUND?
SURE, KID, SURE. MY SON WILL SHOW YOU WHERE YOU CAN GET STARTED.
COLLEGE-EDUCATED PIPSQUEAK THINKS HE CAN INTERRUPT ME. DOES HE HAVE *ANY* IDEA WHO HE'S TALKING TO?
A MILLION DOLLARS, HUH?
WRITE UP THE CONTRACT, MAKE IT TIGHT. APPARENTLY THEY DIDN'T GIVE HIM A SENSE OF HUMOR AT THAT FANCY SCHOOL HE WENT TO.

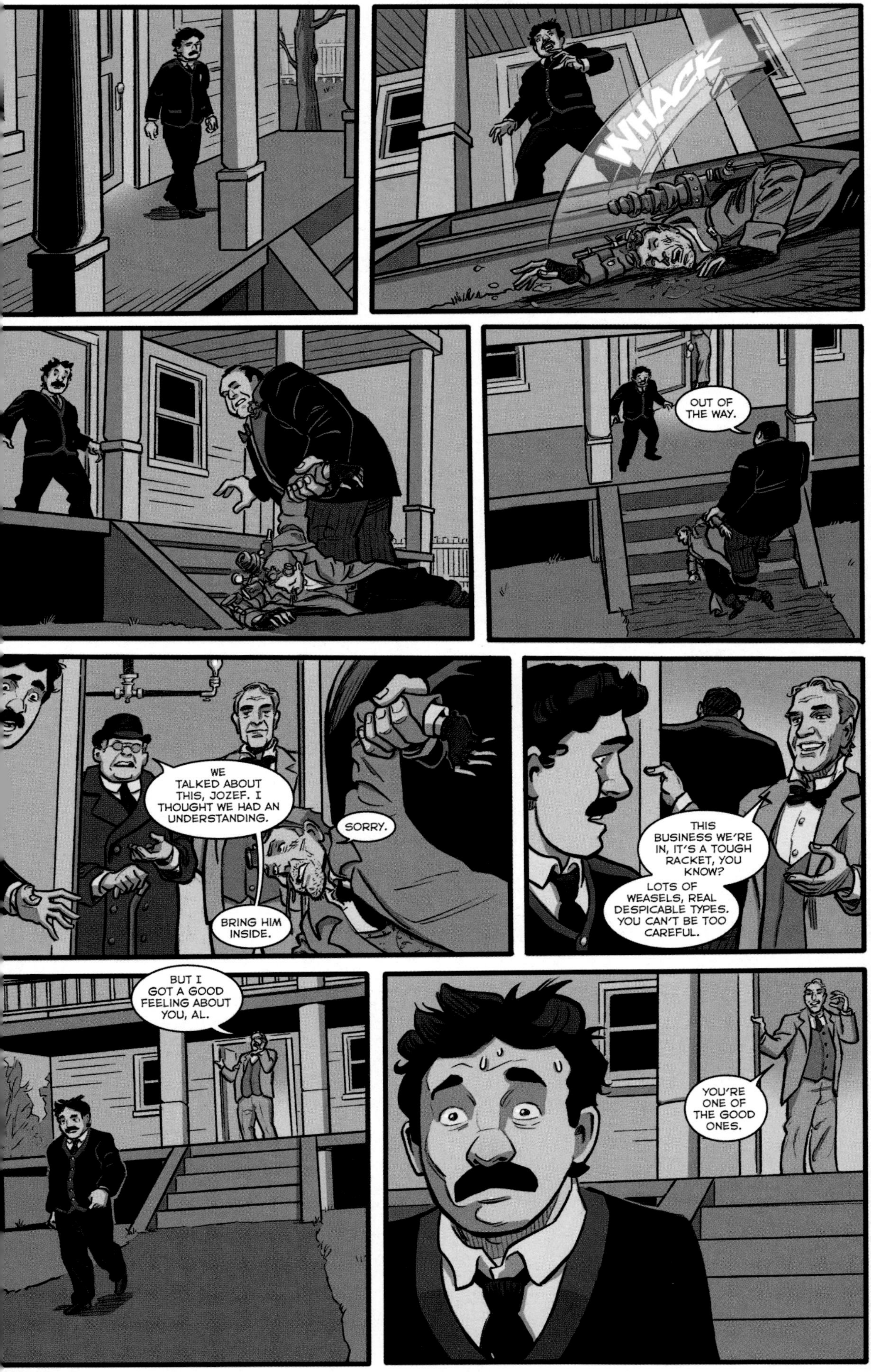
WHACK
OUT OF THE WAY.
WE TALKED ABOUT THIS, JOZEF. I THOUGHT WE HAD AN UNDERSTANDING.
SORRY.
BRING HIM INSIDE.
THIS BUSINESS WE'RE IN, IT'S A TOUGH RACKET, YOU KNOW?
LOTS OF WEASELS, REAL DESPICABLE TYPES. YOU CAN'T BE TOO CAREFUL.
BUT I GOT A GOOD FEELING ABOUT YOU, AL.
YOU'RE ONE OF THE GOOD ONES.

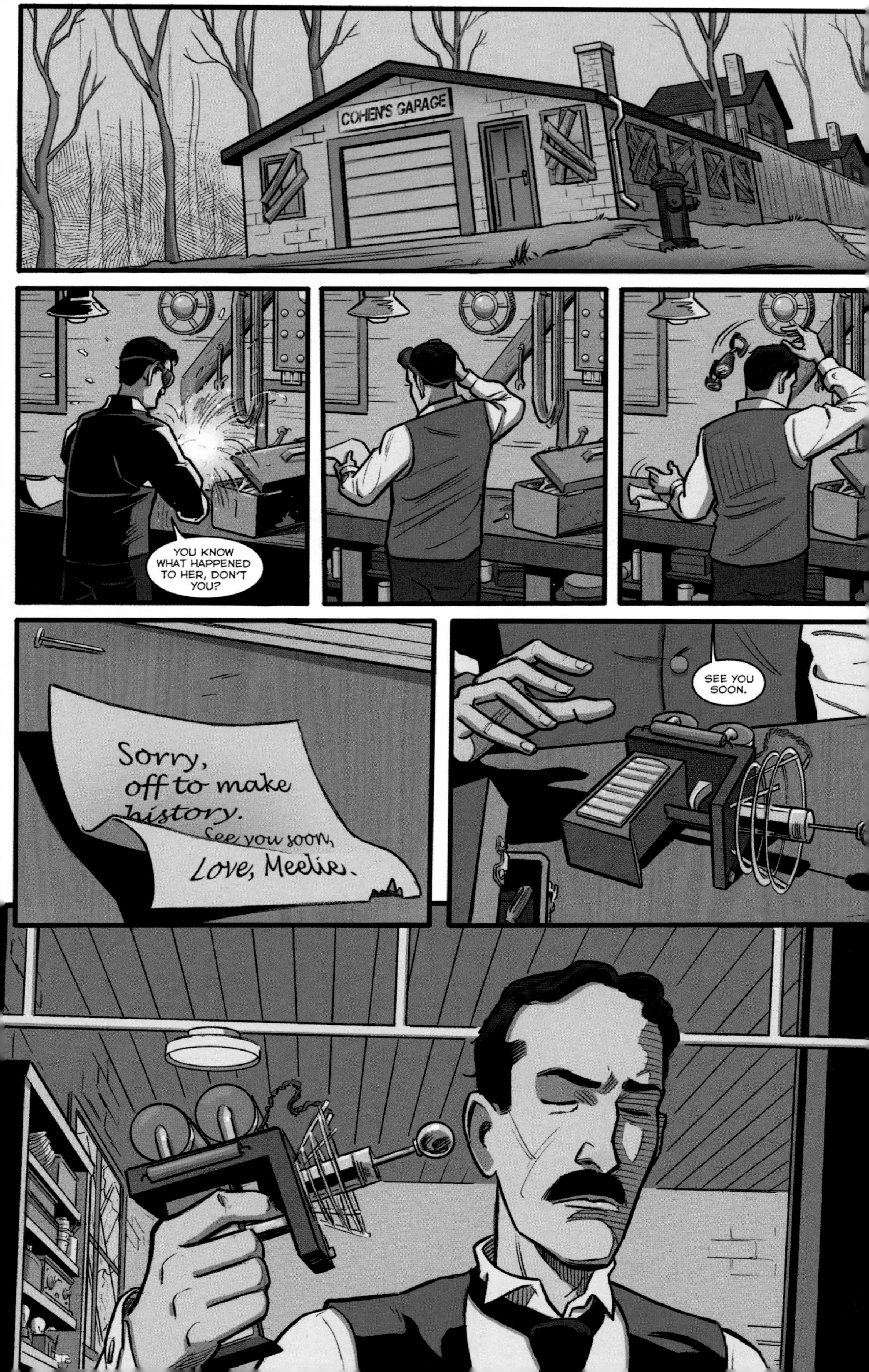
COHEN'S GARAGE
YOU KNOW WHAT HAPPENED TO HER, DON'T YOU?
Sorry, off to make history. See you soon, Love, Meelie.
SEE YOU SOON.

NIK, THERE YOU ARE! EXCELLENT.

SAM? WHAT'S GOING ON?

I WANTED TO SEE HOW YOU WERE DOING, BUT IT SEEMS YOU'VE MADE THE RIGHT CHOICE.

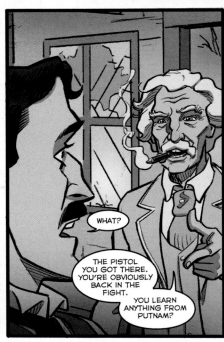

WHAT?

THE PISTOL YOU GOT THERE. YOU'RE OBVIOUSLY BACK IN THE FIGHT. YOU LEARN ANYTHING FROM PUTNAM?

YEAH.

I MEAN, NO. NO. IT WAS A WASTE OF TIME.

DOESN'T MATTER. WHILE YOU WERE OUT RUINING THE RESALE VALUE OF MY AUTOMOBILE, I HAD A TALK WITH MR. LOVECRAFT. TURNS OUT, WE MIGHT BE ABLE TO CONTACT AMELIA.

WHAT? HOW?

DREAMS, NIK. DREAMS.

I DON'T FOLLOW.

LOVECRAFT IS UNDER THE BIZARRE IMPRESSION THAT THERE IS A WORLD OF DREAMS WHERE A PERSON ALWAYS EXISTS, BETTER OR WORSE, RICHER OR POORER.

HE SAYS YOU'VE GOT TO BUILD SOMETHING, BUT YOU COULD SPEAK WITH HER, NIK!

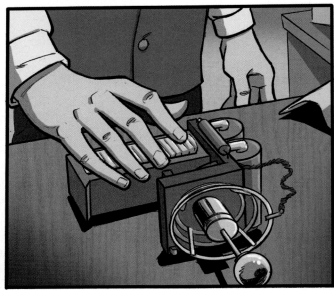

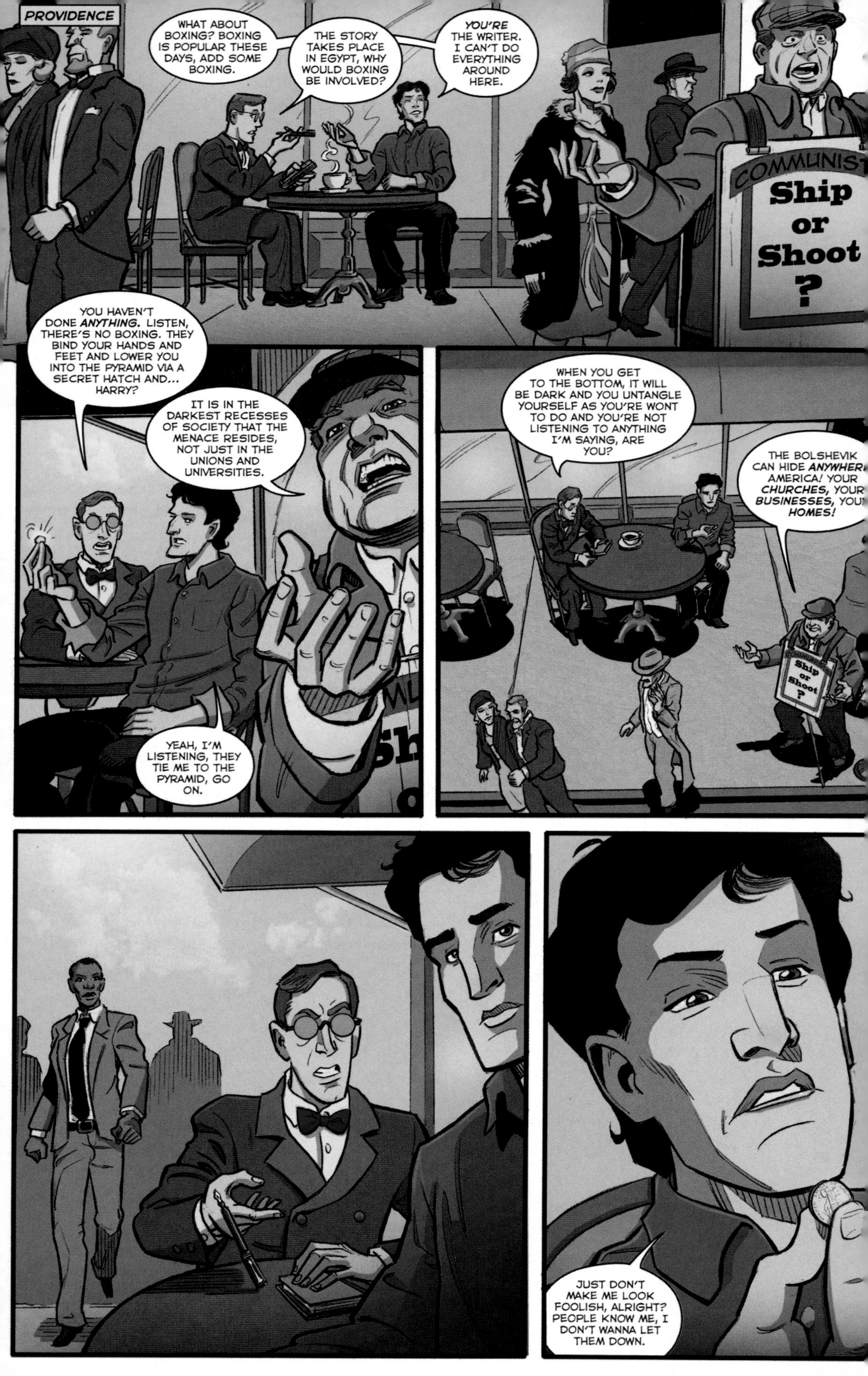

PROVIDENCE
WHAT ABOUT BOXING? BOXING IS POPULAR THESE DAYS, ADD SOME BOXING.
THE STORY TAKES PLACE IN EGYPT, WHY WOULD BOXING BE INVOLVED?
YOU'RE THE WRITER. I CAN'T DO EVERYTHING AROUND HERE.
COMMUNIST
Ship or Shoot ?
YOU HAVEN'T DONE ANYTHING. LISTEN, THERE'S NO BOXING. THEY BIND YOUR HANDS AND FEET AND LOWER YOU INTO THE PYRAMID VIA A SECRET HATCH AND... HARRY?
IT IS IN THE DARKEST RECESSES OF SOCIETY THAT THE MENACE RESIDES, NOT JUST IN THE UNIONS AND UNIVERSITIES.
YEAH, I'M LISTENING, THEY TIE ME TO THE PYRAMID, GO ON.
WHEN YOU GET TO THE BOTTOM, IT WILL BE DARK AND YOU UNTANGLE YOURSELF AS YOU'RE WONT TO DO AND YOU'RE NOT LISTENING TO ANYTHING I'M SAYING, ARE YOU?
THE BOLSHEVIK CAN HIDE ANYWHERE AMERICA! YOUR CHURCHES, YOUR BUSINESSES, YOUR HOMES!
JUST DON'T MAKE ME LOOK FOOLISH, ALRIGHT? PEOPLE KNOW ME, I DON'T WANNA LET THEM DOWN.

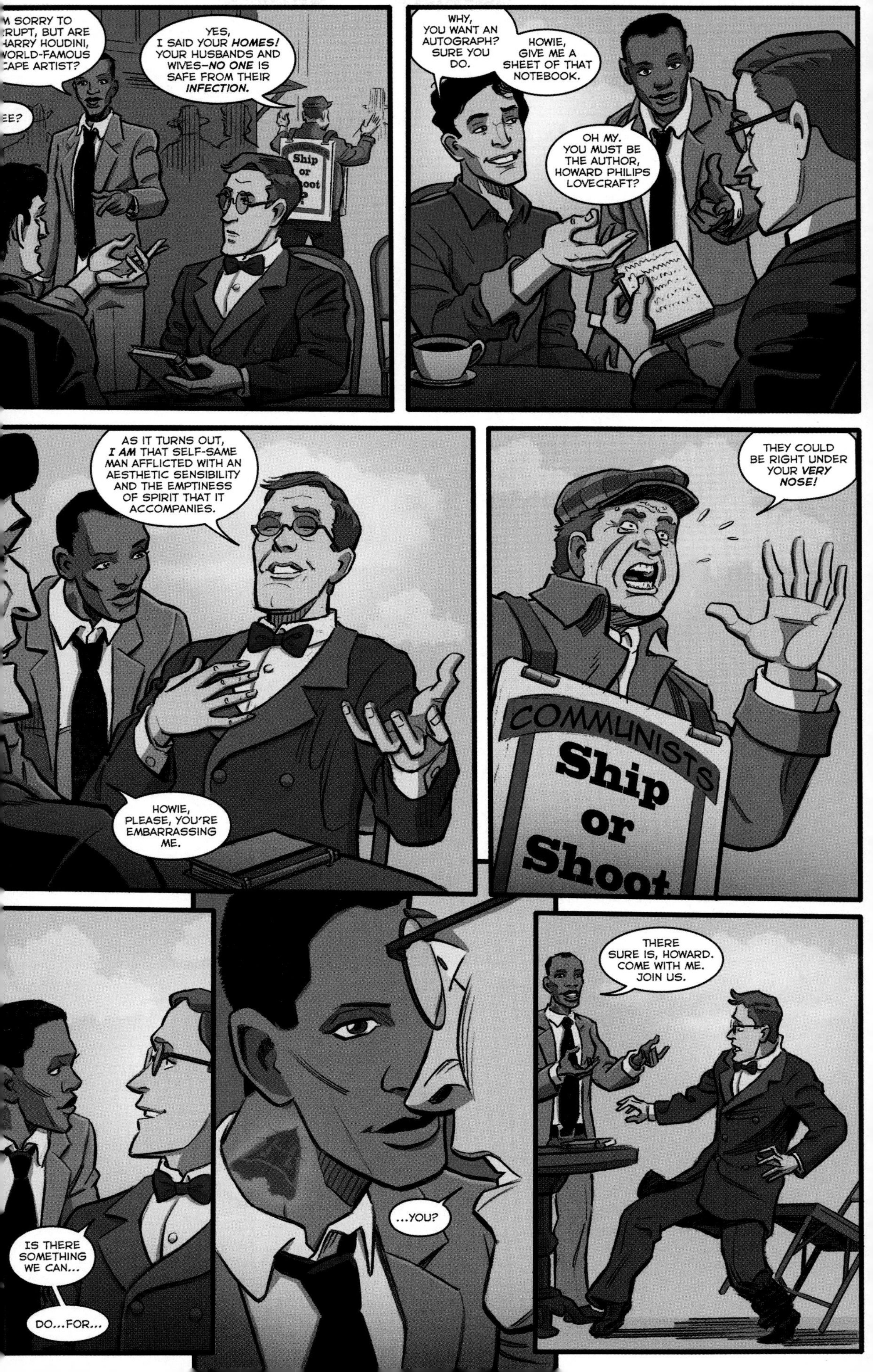
'M SORRY TO
'RUPT, BUT ARE
HARRY HOUDINI,
WORLD-FAMOUS
CAPE ARTIST?
YES, I SAID YOUR HOMES! YOUR HUSBANDS AND WIVES–NO ONE IS SAFE FROM THEIR INFECTION.
EE?
COMMUNISTS
Ship
or
WHY, YOU WANT AN AUTOGRAPH? SURE YOU DO.
HOWIE, GIVE ME A SHEET OF THAT NOTEBOOK.
OH MY. YOU MUST BE THE AUTHOR, HOWARD PHILIPS LOVECRAFT?
AS IT TURNS OUT, I AM THAT SELF-SAME MAN AFFLICTED WITH AN AESTHETIC SENSIBILITY AND THE EMPTINESS OF SPIRIT THAT IT ACCOMPANIES.
HOWIE, PLEASE, YOU'RE EMBARRASSING ME.
THEY COULD BE RIGHT UNDER YOUR VERY NOSE!
COMMUNISTS
Ship
or
Shoot
IS THERE SOMETHING WE CAN...
DO...FOR...
...YOU?
THERE SURE IS, HOWARD. COME WITH ME. JOIN US.

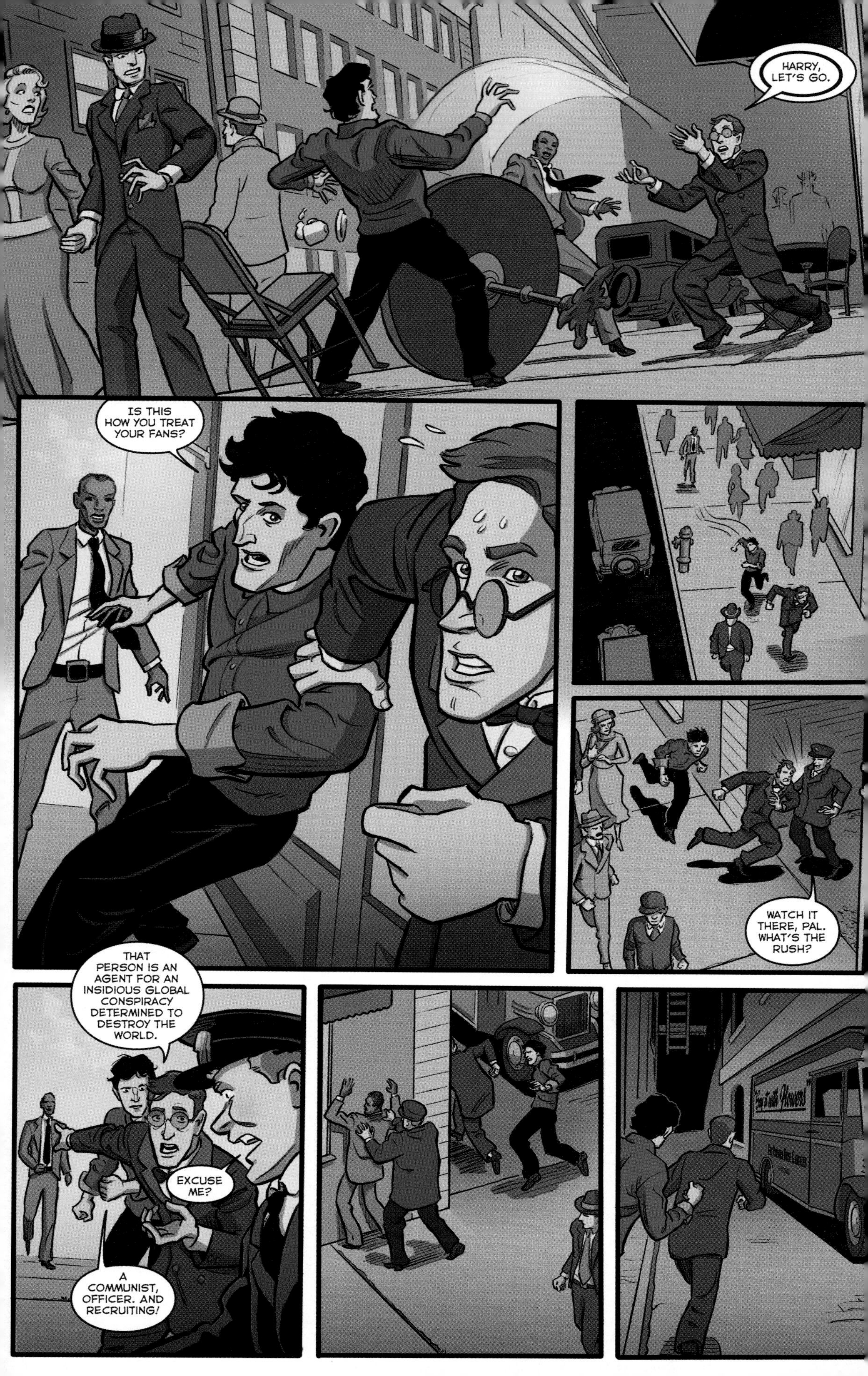
HARRY, LET'S GO.
IS THIS HOW YOU TREAT YOUR FANS?
WATCH IT THERE, PAL. WHAT'S THE RUSH?
THAT PERSON IS AN AGENT FOR AN INSIDIOUS GLOBAL CONSPIRACY DETERMINED TO DESTROY THE WORLD.
EXCUSE ME?
A COMMUNIST, OFFICER. AND RECRUITING!

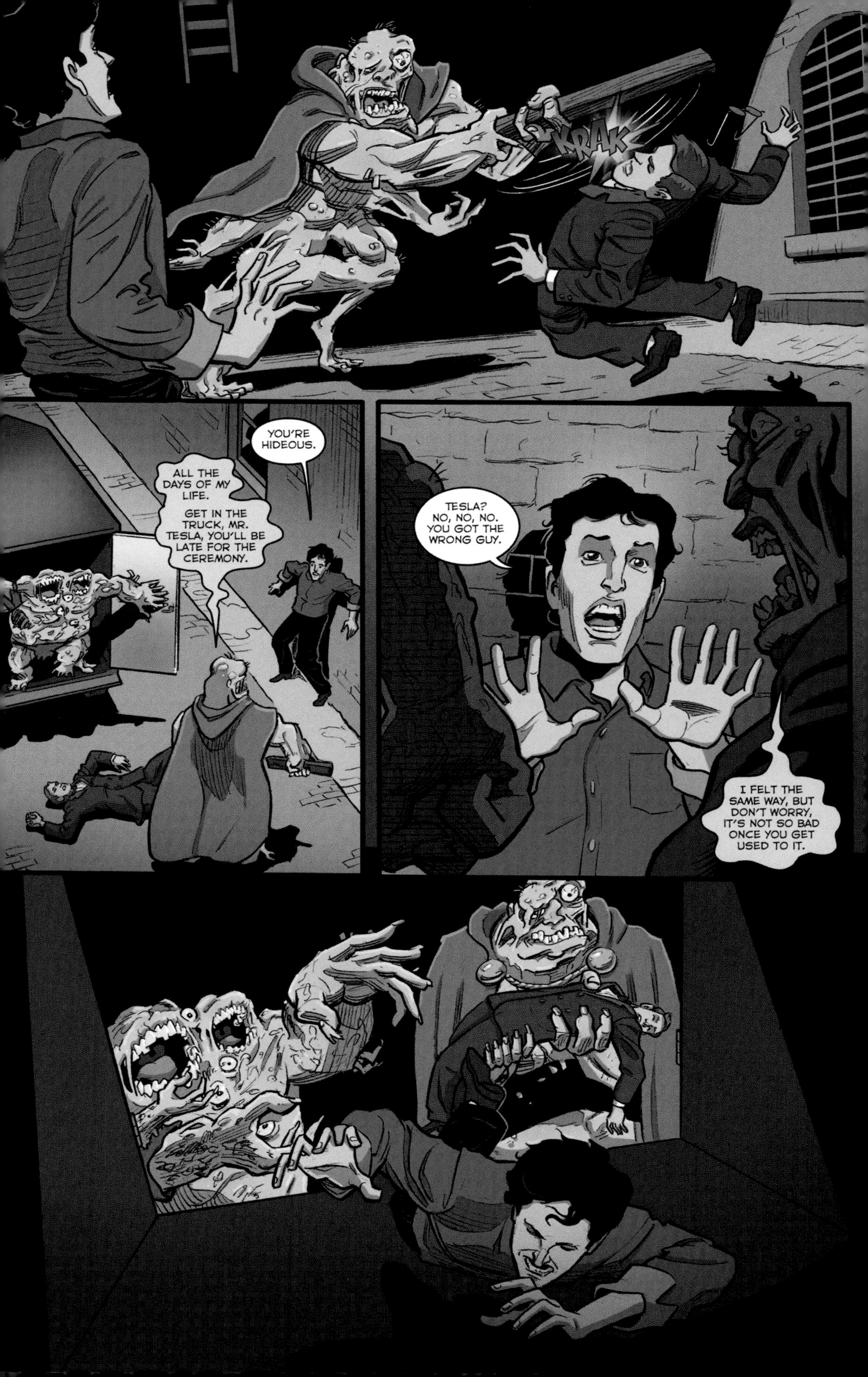
KRAK
ALL THE DAYS OF MY LIFE.
GET IN THE TRUCK, MR. TESLA, YOU'LL BE LATE FOR THE CEREMONY.
YOU'RE HIDEOUS.
TESLA? NO, NO, NO. YOU GOT THE WRONG GUY.
I FELT THE SAME WAY, BUT DON'T WORRY, IT'S NOT SO BAD ONCE YOU GET USED TO IT.

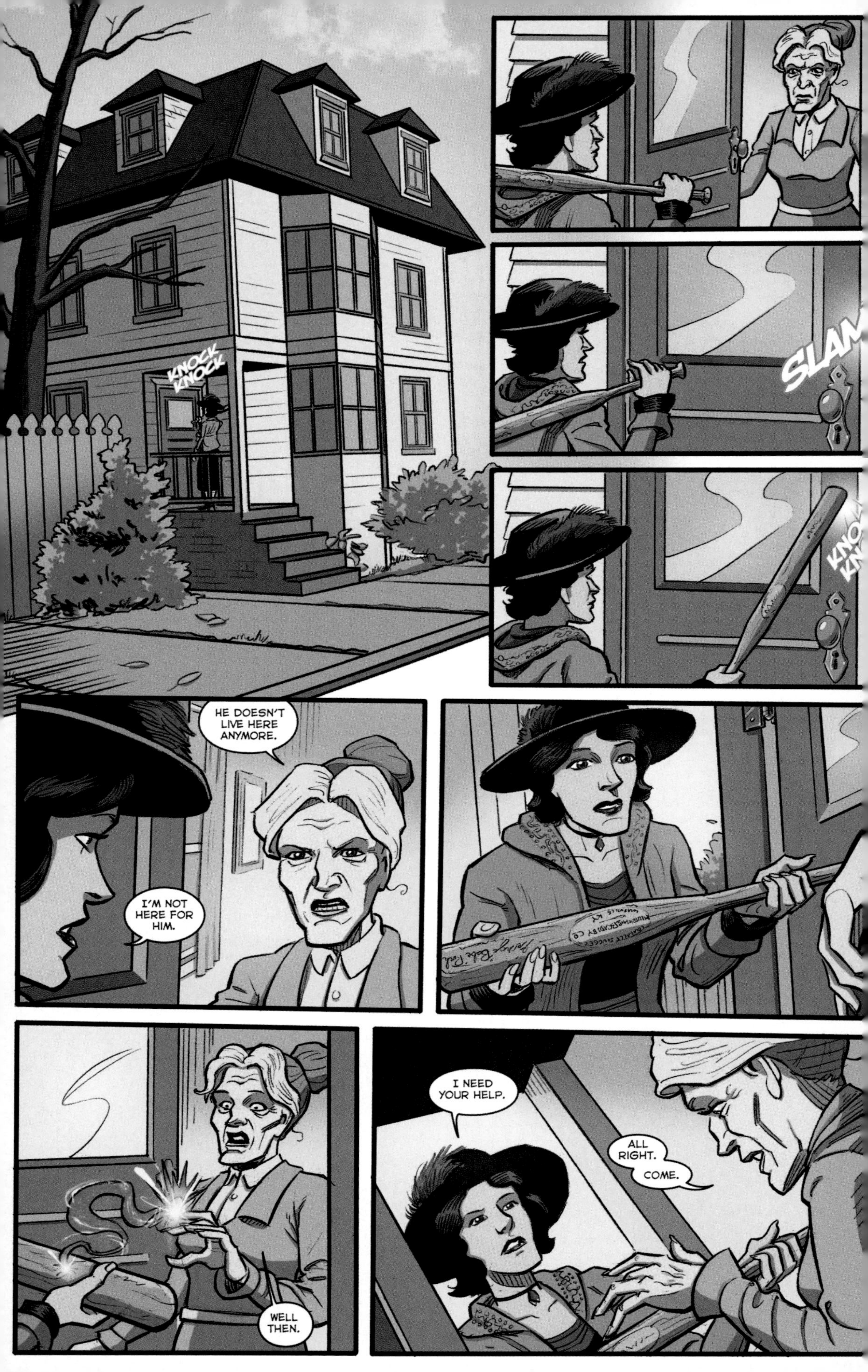
KNOCK KNOCK
SLAM
KNOCK KNOCK
HE DOESN'T LIVE HERE ANYMORE.
I'M NOT HERE FOR HIM.
WELL THEN.
I NEED YOUR HELP.
ALL RIGHT.
COME.

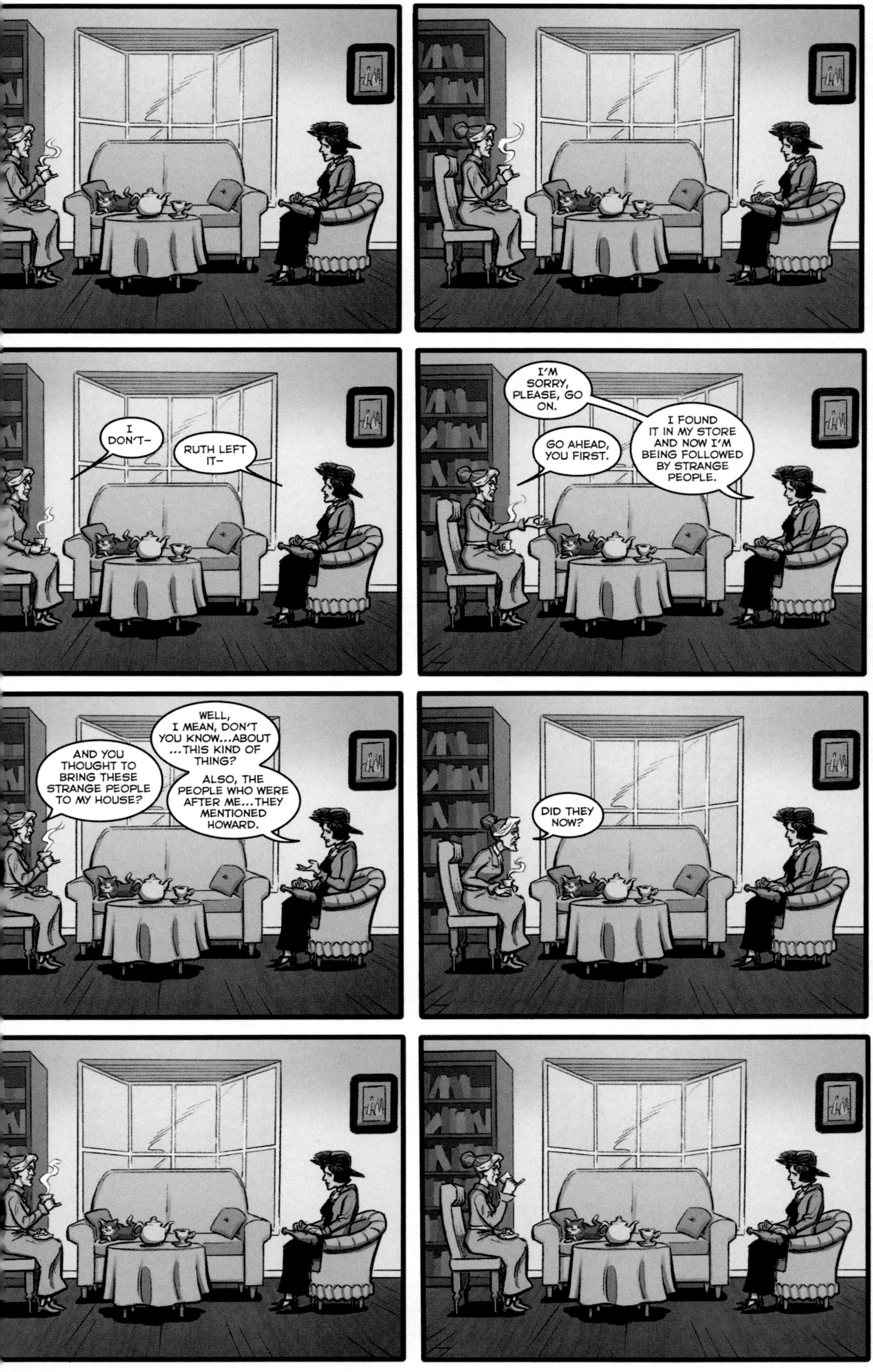
I DON'T–
RUTH LEFT IT–
I'M SORRY, PLEASE, GO ON.
GO AHEAD, YOU FIRST.
I FOUND IT IN MY STORE AND NOW I'M BEING FOLLOWED BY STRANGE PEOPLE.
AND YOU THOUGHT TO BRING THESE STRANGE PEOPLE TO MY HOUSE?
WELL, I MEAN, DON'T YOU KNOW...ABOUT ...THIS KIND OF THING?
ALSO, THE PEOPLE WHO WERE AFTER ME...THEY MENTIONED HOWARD.
DID THEY NOW?

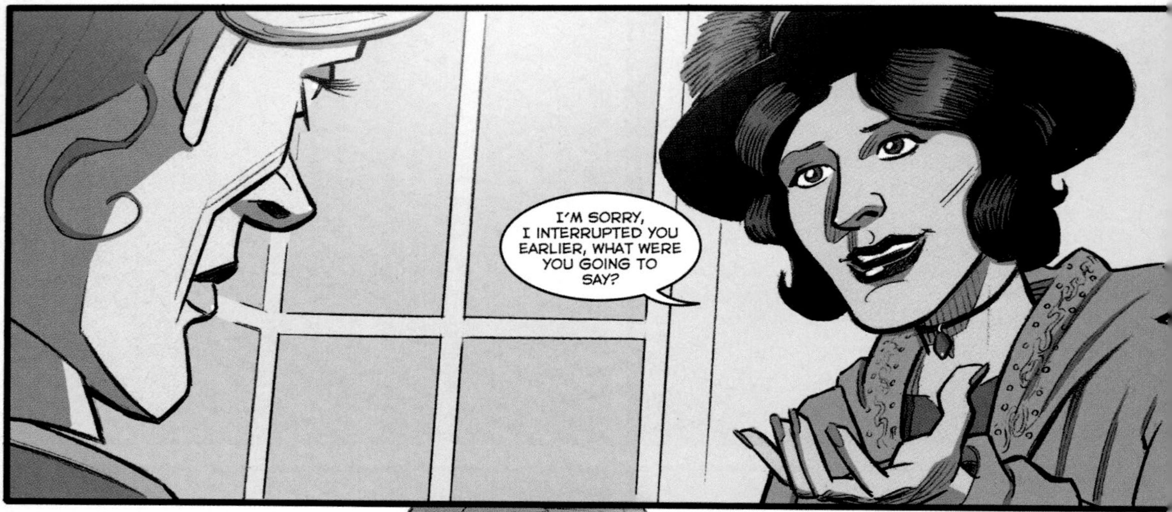
I'M SORRY, I INTERRUPTED YOU EARLIER, WHAT WERE YOU GOING TO SAY?

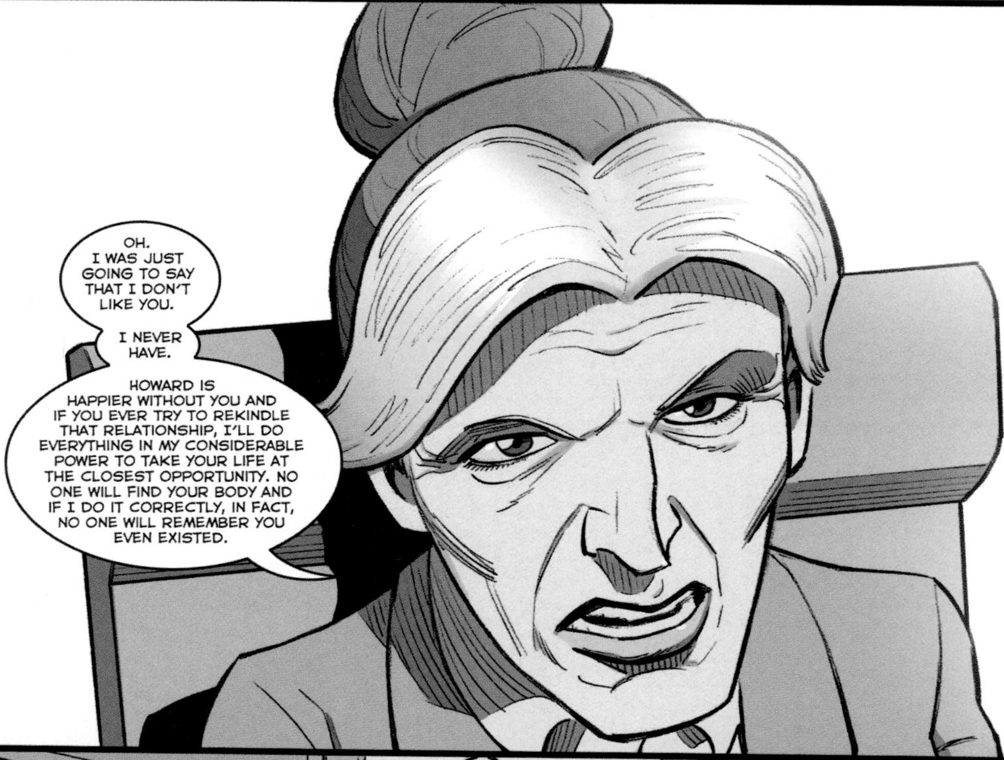
OH. I WAS JUST GOING TO SAY THAT I DON'T LIKE YOU.
I NEVER HAVE.
HOWARD IS HAPPIER WITHOUT YOU AND IF YOU EVER TRY TO REKINDLE THAT RELATIONSHIP, I'LL DO EVERYTHING IN MY CONSIDERABLE POWER TO TAKE YOUR LIFE AT THE CLOSEST OPPORTUNITY. NO ONE WILL FIND YOUR BODY AND IF I DO IT CORRECTLY, IN FACT, NO ONE WILL REMEMBER YOU EVEN EXISTED.

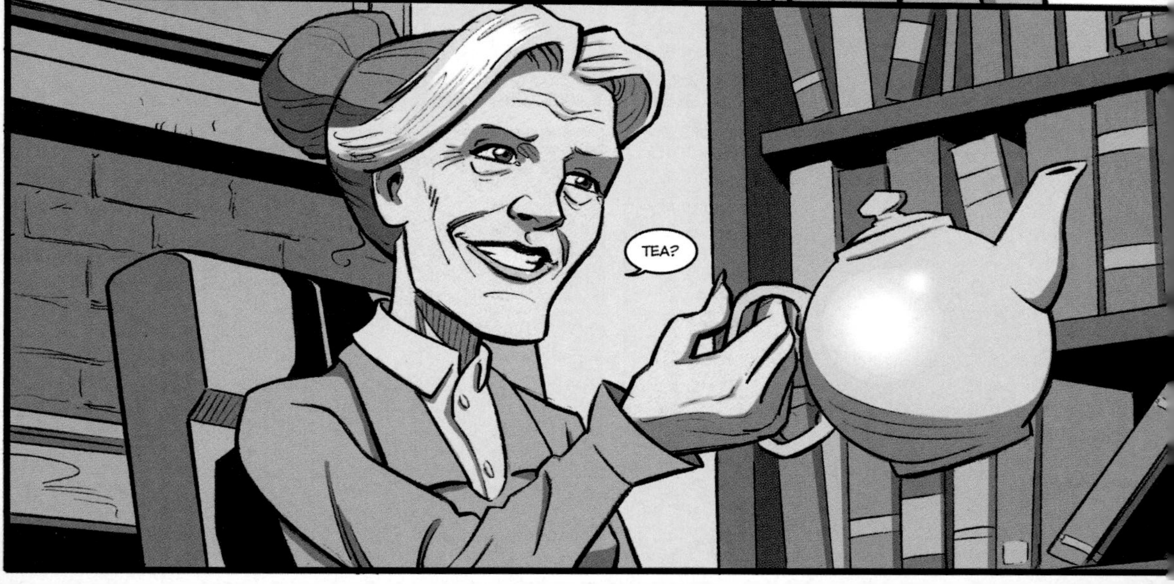
TEA?

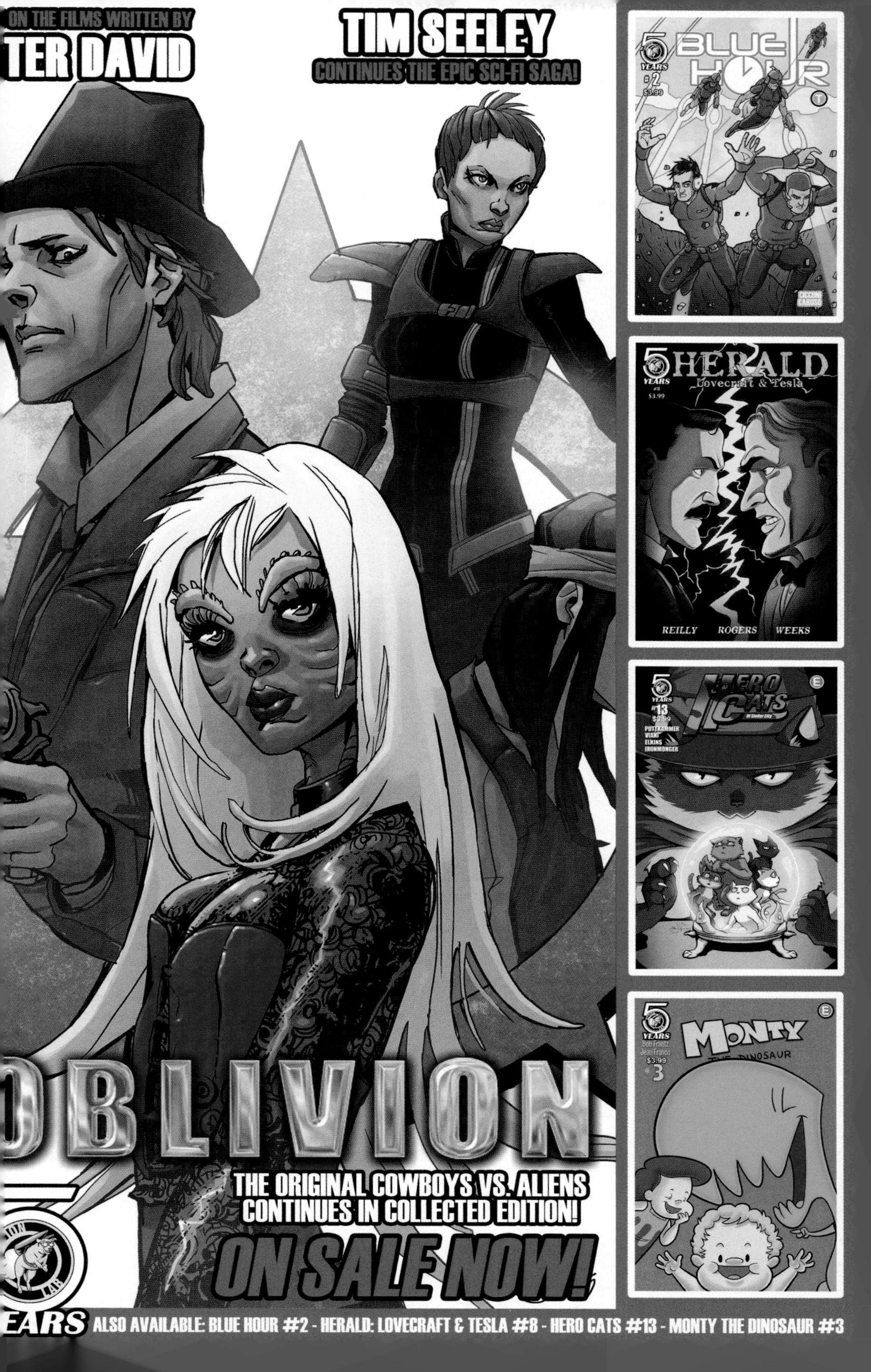
ON THE FILMS WRITTEN BY
TER DAVID
TIM SEELEY
CONTINUES THE EPIC SCI-FI SAGA!
5 YEARS
BLUE HOUR
#2
$3.99
CICCONE
CARUSO
5 YEARS
HERALD
Lovecraft & Tesla
#8
$3.99
REILLY ROGERS WEEKS
5 YEARS
HERO CATS
#13
$3.99
PUTTKAMMER
VIANI
ELKINS
IRONMONGER
5 YEARS
MONTY
THE DINOSAUR
Bob Frantz
Jean Franco
$3.99
#3
OBLIVION
THE ORIGINAL COWBOYS VS. ALIENS
CONTINUES IN COLLECTED EDITION!
ON SALE NOW!
EARS ALSO AVAILABLE: BLUE HOUR #2 - HERALD: LOVECRAFT & TESLA #8 - HERO CATS #13 - MONTY THE DINOSAUR #3

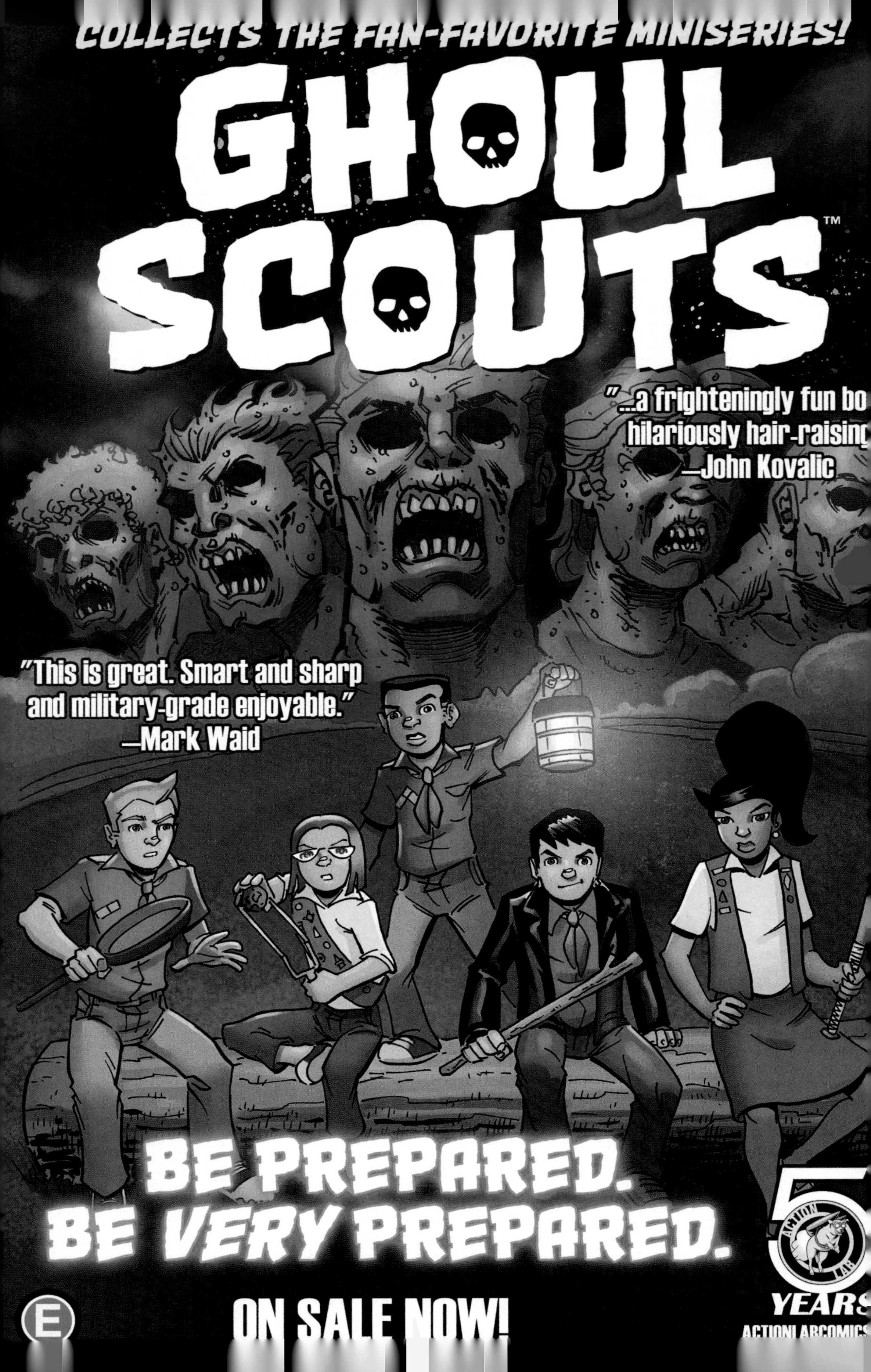
COLLECTS THE FAN-FAVORITE MINISERIES!
GHOUL SCOUTS™
"...a frighteningly fun bo
hilariously hair-raising
—John Kovalic
"This is great. Smart and sharp and military-grade enjoyable."
—Mark Waid
BE PREPARED.
BE VERY PREPARED.
E
ON SALE NOW!
5 YEARS
ACTION LAB
ACTIONLABCOMICS

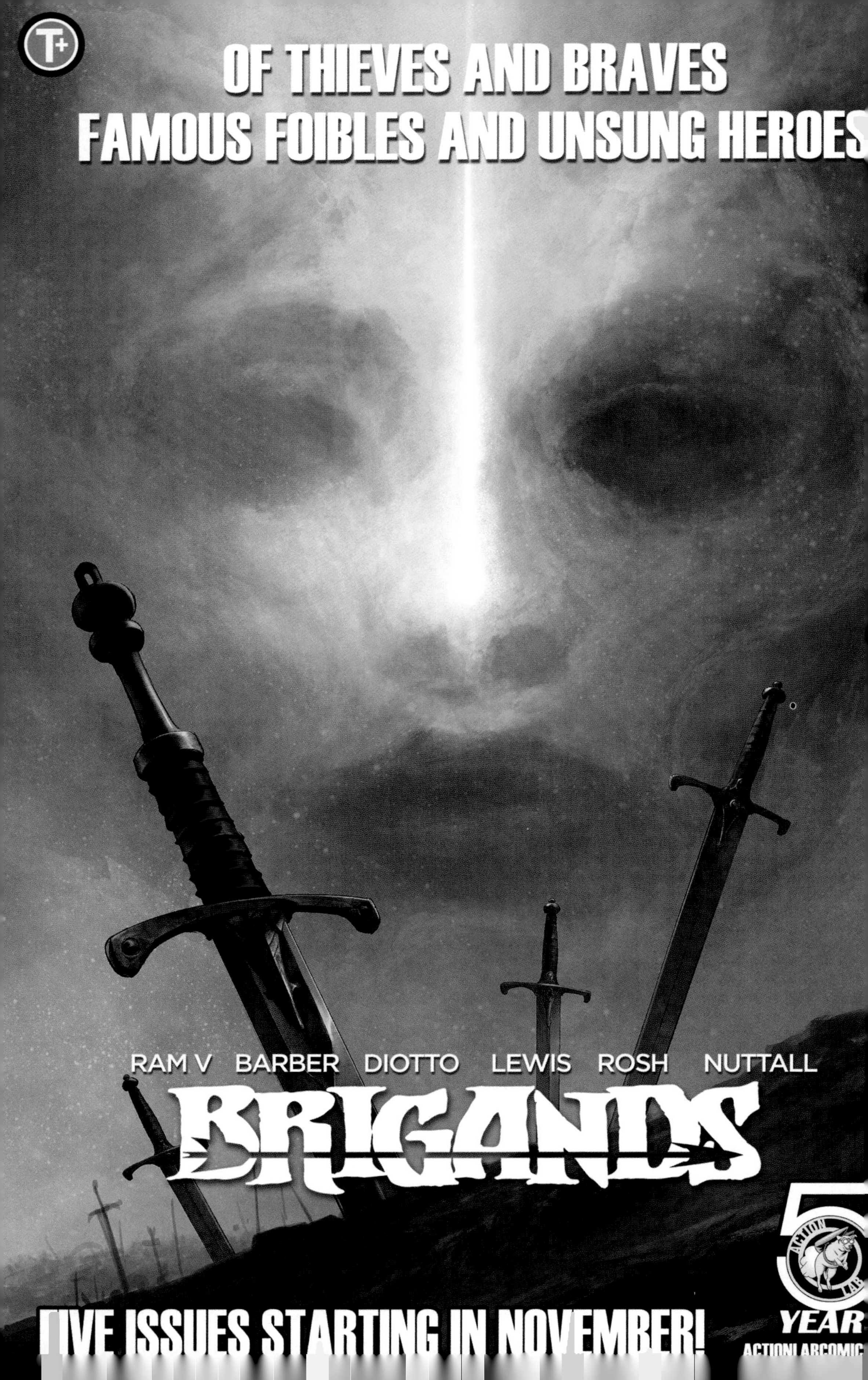
T+
OF THIEVES AND BRAVES
FAMOUS FOIBLES AND UNSUNG HEROES
RAM V BARBER DIOTTO LEWIS ROSH NUTTALL
BRIGANDS
FIVE ISSUES STARTING IN NOVEMBER!
5 YEAR
ACTION LAB

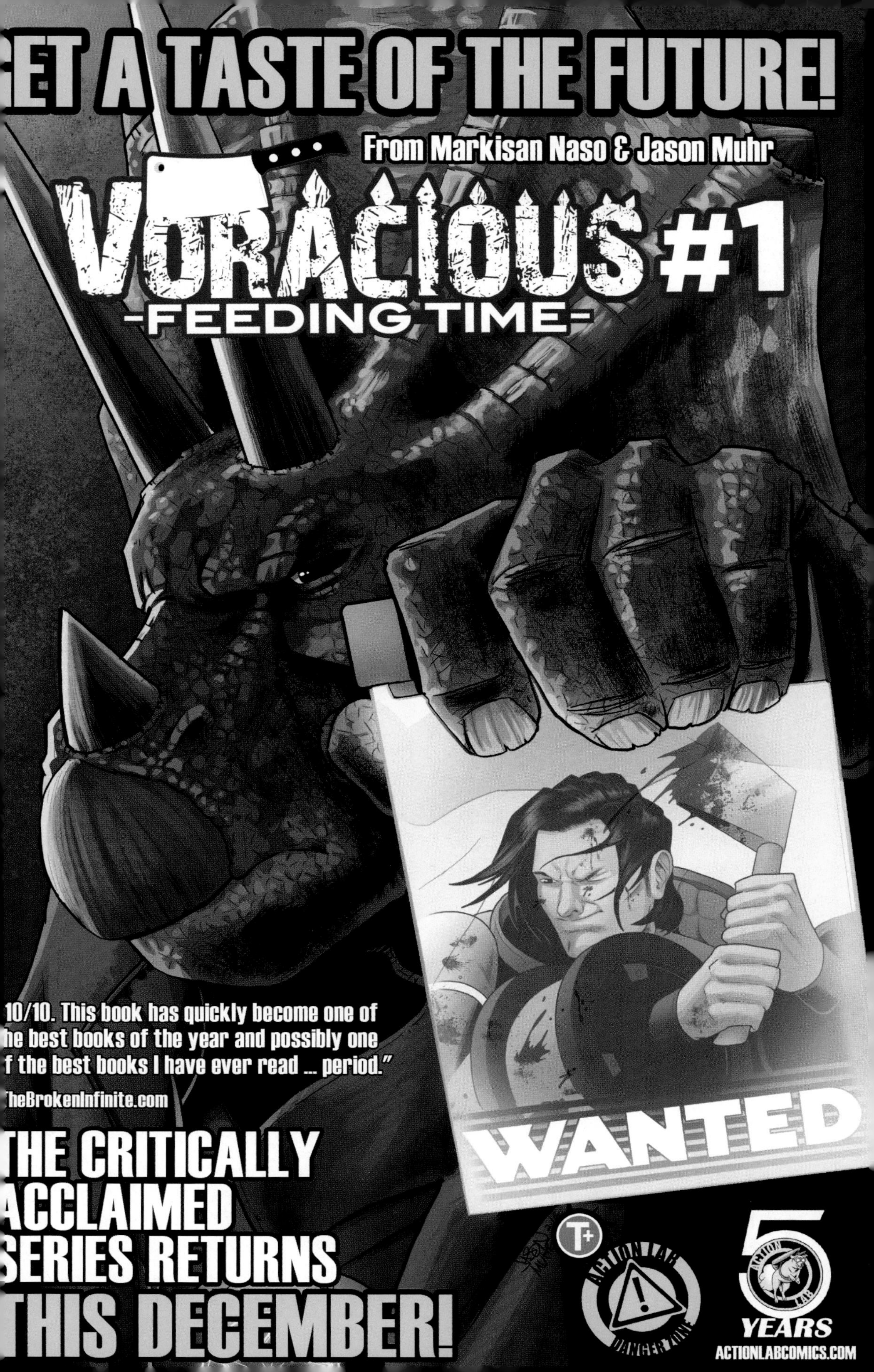

ET A TASTE OF THE FUTURE!
From Markisan Naso & Jason Muhr
VORACIOUS #1
-FEEDING TIME-
10/10. This book has quickly become one of
he best books of the year and possibly one
f the best books I have ever read ... period.”
heBrokenInfinite.com
WANTED
HE CRITICALLY
CCLAIMED
SERIES RETURNS
THIS DECEMBER!
T+
ACTION LAB
DANGER ZONE
5 YEARS
ACTIONLABCOMICS.COM

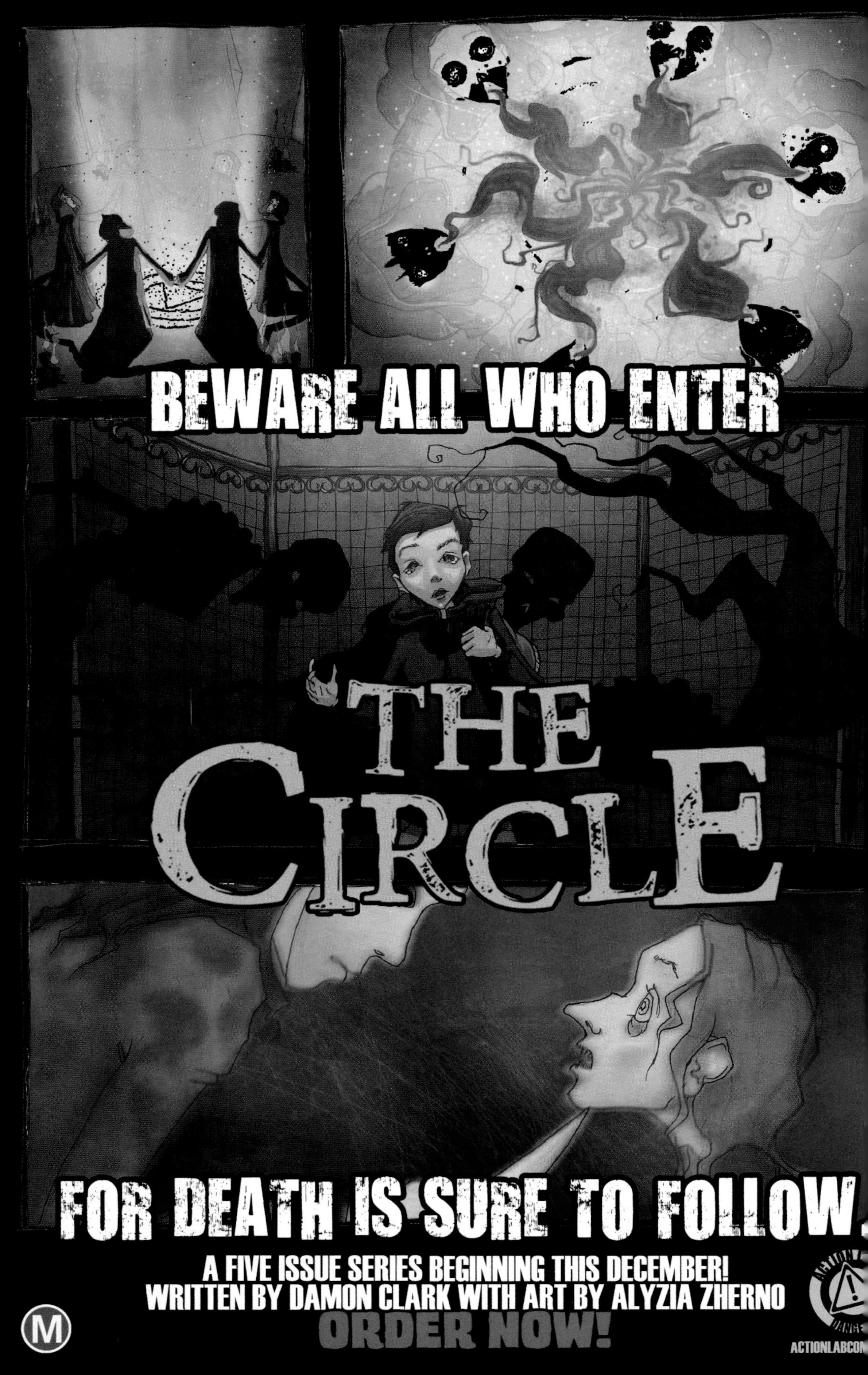

BEWARE ALL WHO ENTER

THE CIRCLE

FOR DEATH IS SURE TO FOLLOW.

A FIVE ISSUE SERIES BEGINNING THIS DECEMBER!
WRITTEN BY DAMON CLARK WITH ART BY ALYZIA ZHERNO
ORDER NOW!

ACTIONLABCOM

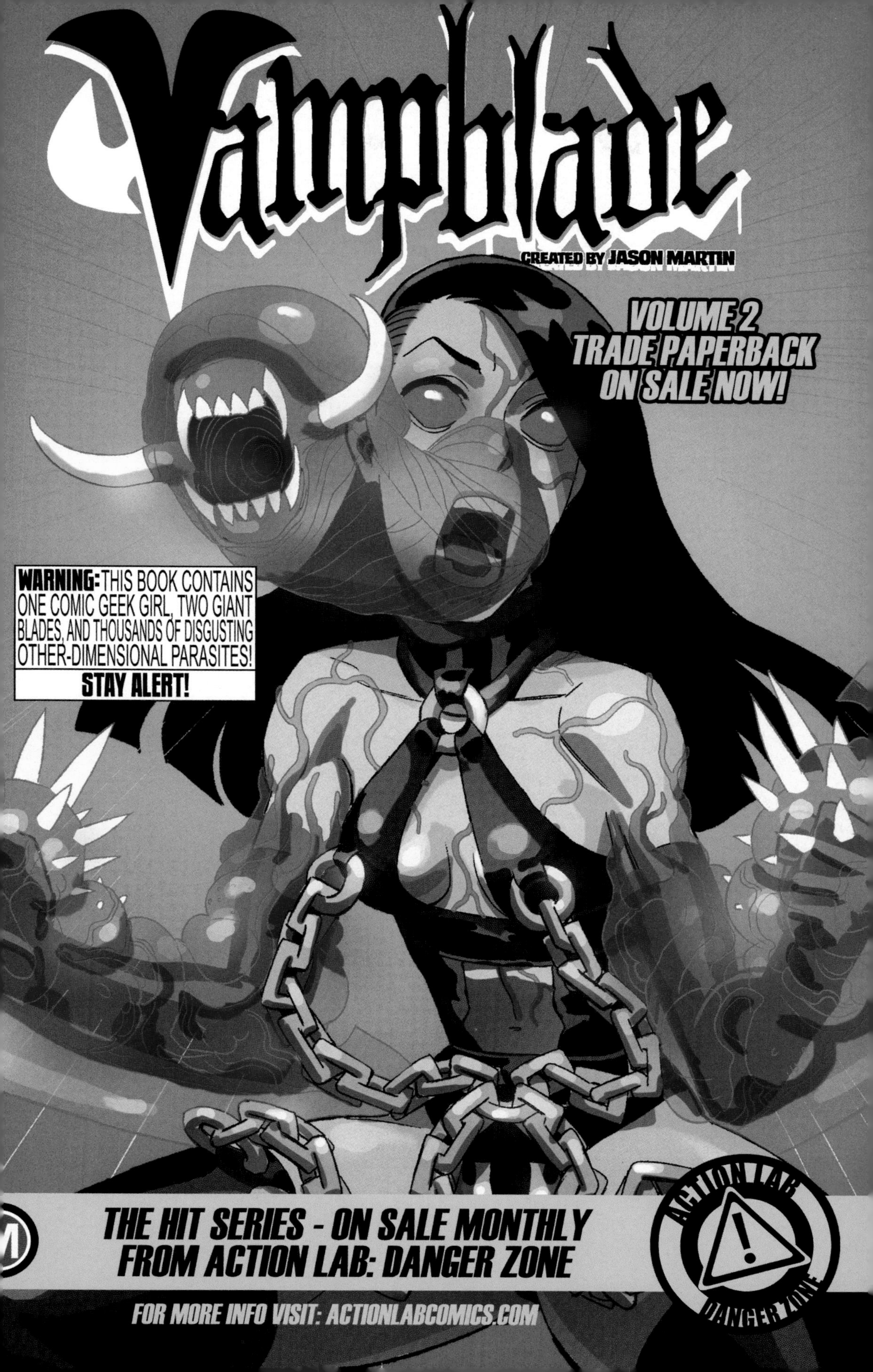
Vampblade
CREATED BY JASON MARTIN
VOLUME 2 TRADE PAPERBACK ON SALE NOW!
WARNING: THIS BOOK CONTAINS ONE COMIC GEEK GIRL, TWO GIANT BLADES, AND THOUSANDS OF DISGUSTING OTHER-DIMENSIONAL PARASITES!
STAY ALERT!
THE HIT SERIES - ON SALE MONTHLY FROM ACTION LAB: DANGER ZONE
ACTION LAB DANGER ZONE
FOR MORE INFO VISIT: ACTIONLABCOMICS.COM

READ MORE NOW

ACTIONLABCOMICS.COM

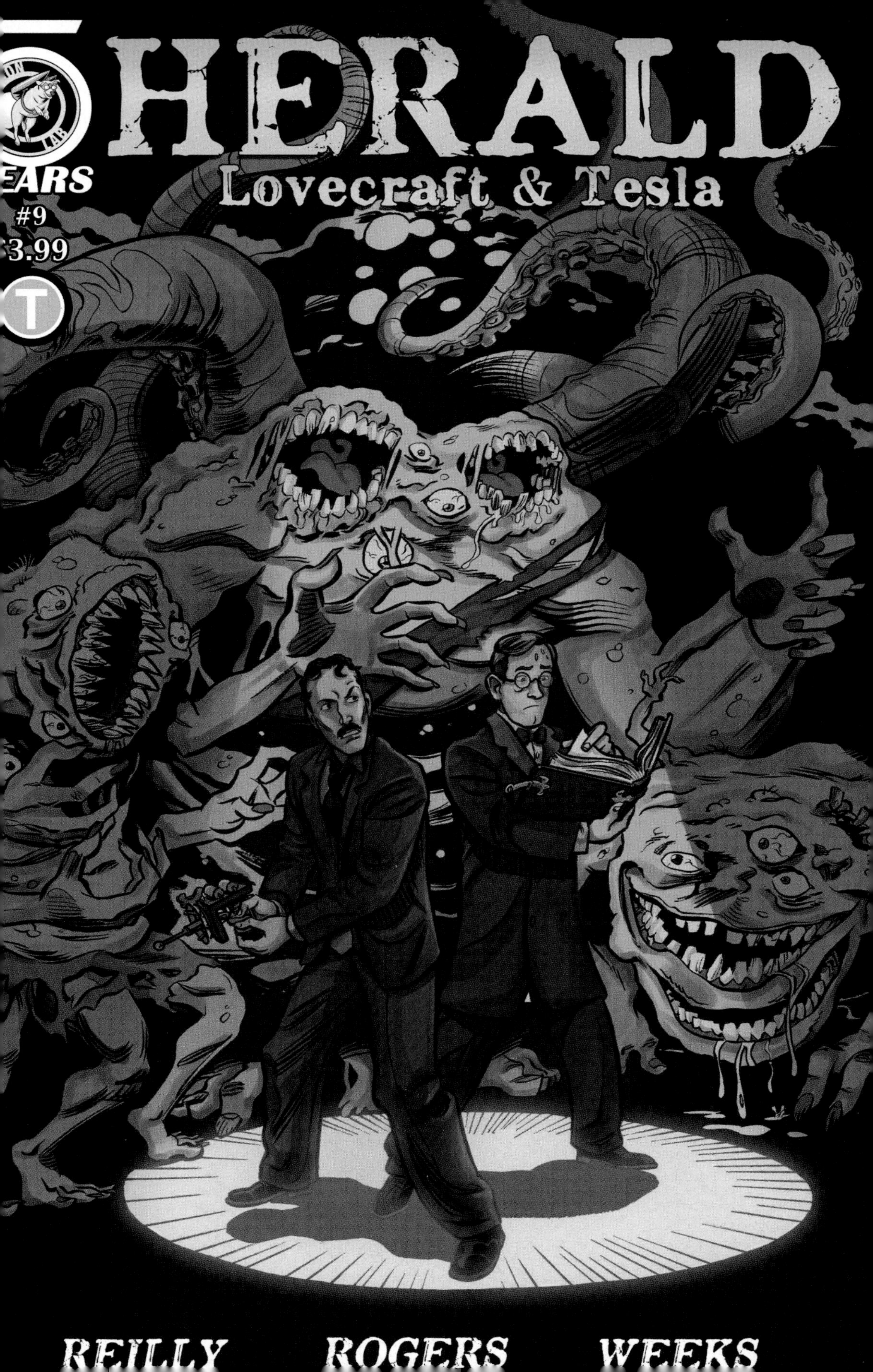
HERALD
Lovecraft & Tesla
#9
3.99
REILLY ROGERS WEEKS

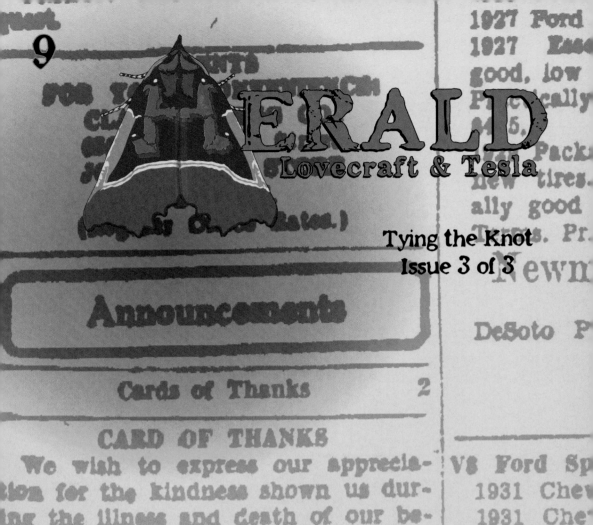

HERALD
Lovecraft & Tesla

Tying the Knot
Issue 3 of 3

Written by **John Reilly**   Pencils by **Tom Rogers**   Color, Letters by **Dexter Weeks**

Cover Colors by **Zach Clarkson**

Action Lab Comics

Publisher - Bryan Seaton   President - Kevin Freeman   Creative Director - Dave Dwonch

Editor-in-Chief - Shawn Gabborin   Co-Directors of Marketing - Jamal Igle & Kelly Dale

Social Media Director - Jim Dietz   Education Outreach Director - Jeremey Whitley

Associate Editors - Chad Cicconi & Colleen Boyd

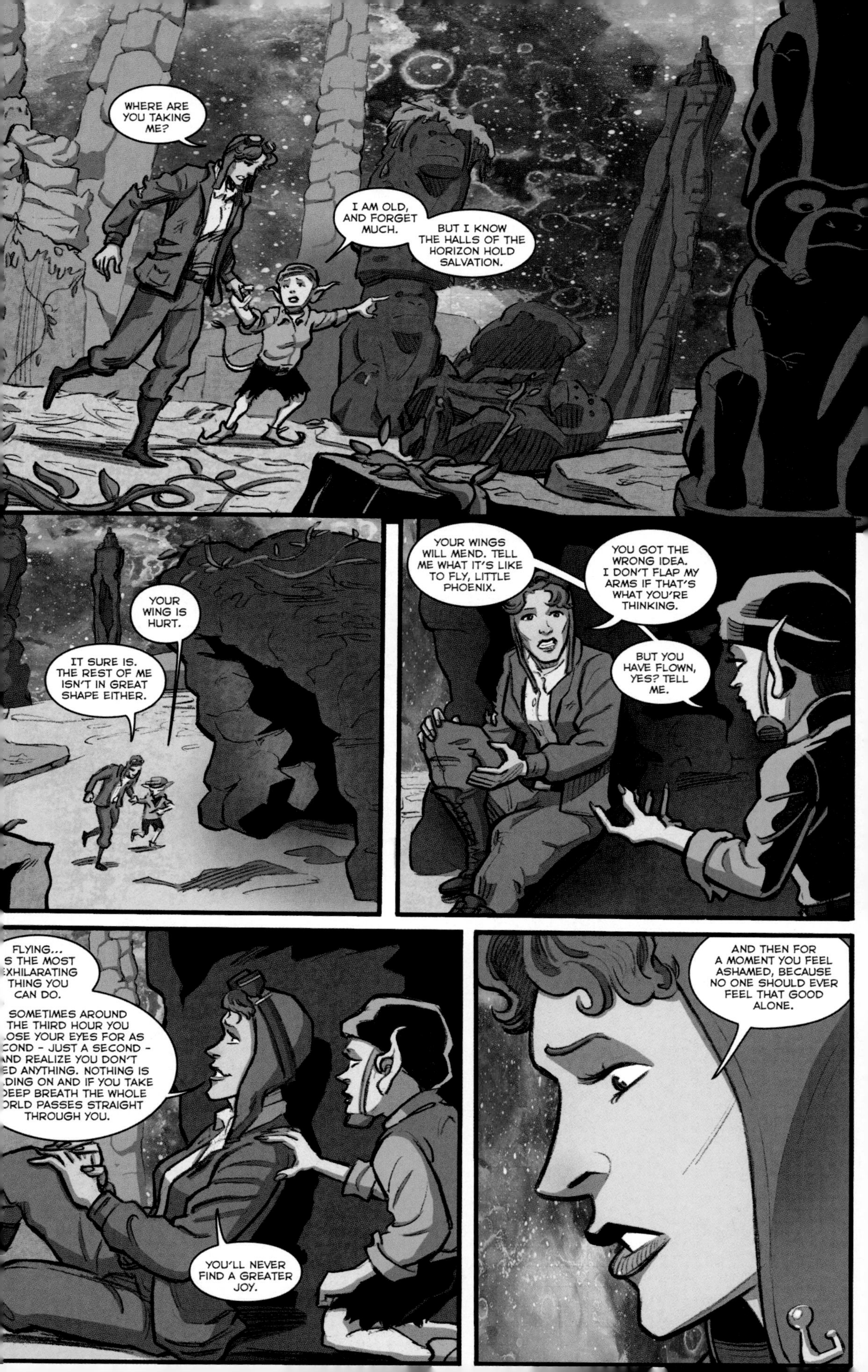
WHERE ARE YOU TAKING ME?
I AM OLD, AND FORGET MUCH.
BUT I KNOW THE HALLS OF THE HORIZON HOLD SALVATION.
YOUR WING IS HURT.
IT SURE IS. THE REST OF ME ISN'T IN GREAT SHAPE EITHER.
YOUR WINGS WILL MEND. TELL ME WHAT IT'S LIKE TO FLY, LITTLE PHOENIX.
YOU GOT THE WRONG IDEA. I DON'T FLAP MY ARMS IF THAT'S WHAT YOU'RE THINKING.
BUT YOU HAVE FLOWN, YES? TELL ME.
FLYING... S THE MOST EXHILARATING THING YOU CAN DO.
SOMETIMES AROUND THE THIRD HOUR YOU OSE YOUR EYES FOR AS COND - JUST A SECOND - ND REALIZE YOU DON'T ED ANYTHING. NOTHING IS DING ON AND IF YOU TAKE DEEP BREATH THE WHOLE ORLD PASSES STRAIGHT THROUGH YOU.
YOU'LL NEVER FIND A GREATER JOY.
AND THEN FOR A MOMENT YOU FEEL ASHAMED, BECAUSE NO ONE SHOULD EVER FEEL THAT GOOD ALONE.

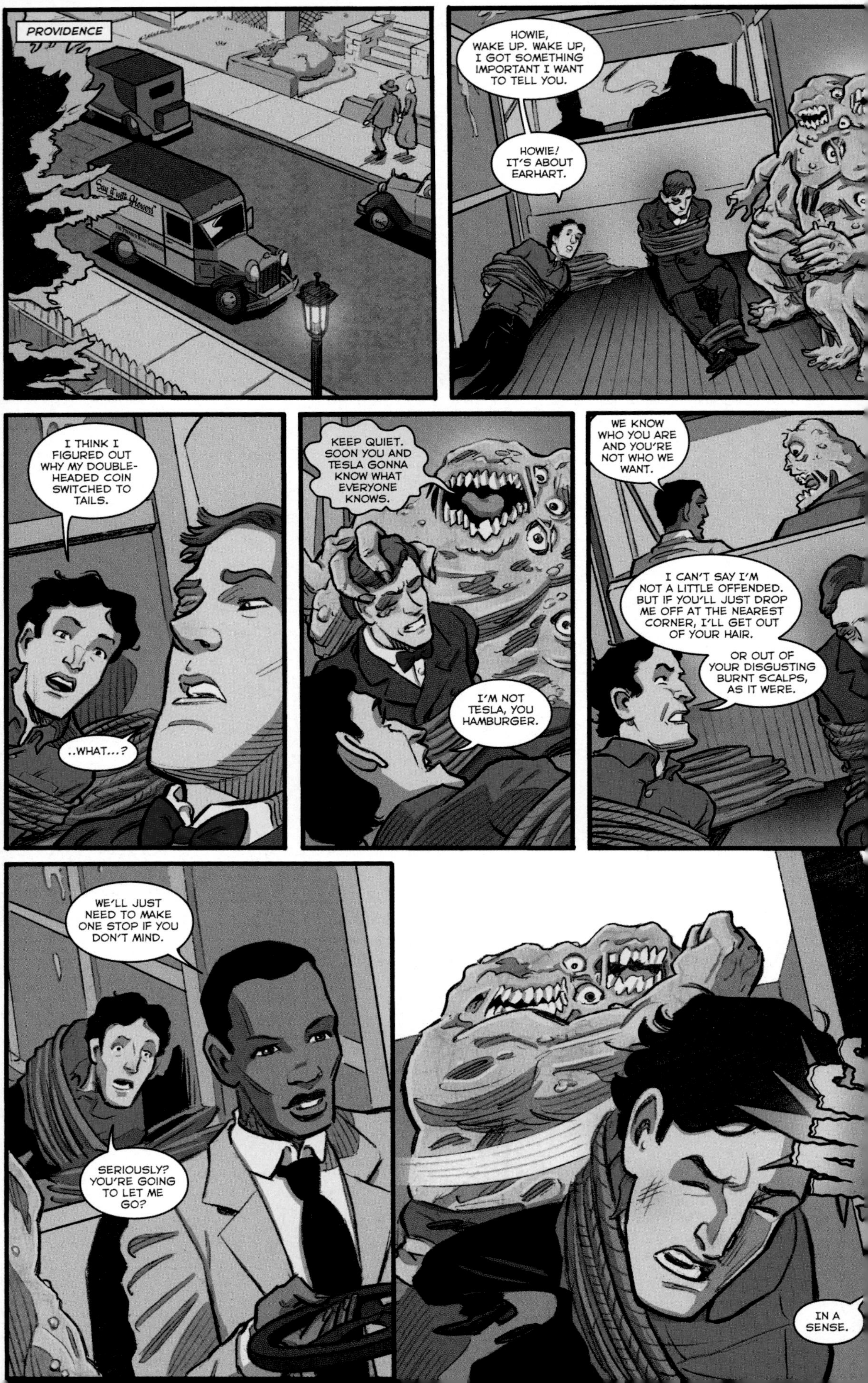
PROVIDENCE
Say it with Flowers
HOWIE, WAKE UP. WAKE UP, I GOT SOMETHING IMPORTANT I WANT TO TELL YOU.
HOWIE! IT'S ABOUT EARHART.
I THINK I FIGURED OUT WHY MY DOUBLE-HEADED COIN SWITCHED TO TAILS.
..WHAT...?
KEEP QUIET. SOON YOU AND TESLA GONNA KNOW WHAT EVERYONE KNOWS.
I'M NOT TESLA, YOU HAMBURGER.
WE KNOW WHO YOU ARE AND YOU'RE NOT WHO WE WANT.
I CAN'T SAY I'M NOT A LITTLE OFFENDED. BUT IF YOU'LL JUST DROP ME OFF AT THE NEAREST CORNER, I'LL GET OUT OF YOUR HAIR.
OR OUT OF YOUR DISGUSTING BURNT SCALPS, AS IT WERE.
WE'LL JUST NEED TO MAKE ONE STOP IF YOU DON'T MIND.
SERIOUSLY? YOU'RE GOING TO LET ME GO?
IN A SENSE.

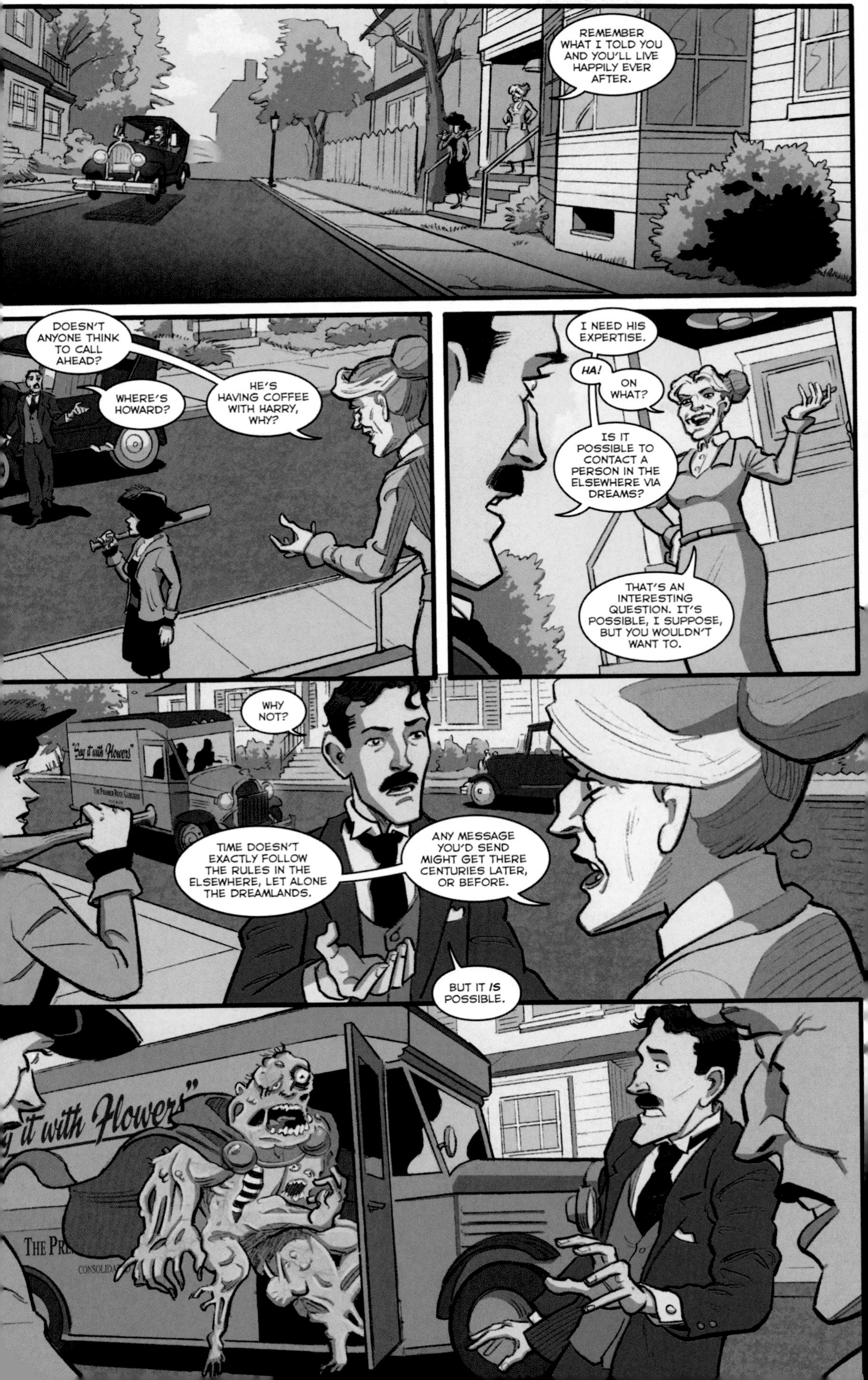
REMEMBER WHAT I TOLD YOU AND YOU'LL LIVE HAPPILY EVER AFTER.
DOESN'T ANYONE THINK TO CALL AHEAD?
WHERE'S HOWARD?
HE'S HAVING COFFEE WITH HARRY, WHY?
I NEED HIS EXPERTISE.
HA!
ON WHAT?
IS IT POSSIBLE TO CONTACT A PERSON IN THE ELSEWHERE VIA DREAMS?
THAT'S AN INTERESTING QUESTION. IT'S POSSIBLE, I SUPPOSE, BUT YOU WOULDN'T WANT TO.
WHY NOT?
"Say it with Flowers"
TIME DOESN'T EXACTLY FOLLOW THE RULES IN THE ELSEWHERE, LET ALONE THE DREAMLANDS.
ANY MESSAGE YOU'D SEND MIGHT GET THERE CENTURIES LATER, OR BEFORE.
BUT IT *IS* POSSIBLE.

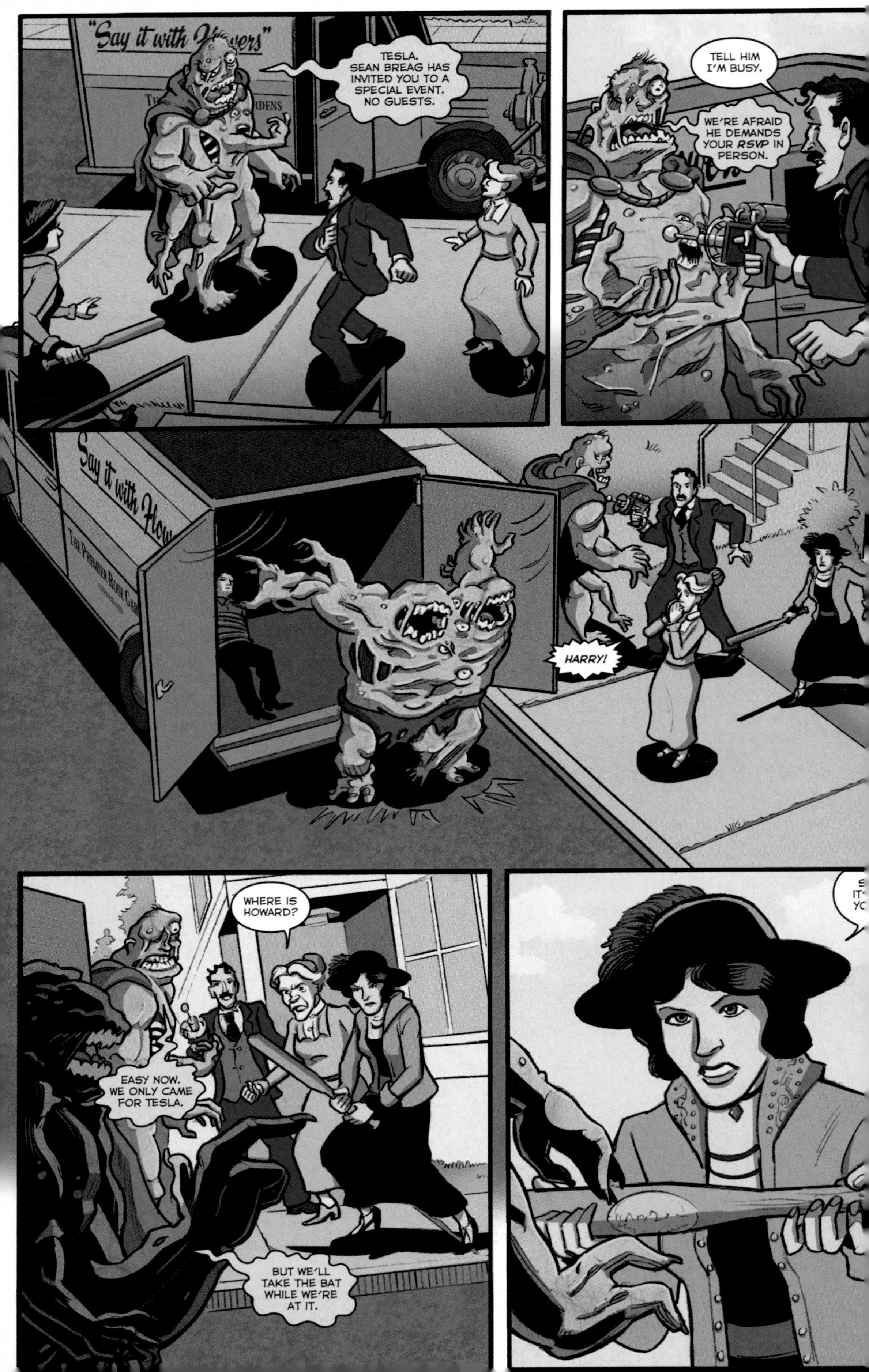

TESLA. SEAN BREAG HAS INVITED YOU TO A SPECIAL EVENT. NO GUESTS.
TELL HIM I'M BUSY.
WE'RE AFRAID HE DEMANDS YOUR *RSVP* IN PERSON.
HARRY!
WHERE IS HOWARD?
EASY NOW. WE ONLY CAME FOR TESLA.
BUT WE'LL TAKE THE BAT WHILE WE'RE AT IT.

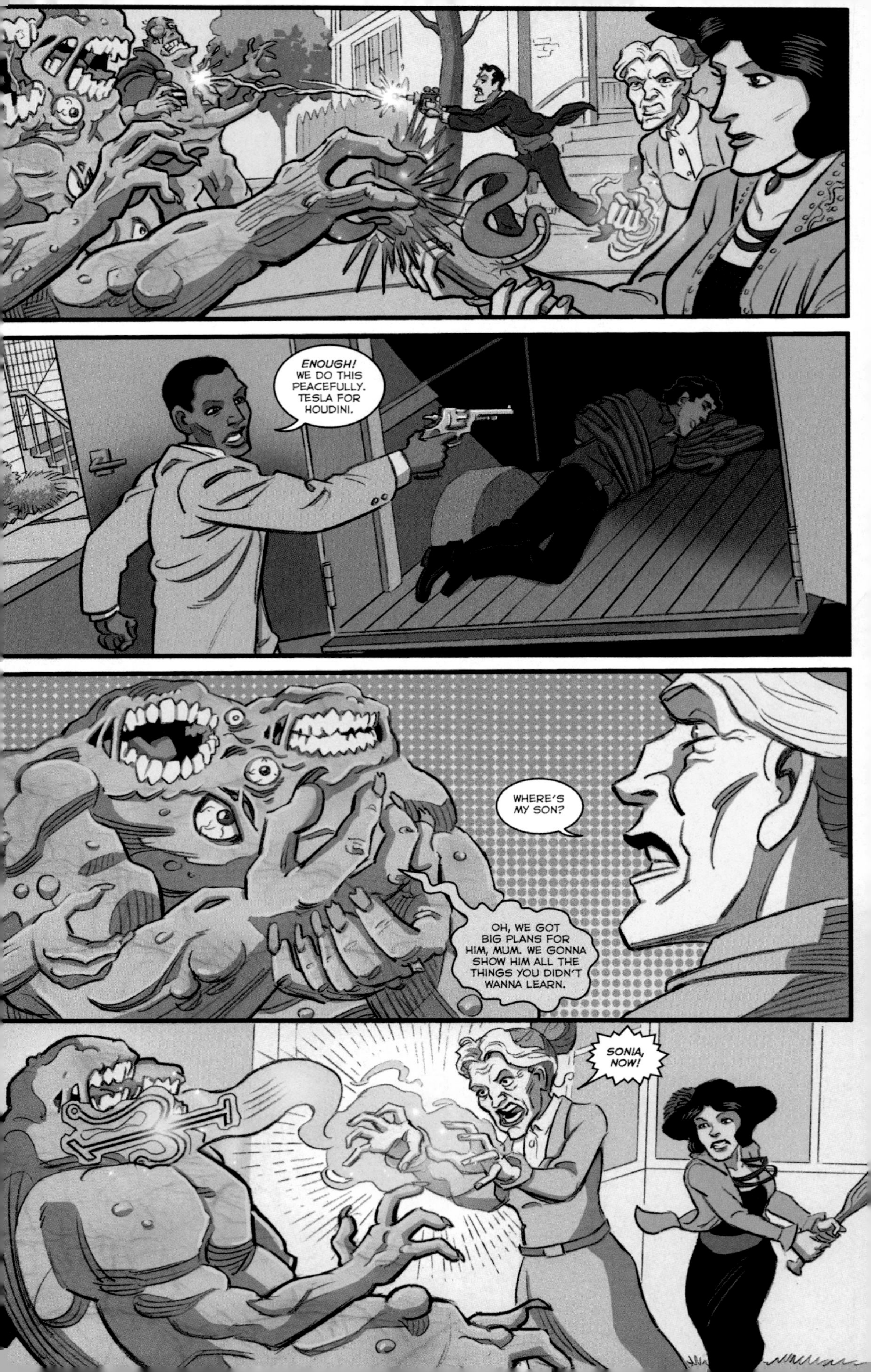
ENOUGH! WE DO THIS PEACEFULLY. TESLA FOR HOUDINI.
WHERE'S MY SON?
OH, WE GOT BIG PLANS FOR HIM, MUM. WE GONNA SHOW HIM ALL THE THINGS YOU DIDN'T WANNA LEARN.
SONIA, NOW!

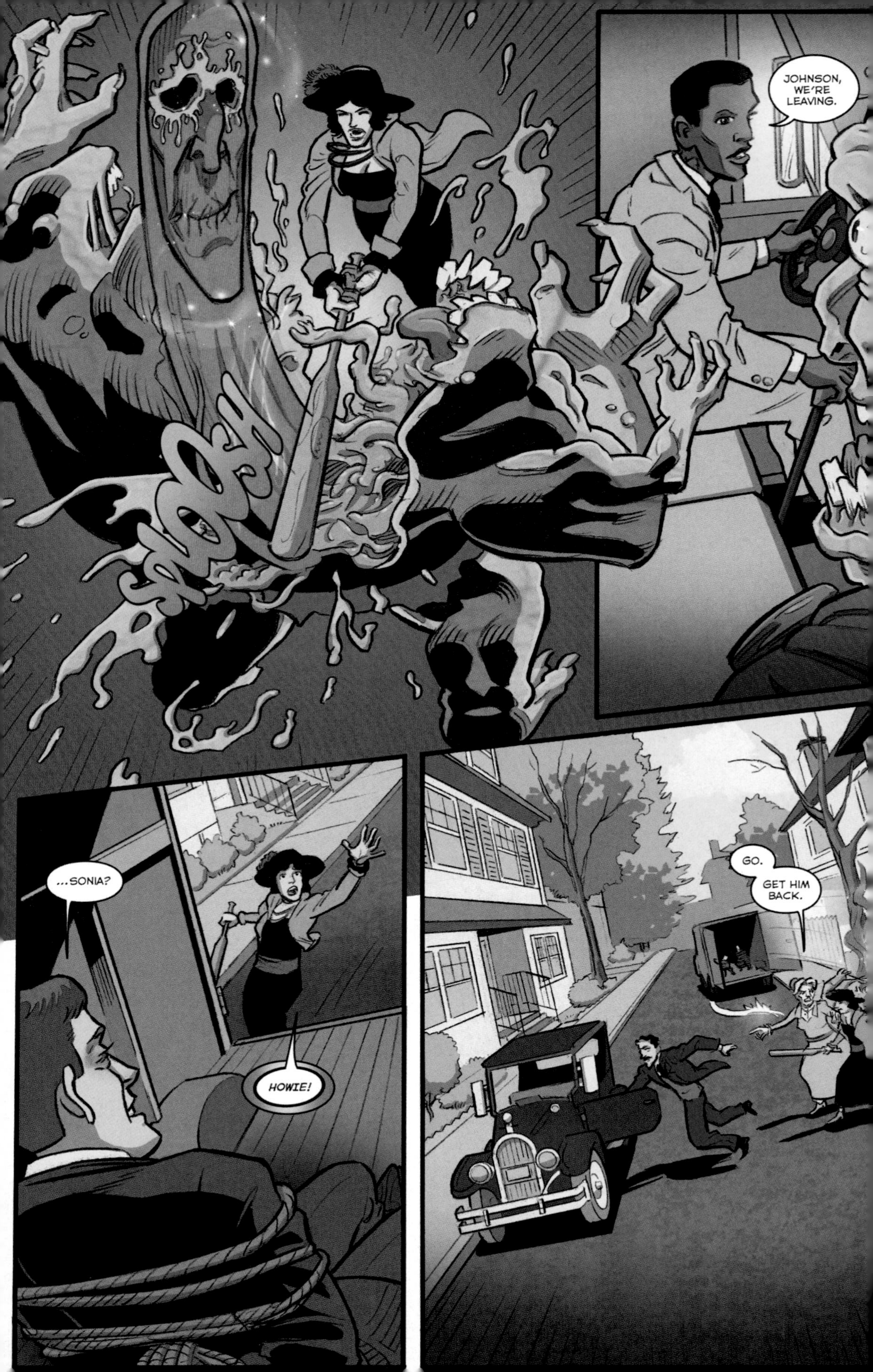
SHLOOSH
JOHNSON, WE'RE LEAVING.
...SONIA?
HOWIE!
GO.
GET HIM BACK.

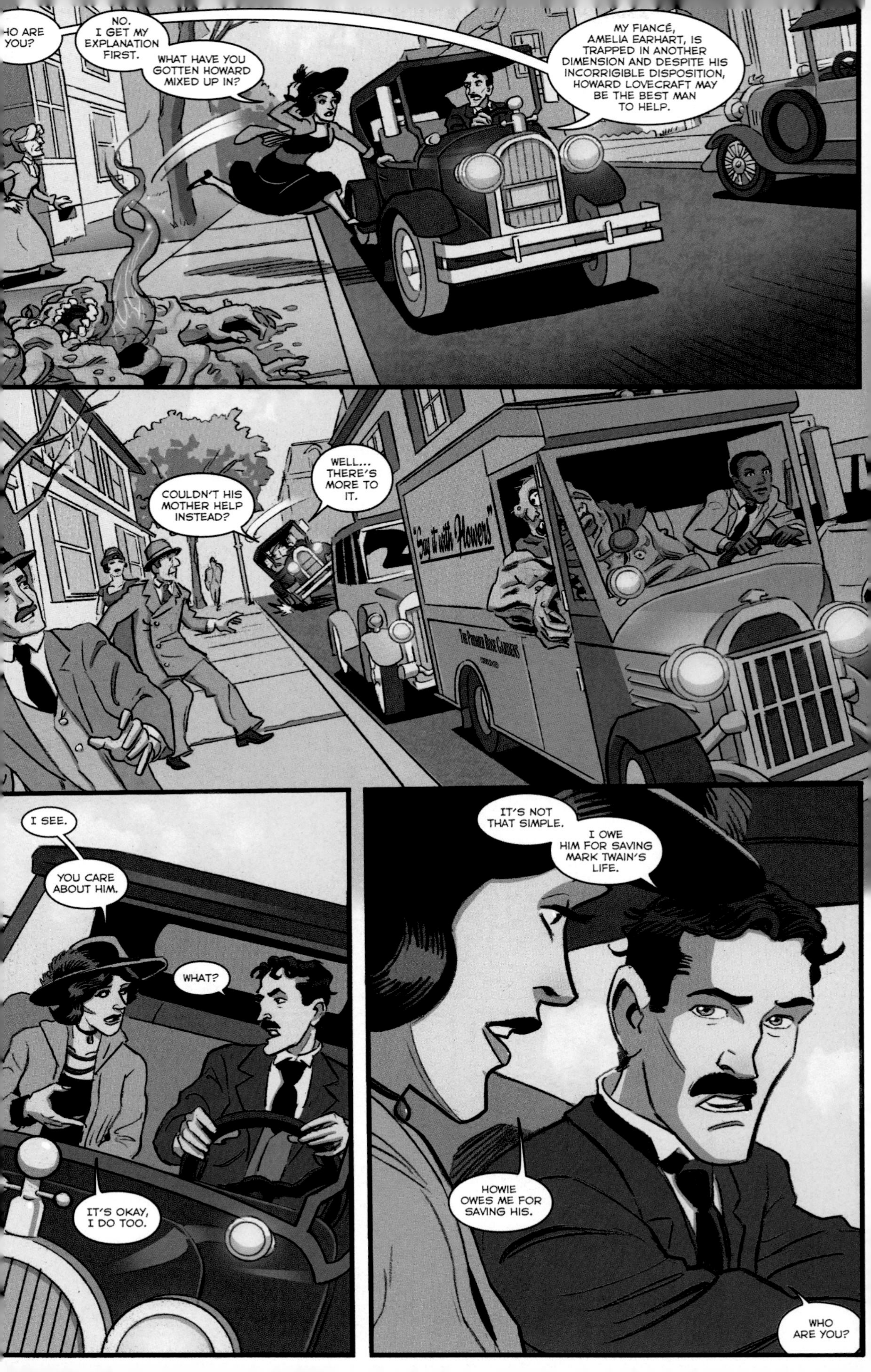
HO ARE YOU?
NO. I GET MY EXPLANATION FIRST.
WHAT HAVE YOU GOTTEN HOWARD MIXED UP IN?
MY FIANCÉ, AMELIA EARHART, IS TRAPPED IN ANOTHER DIMENSION AND DESPITE HIS INCORRIGIBLE DISPOSITION, HOWARD LOVECRAFT MAY BE THE BEST MAN TO HELP.
COULDN'T HIS MOTHER HELP INSTEAD?
WELL... THERE'S MORE TO IT.
"Say it with Flowers"
THE PREMIER ROSE GARDENS
I SEE.
YOU CARE ABOUT HIM.
WHAT?
IT'S OKAY, I DO TOO.
IT'S NOT THAT SIMPLE.
I OWE HIM FOR SAVING MARK TWAIN'S LIFE.
HOWIE OWES ME FOR SAVING HIS.
WHO ARE YOU?

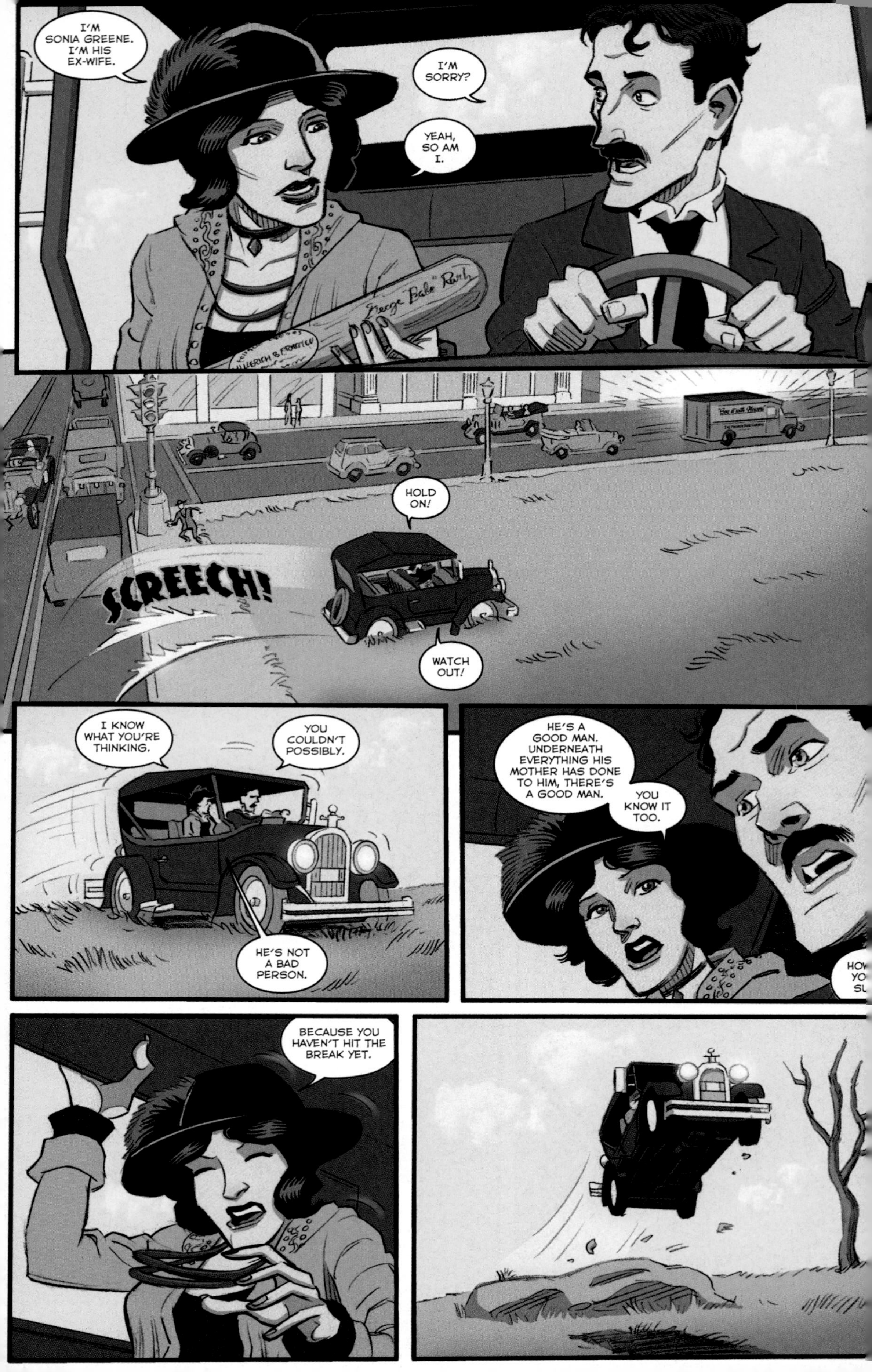
I'M SONIA GREENE. I'M HIS EX-WIFE.
I'M SORRY?
YEAH, SO AM I.
HOLD ON!
SCREECH!
WATCH OUT!
I KNOW WHAT YOU'RE THINKING.
YOU COULDN'T POSSIBLY.
HE'S NOT A BAD PERSON.
HE'S A GOOD MAN. UNDERNEATH EVERYTHING HIS MOTHER HAS DONE TO HIM, THERE'S A GOOD MAN.
YOU KNOW IT TOO.
BECAUSE YOU HAVEN'T HIT THE BREAK YET.

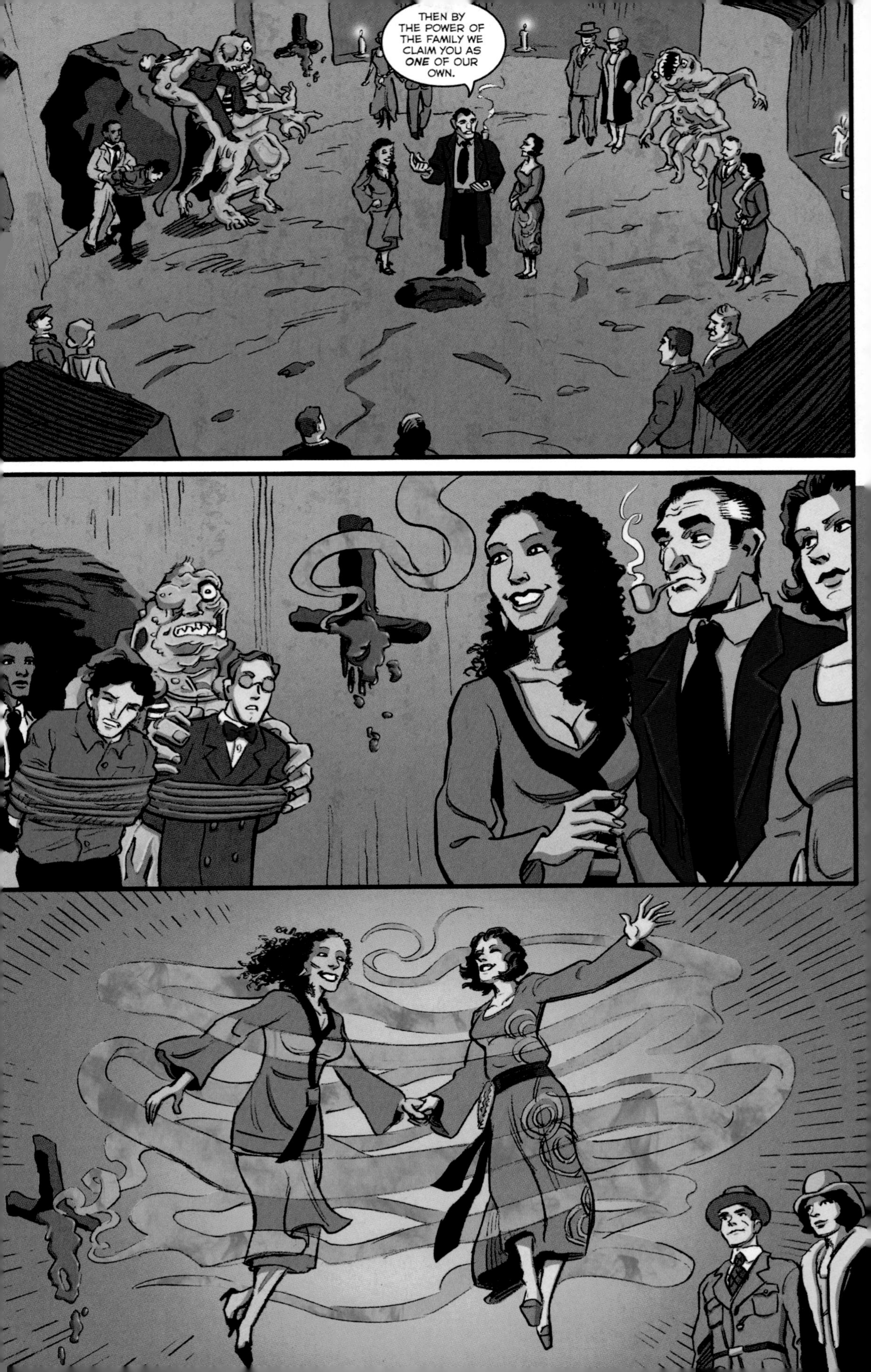
THEN BY THE POWER OF THE FAMILY WE CLAIM YOU AS ONE OF OUR OWN.

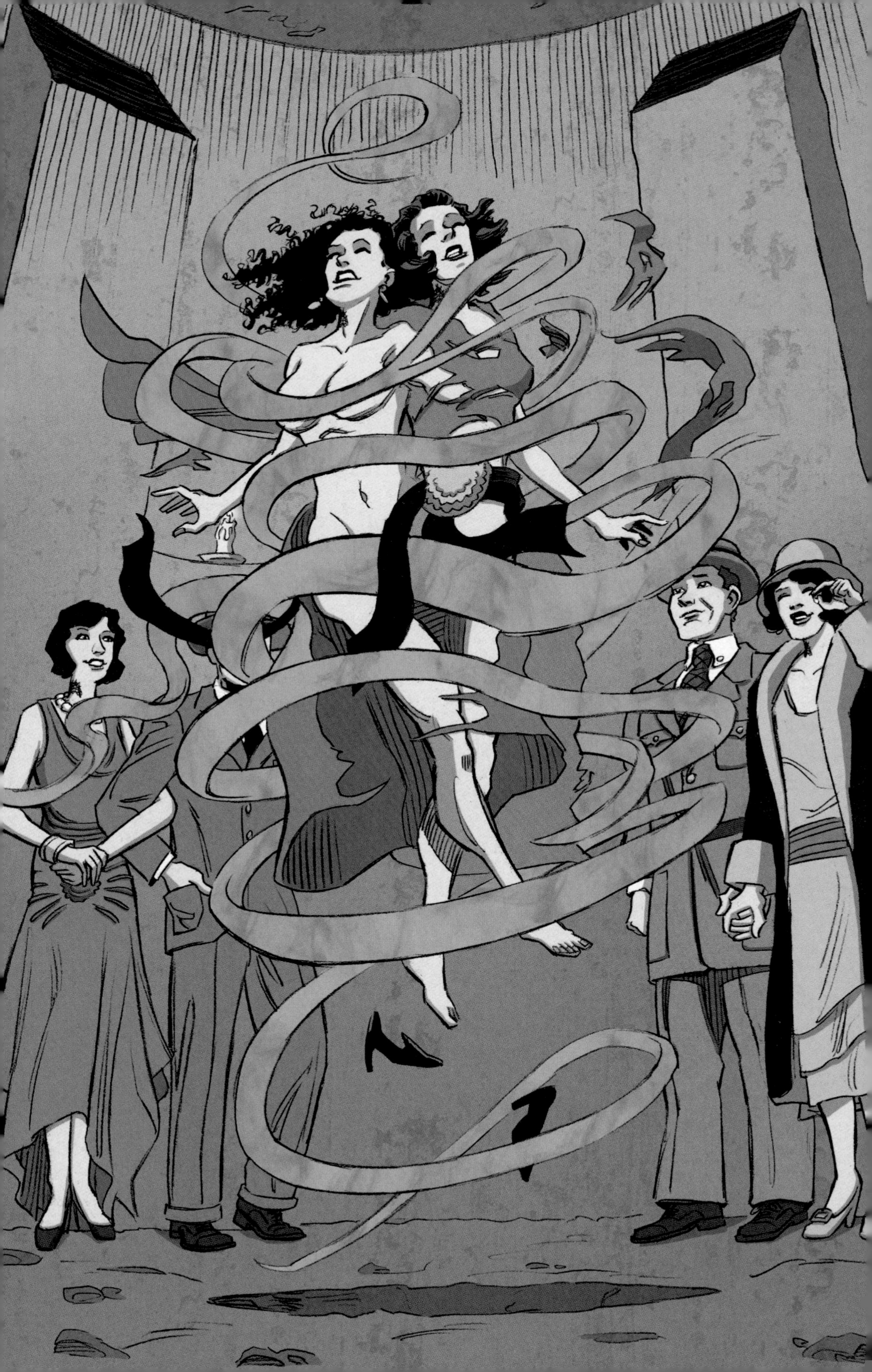

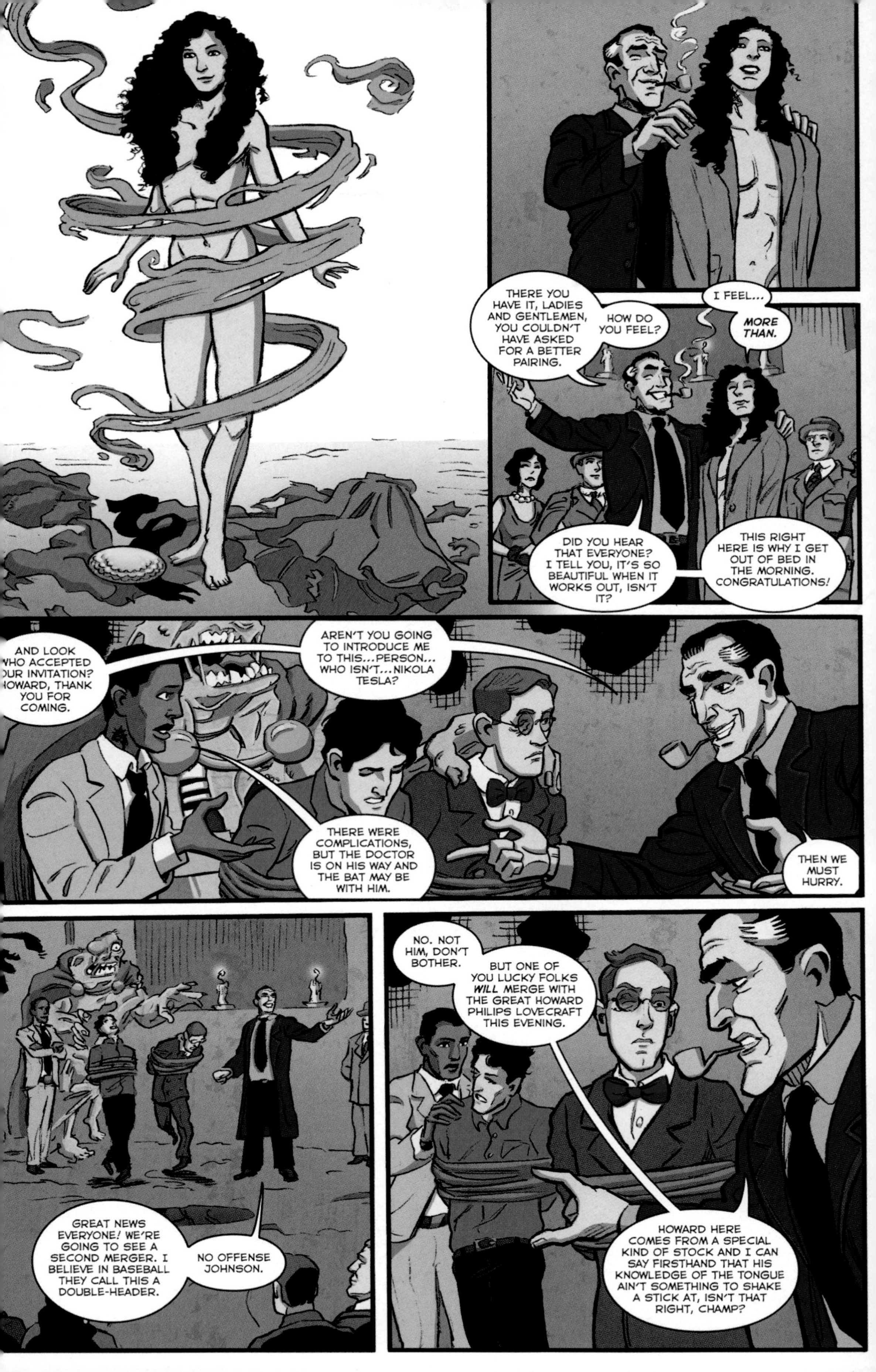
THERE YOU HAVE IT, LADIES AND GENTLEMEN, YOU COULDN'T HAVE ASKED FOR A BETTER PAIRING.
HOW DO YOU FEEL?
I FEEL...
MORE THAN.
DID YOU HEAR THAT EVERYONE? I TELL YOU, IT'S SO BEAUTIFUL WHEN IT WORKS OUT, ISN'T IT?
THIS RIGHT HERE IS WHY I GET OUT OF BED IN THE MORNING. CONGRATULATIONS!
AND LOOK WHO ACCEPTED OUR INVITATION? HOWARD, THANK YOU FOR COMING.
AREN'T YOU GOING TO INTRODUCE ME TO THIS...PERSON... WHO ISN'T...NIKOLA TESLA?
THERE WERE COMPLICATIONS, BUT THE DOCTOR IS ON HIS WAY AND THE BAT MAY BE WITH HIM.
THEN WE MUST HURRY.
GREAT NEWS EVERYONE! WE'RE GOING TO SEE A SECOND MERGER. I BELIEVE IN BASEBALL THEY CALL THIS A DOUBLE-HEADER.
NO OFFENSE JOHNSON.
NO. NOT HIM, DON'T BOTHER.
BUT ONE OF YOU LUCKY FOLKS WILL MERGE WITH THE GREAT HOWARD PHILIPS LOVECRAFT THIS EVENING.
HOWARD HERE COMES FROM A SPECIAL KIND OF STOCK AND I CAN SAY FIRSTHAND THAT HIS KNOWLEDGE OF THE TONGUE AIN'T SOMETHING TO SHAKE A STICK AT, ISN'T THAT RIGHT, CHAMP?

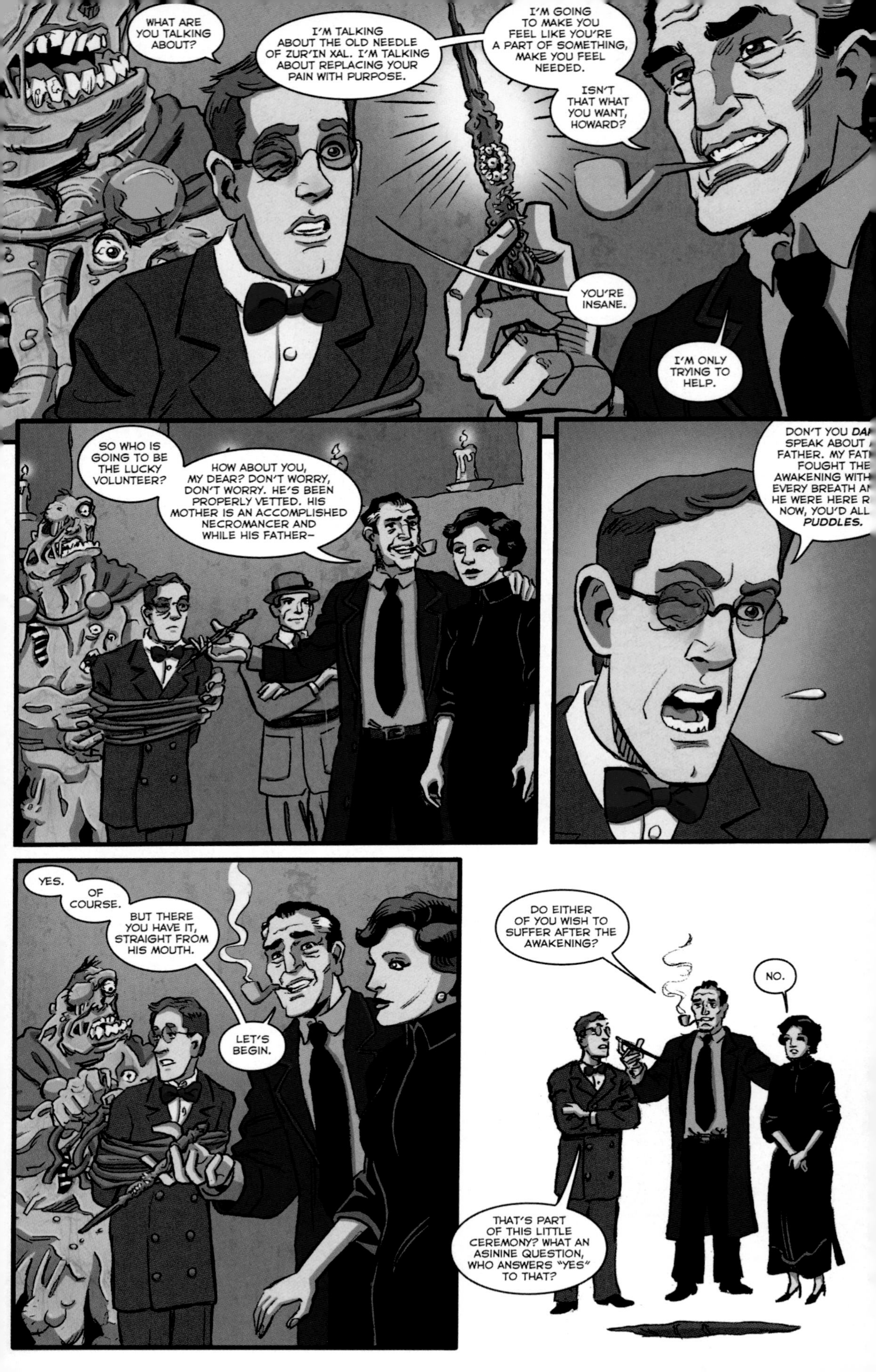
WHAT ARE YOU TALKING ABOUT?
I'M TALKING ABOUT THE OLD NEEDLE OF ZUR'IN XAL. I'M TALKING ABOUT REPLACING YOUR PAIN WITH PURPOSE.
I'M GOING TO MAKE YOU FEEL LIKE YOU'RE A PART OF SOMETHING, MAKE YOU FEEL NEEDED.
ISN'T THAT WHAT YOU WANT, HOWARD?
YOU'RE INSANE.
I'M ONLY TRYING TO HELP.
SO WHO IS GOING TO BE THE LUCKY VOLUNTEER?
HOW ABOUT YOU, MY DEAR? DON'T WORRY, DON'T WORRY. HE'S BEEN PROPERLY VETTED. HIS MOTHER IS AN ACCOMPLISHED NECROMANCER AND WHILE HIS FATHER–
YES.
OF COURSE.
BUT THERE YOU HAVE IT, STRAIGHT FROM HIS MOUTH.
LET'S BEGIN.
DO EITHER OF YOU WISH TO SUFFER AFTER THE AWAKENING?
NO.
THAT'S PART OF THIS LITTLE CEREMONY? WHAT AN ASININE QUESTION, WHO ANSWERS "YES" TO THAT?

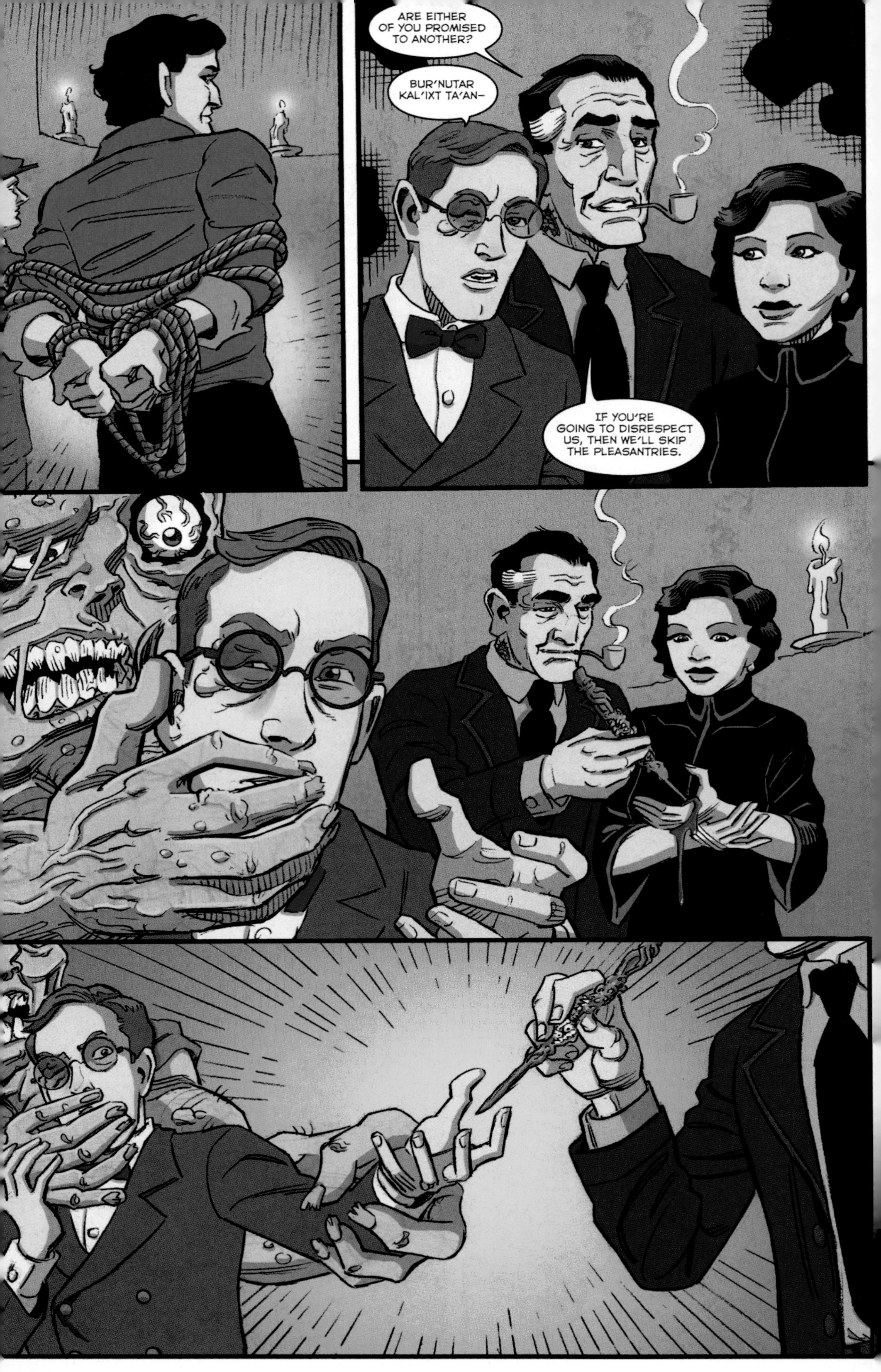

ARE EITHER OF YOU PROMISED TO ANOTHER?
BUR'NUTAR KAL'IXT TA'AN–
IF YOU'RE GOING TO DISRESPECT US, THEN WE'LL SKIP THE PLEASANTRIES.

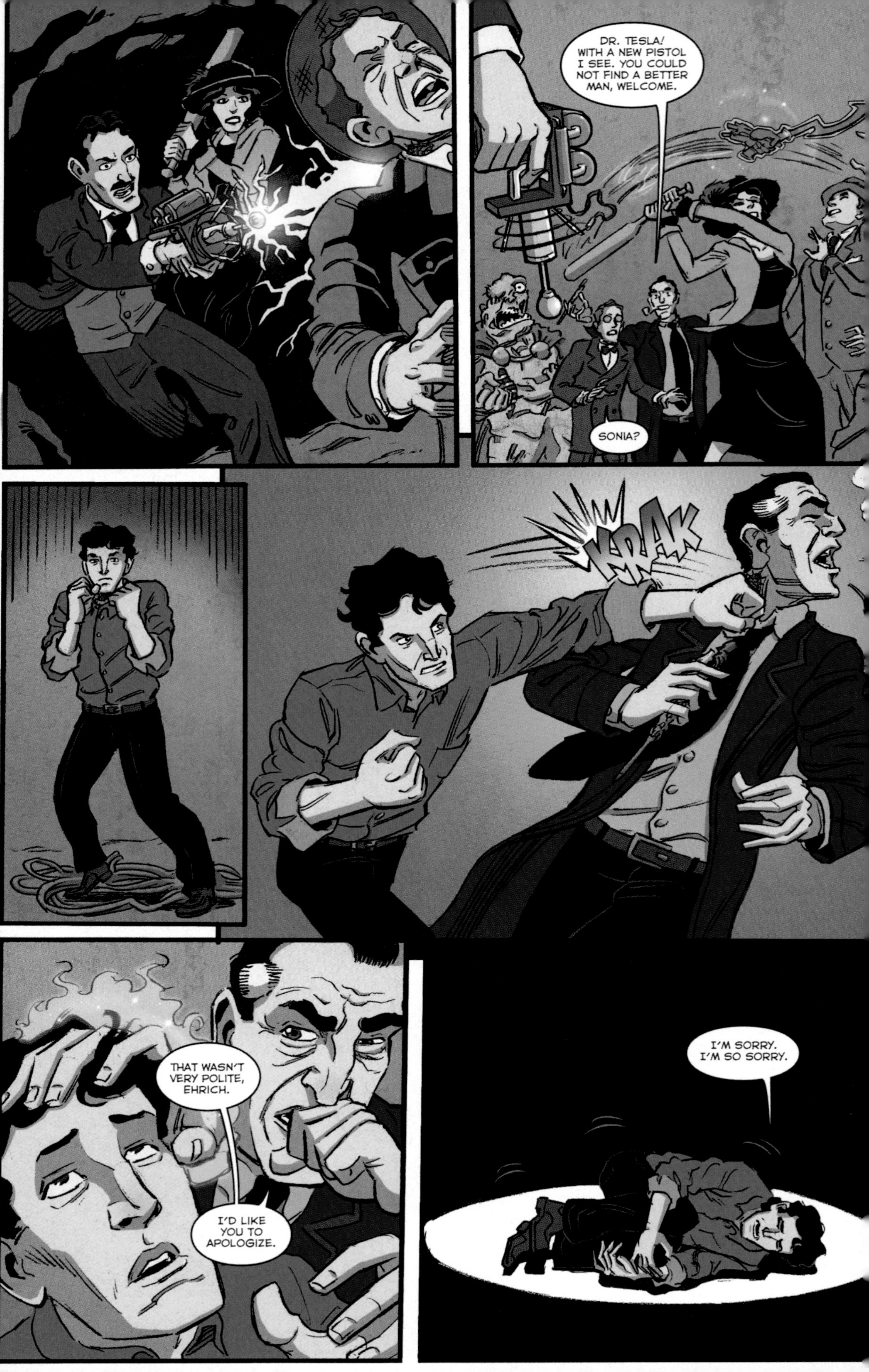
DR. TESLA! WITH A NEW PISTOL I SEE. YOU COULD NOT FIND A BETTER MAN, WELCOME.
SONIA?
KRAK
THAT WASN'T VERY POLITE, EHRICH.
I'D LIKE YOU TO APOLOGIZE.
I'M SORRY. I'M SO SORRY.

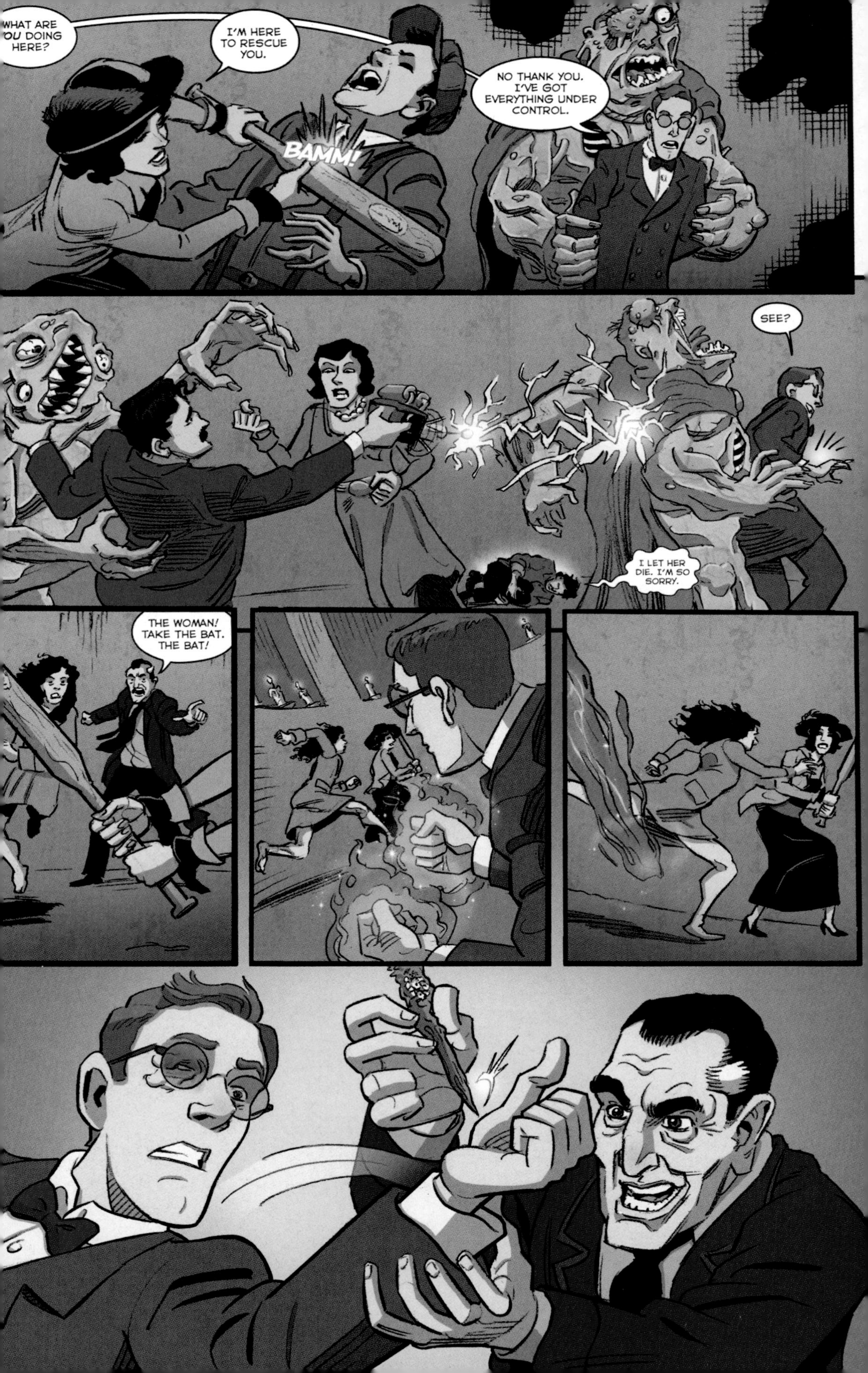
WHAT ARE YOU DOING HERE?
I'M HERE TO RESCUE YOU.
BAMM!
NO THANK YOU. I'VE GOT EVERYTHING UNDER CONTROL.
SEE?
I LET HER DIE. I'M SO SORRY.
THE WOMAN! TAKE THE BAT. THE BAT!

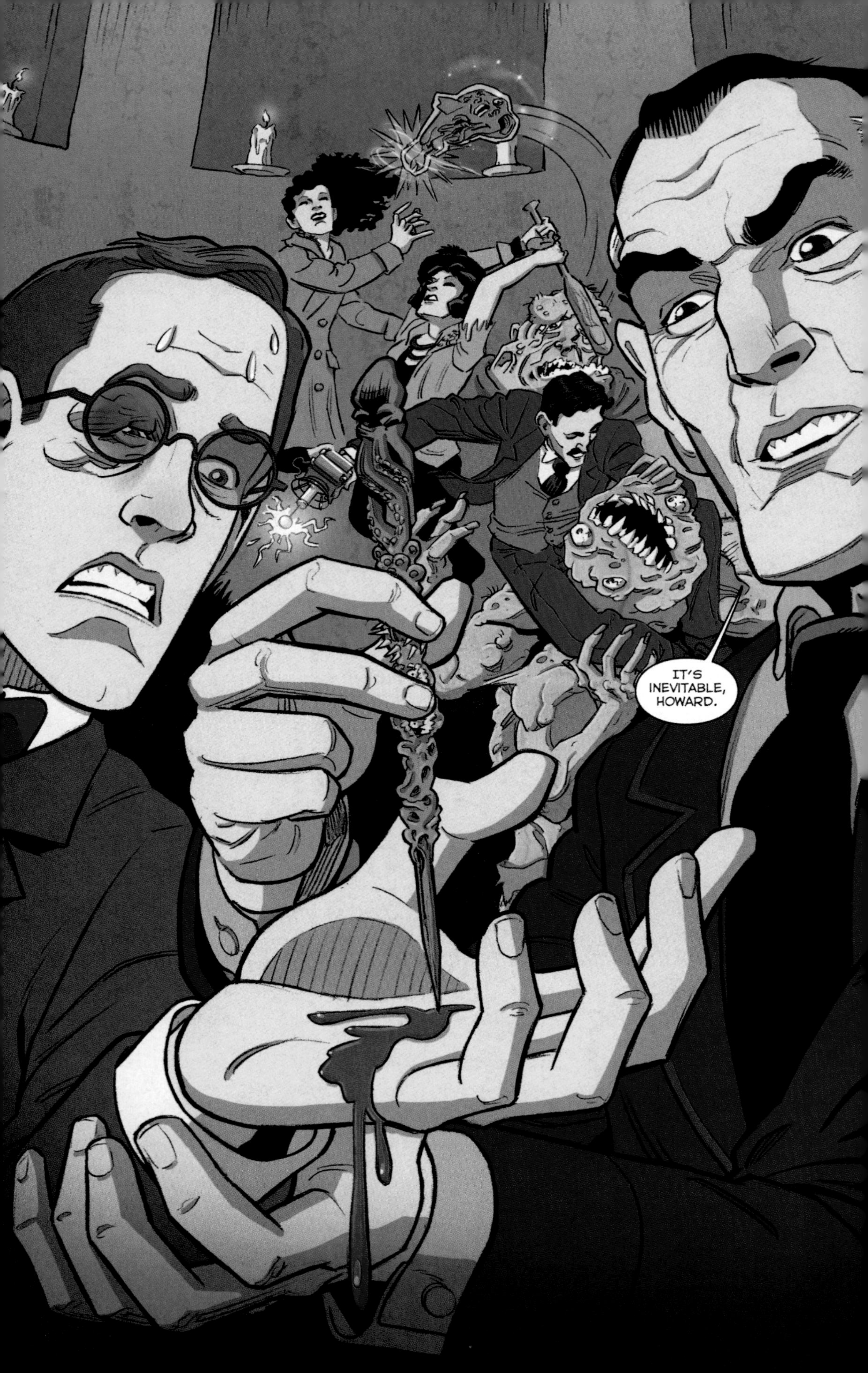
IT'S INEVITABLE, HOWARD.

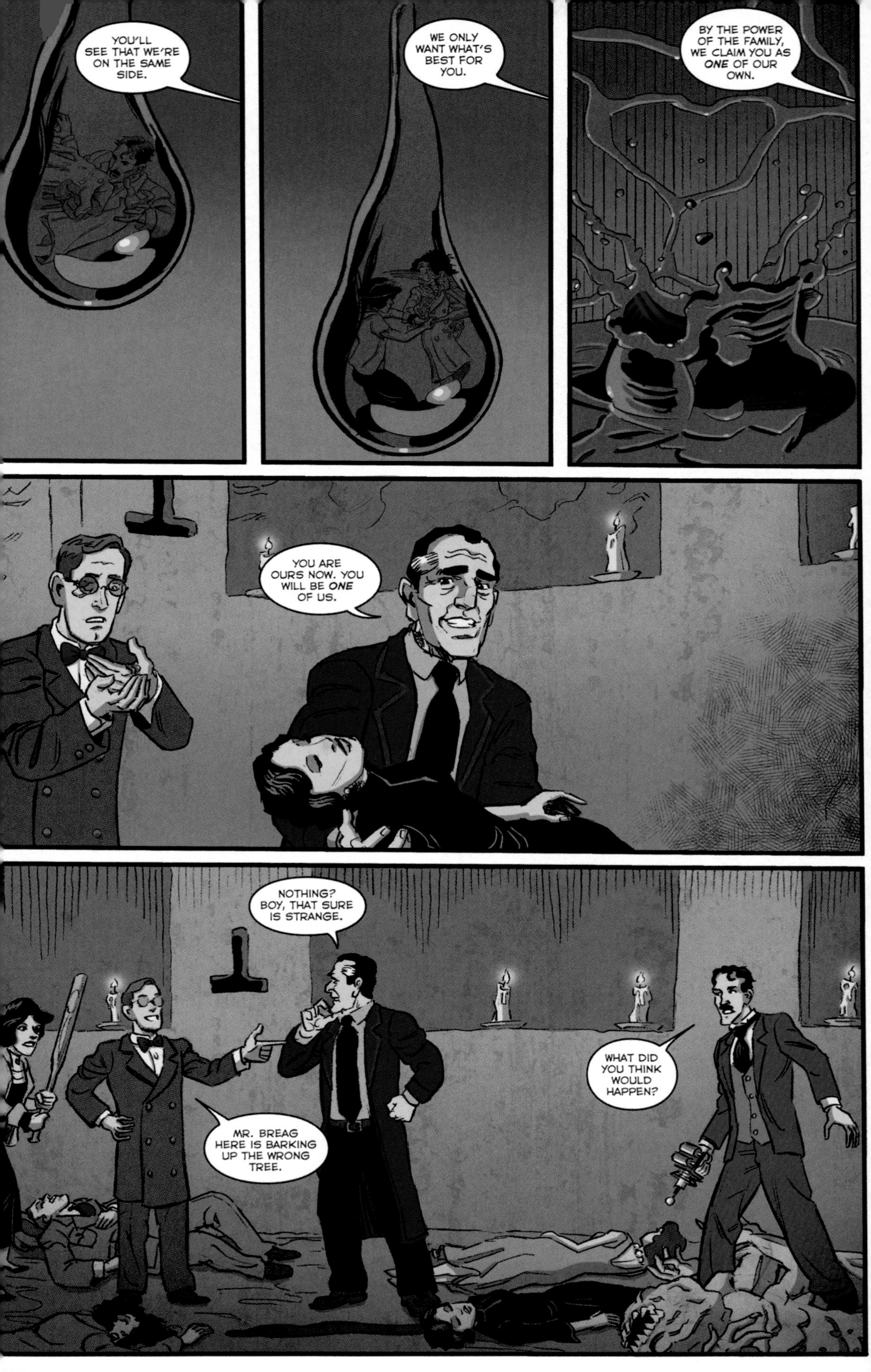
YOU'LL SEE THAT WE'RE ON THE SAME SIDE.
WE ONLY WANT WHAT'S BEST FOR YOU.
BY THE POWER OF THE FAMILY, WE CLAIM YOU AS *ONE* OF OUR OWN.
YOU ARE OURS NOW. YOU WILL BE *ONE* OF US.
NOTHING? BOY, THAT SURE IS STRANGE.
MR. BREAG HERE IS BARKING UP THE WRONG TREE.
WHAT DID YOU THINK WOULD HAPPEN?

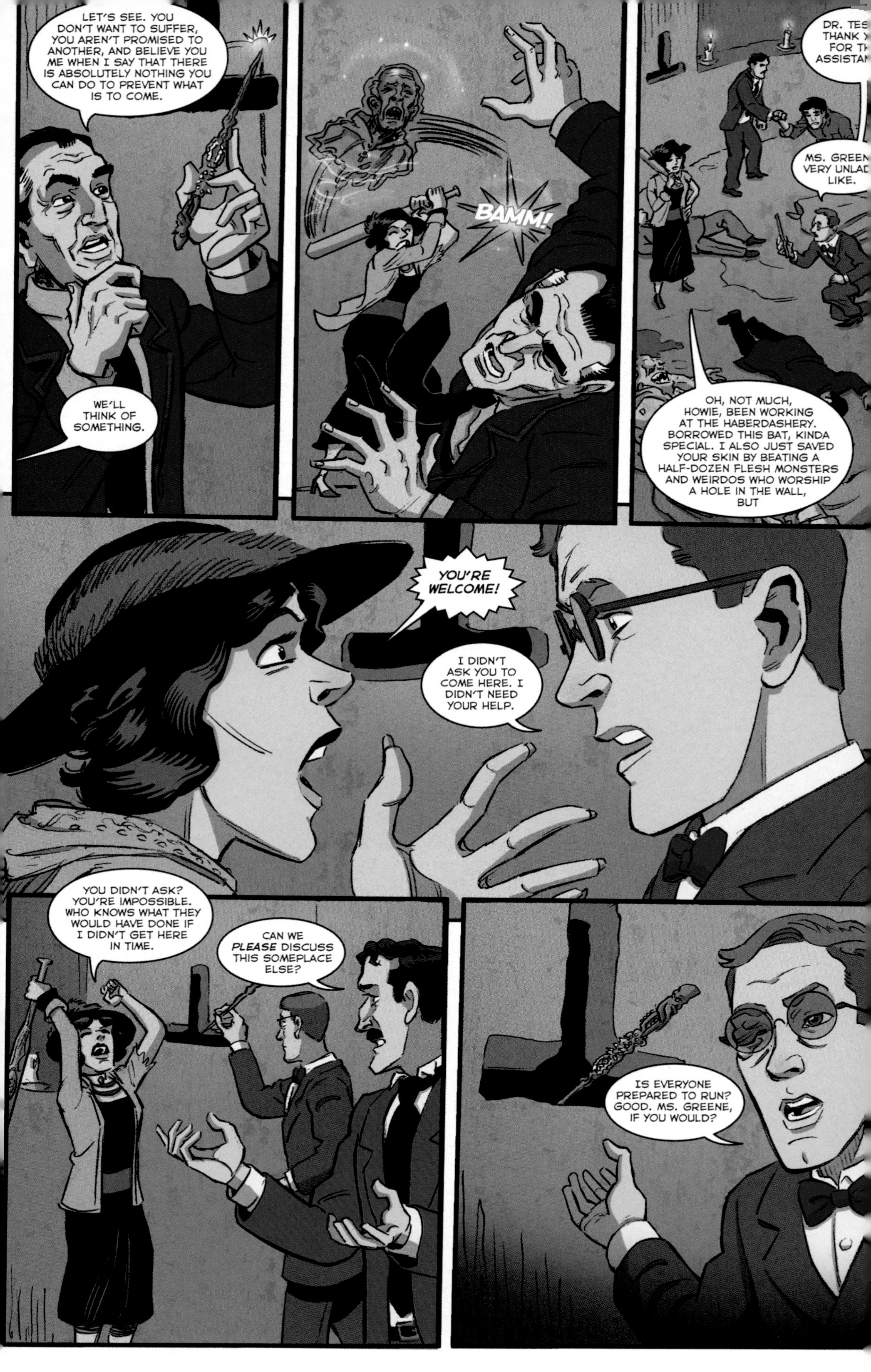
LET'S SEE. YOU DON'T WANT TO SUFFER, YOU AREN'T PROMISED TO ANOTHER, AND BELIEVE YOU ME WHEN I SAY THAT THERE IS ABSOLUTELY NOTHING YOU CAN DO TO PREVENT WHAT IS TO COME.
WE'LL THINK OF SOMETHING.
BAMM!
DR. TES
THANK Y
FOR TH
ASSISTAN
MS. GREEN
VERY UNLAD
LIKE.
OH, NOT MUCH, HOWIE, BEEN WORKING AT THE HABERDASHERY. BORROWED THIS BAT, KINDA SPECIAL. I ALSO JUST SAVED YOUR SKIN BY BEATING A HALF-DOZEN FLESH MONSTERS AND WEIRDOS WHO WORSHIP A HOLE IN THE WALL, BUT
YOU'RE WELCOME!
I DIDN'T ASK YOU TO COME HERE. I DIDN'T NEED YOUR HELP.
YOU DIDN'T ASK? YOU'RE IMPOSSIBLE. WHO KNOWS WHAT THEY WOULD HAVE DONE IF I DIDN'T GET HERE IN TIME.
CAN WE *PLEASE* DISCUSS THIS SOMEPLACE ELSE?
IS EVERYONE PREPARED TO RUN? GOOD. MS. GREENE, IF YOU WOULD?

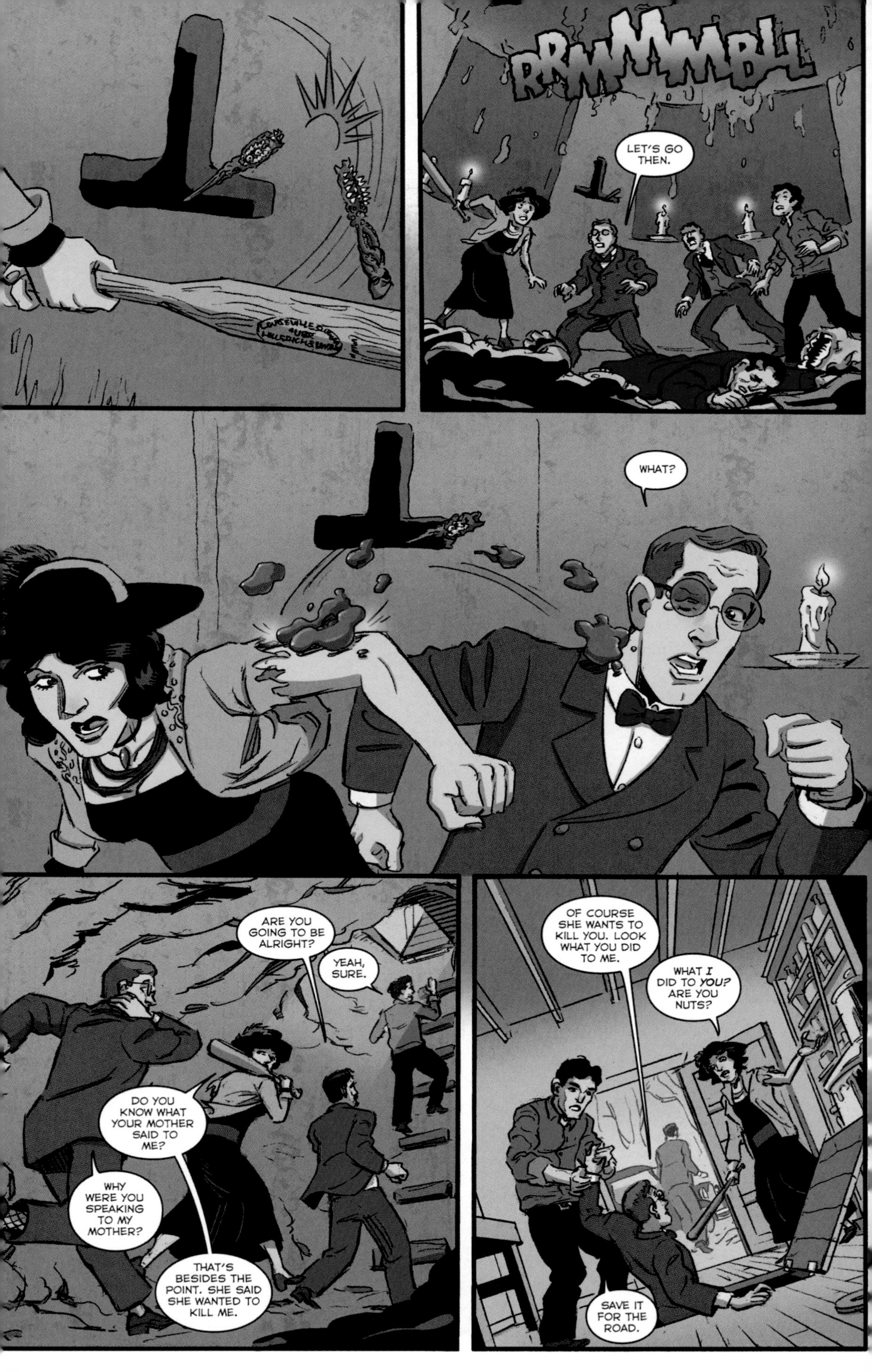
RRMMMBLL
LET'S GO THEN.
WHAT?
ARE YOU GOING TO BE ALRIGHT?
YEAH, SURE.
DO YOU KNOW WHAT YOUR MOTHER SAID TO ME?
WHY WERE YOU SPEAKING TO MY MOTHER?
THAT'S BESIDES THE POINT. SHE SAID SHE WANTED TO KILL ME.
OF COURSE SHE WANTS TO KILL YOU. LOOK WHAT YOU DID TO ME.
WHAT *I* DID TO *YOU?* ARE YOU NUTS?
SAVE IT FOR THE ROAD.

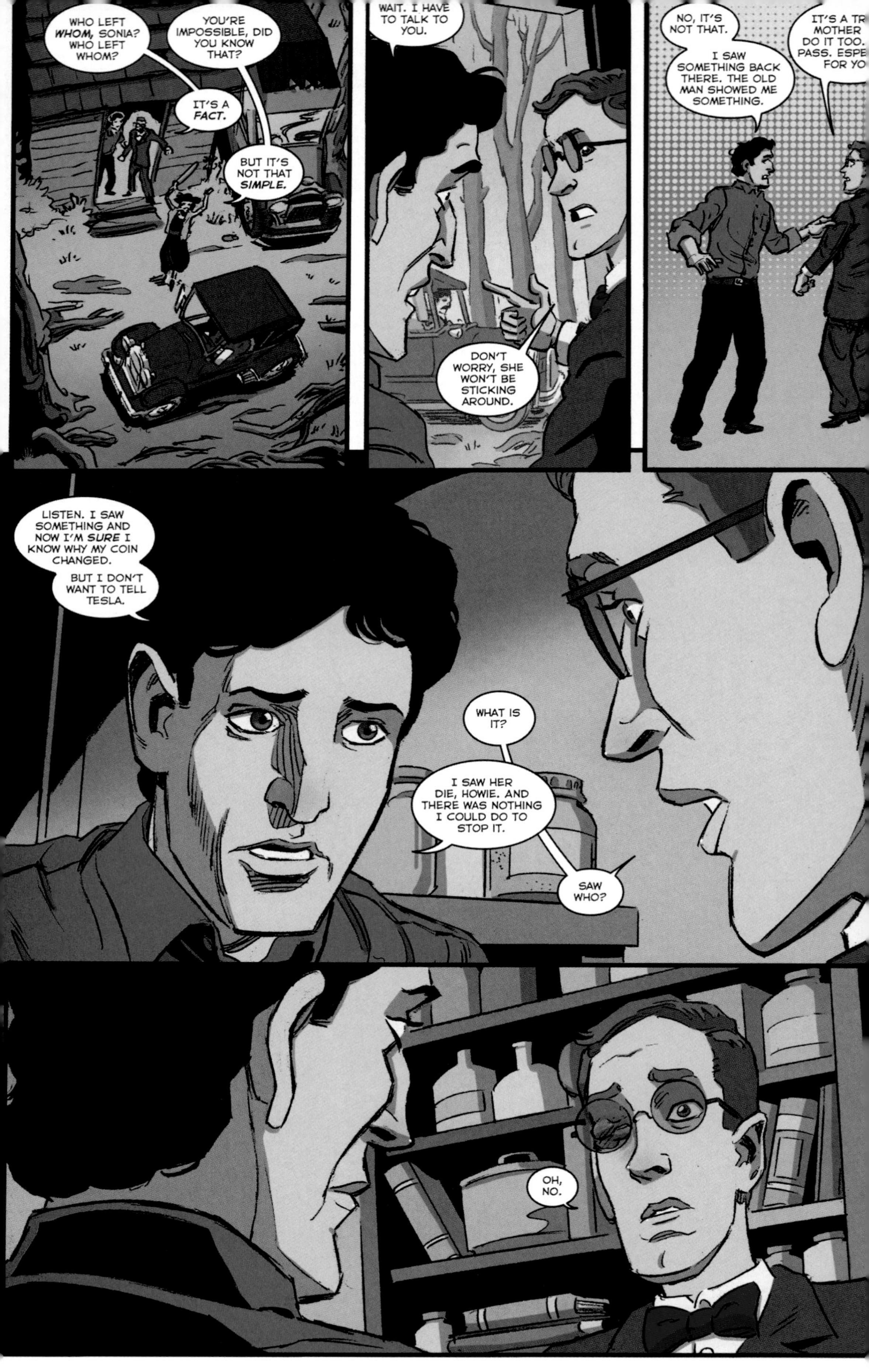
WHO LEFT *WHOM,* SONIA? WHO LEFT WHOM?
YOU'RE IMPOSSIBLE, DID YOU KNOW THAT?
IT'S A *FACT.*
BUT IT'S NOT THAT *SIMPLE.*
WAIT. I HAVE TO TALK TO YOU.
DON'T WORRY, SHE WON'T BE STICKING AROUND.
NO, IT'S NOT THAT.
I SAW SOMETHING BACK THERE. THE OLD MAN SHOWED ME SOMETHING.
LISTEN. I SAW SOMETHING AND NOW I'M *SURE* I KNOW WHY *MY* COIN CHANGED.
BUT I DON'T WANT TO TELL TESLA.
WHAT IS IT?
I SAW HER DIE, HOWIE. AND THERE WAS NOTHING I COULD DO TO STOP IT.
SAW WHO?
OH, NO.

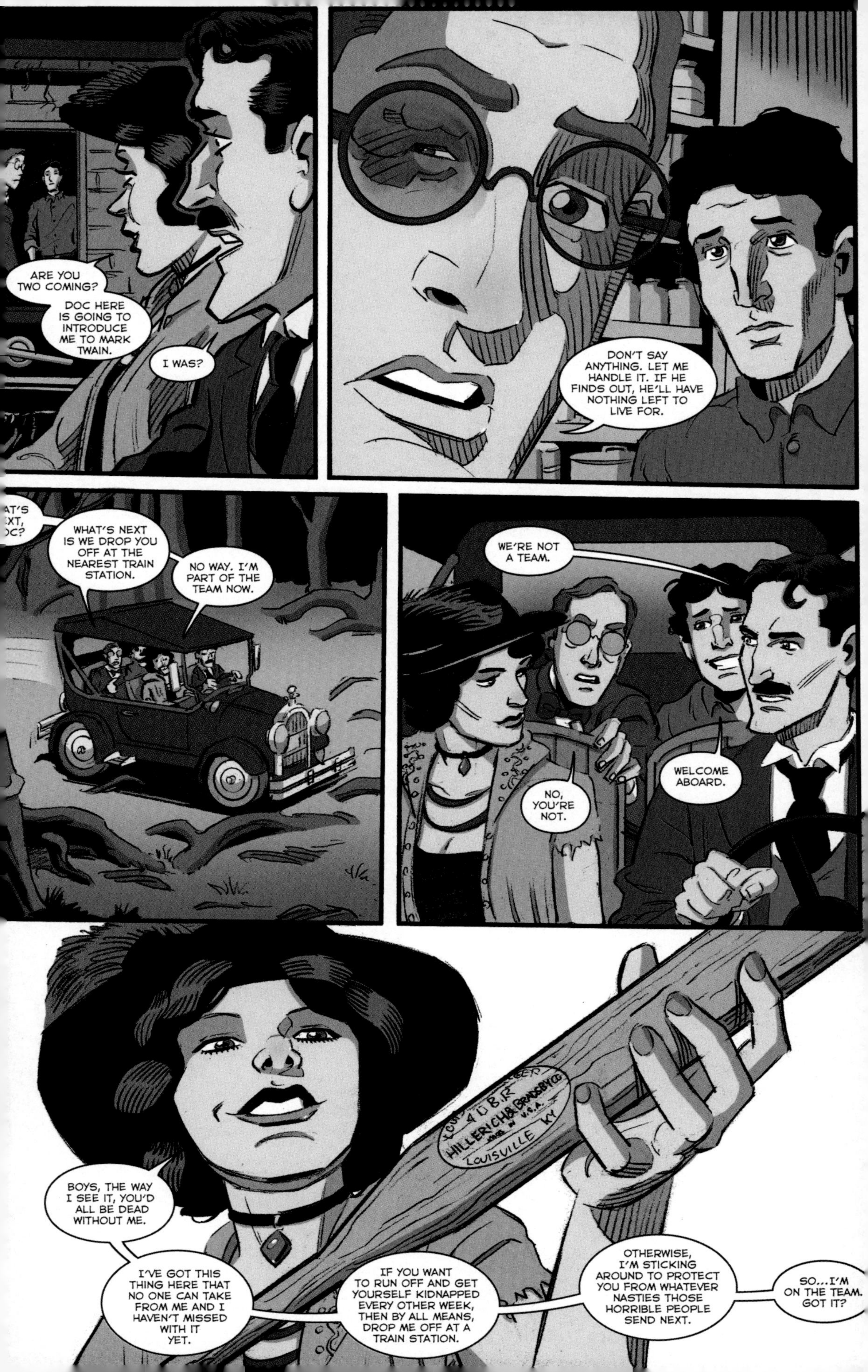
ARE YOU TWO COMING?
DOC HERE IS GOING TO INTRODUCE ME TO MARK TWAIN.
I WAS?
DON'T SAY ANYTHING. LET ME HANDLE IT. IF HE FINDS OUT, HE'LL HAVE NOTHING LEFT TO LIVE FOR.
WHAT'S NEXT IS WE DROP YOU OFF AT THE NEAREST TRAIN STATION.
NO WAY. I'M PART OF THE TEAM NOW.
WE'RE NOT A TEAM.
NO, YOU'RE NOT.
WELCOME ABOARD.
HILLERICH & BRADSBY CO
LOUISVILLE KY
BOYS, THE WAY I SEE IT, YOU'D ALL BE DEAD WITHOUT ME.
I'VE GOT THIS THING HERE THAT NO ONE CAN TAKE FROM ME AND I HAVEN'T MISSED WITH IT YET.
IF YOU WANT TO RUN OFF AND GET YOURSELF KIDNAPPED EVERY OTHER WEEK, THEN BY ALL MEANS, DROP ME OFF AT A TRAIN STATION.
OTHERWISE, I'M STICKING AROUND TO PROTECT YOU FROM WHATEVER NASTIES THOSE HORRIBLE PEOPLE SEND NEXT.
SO...I'M ON THE TEAM. GOT IT?

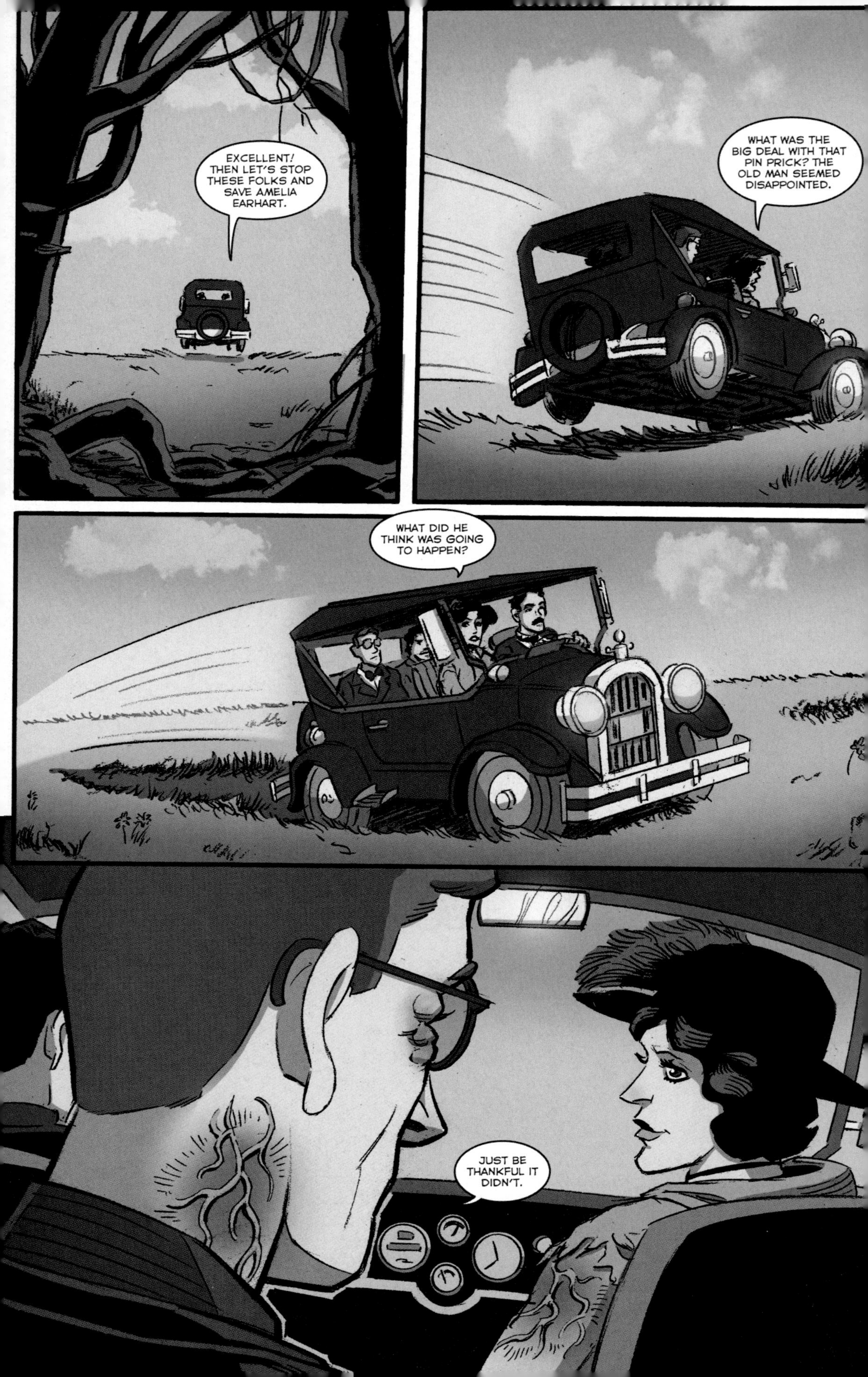
EXCELLENT! THEN LET'S STOP THESE FOLKS AND SAVE AMELIA EARHART.
WHAT WAS THE BIG DEAL WITH THAT PIN PRICK? THE OLD MAN SEEMED DISAPPOINTED.
WHAT DID HE THINK WAS GOING TO HAPPEN?
JUST BE THANKFUL IT DIDN'T.

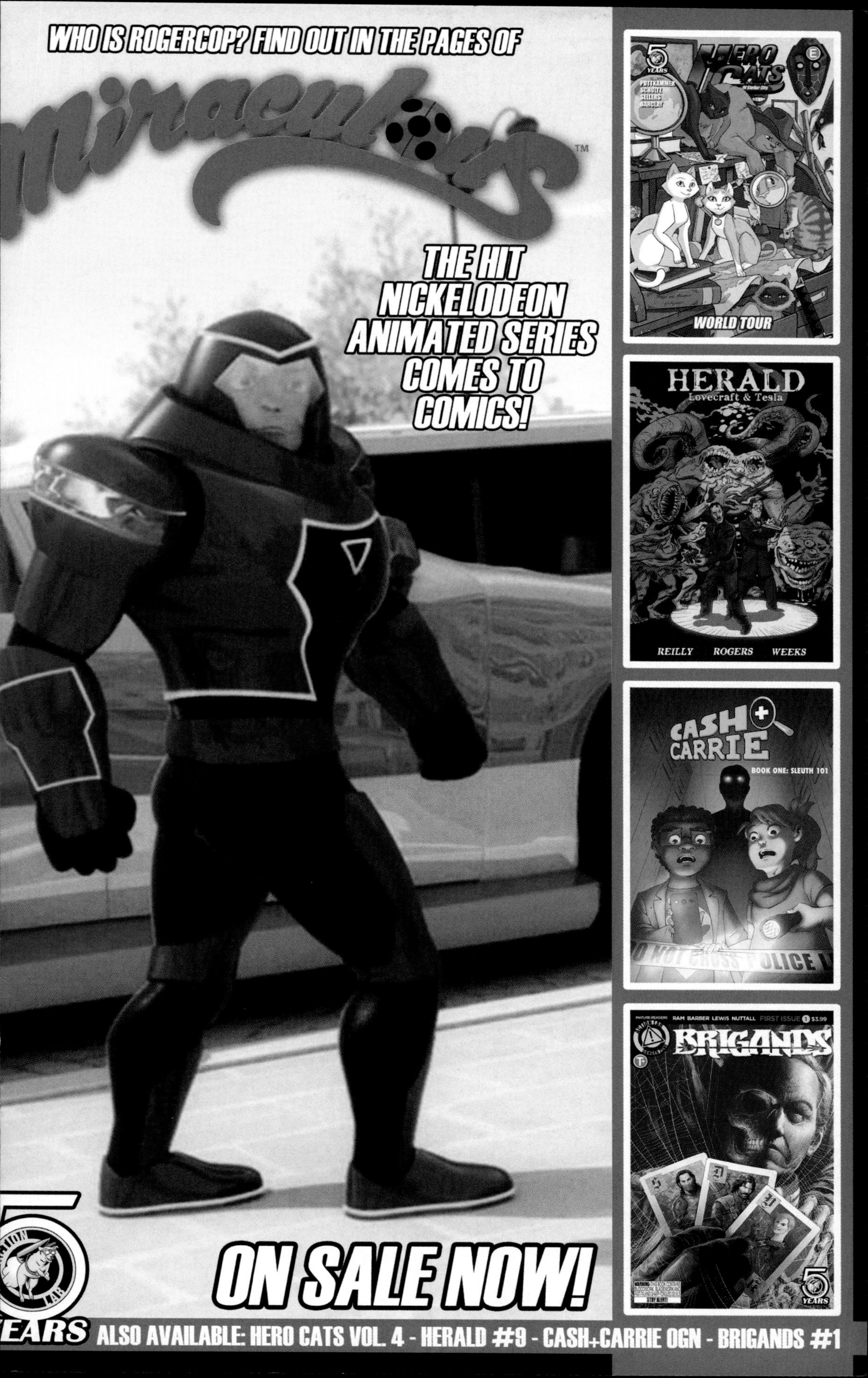

WHO IS ROGERCOP? FIND OUT IN THE PAGES OF
Miraculous™
THE HIT NICKELODEON ANIMATED SERIES COMES TO COMICS!
ON SALE NOW!
5 YEARS
HERO CATS
PUTTKAMMER
SCHULTZ
SELLERS
BARCLAY
WORLD TOUR
HERALD
Lovecraft & Tesla
REILLY ROGERS WEEKS
CASH + CARRIE
BOOK ONE: SLEUTH 101
RAM BARBER LEWIS NUTTALL FIRST ISSUE 1 $3.99
BRIGANDS
STAY ALERT!
5 YEARS
ALSO AVAILABLE: HERO CATS VOL. 4 - HERALD #9 - CASH+CARRIE OGN - BRIGANDS #1

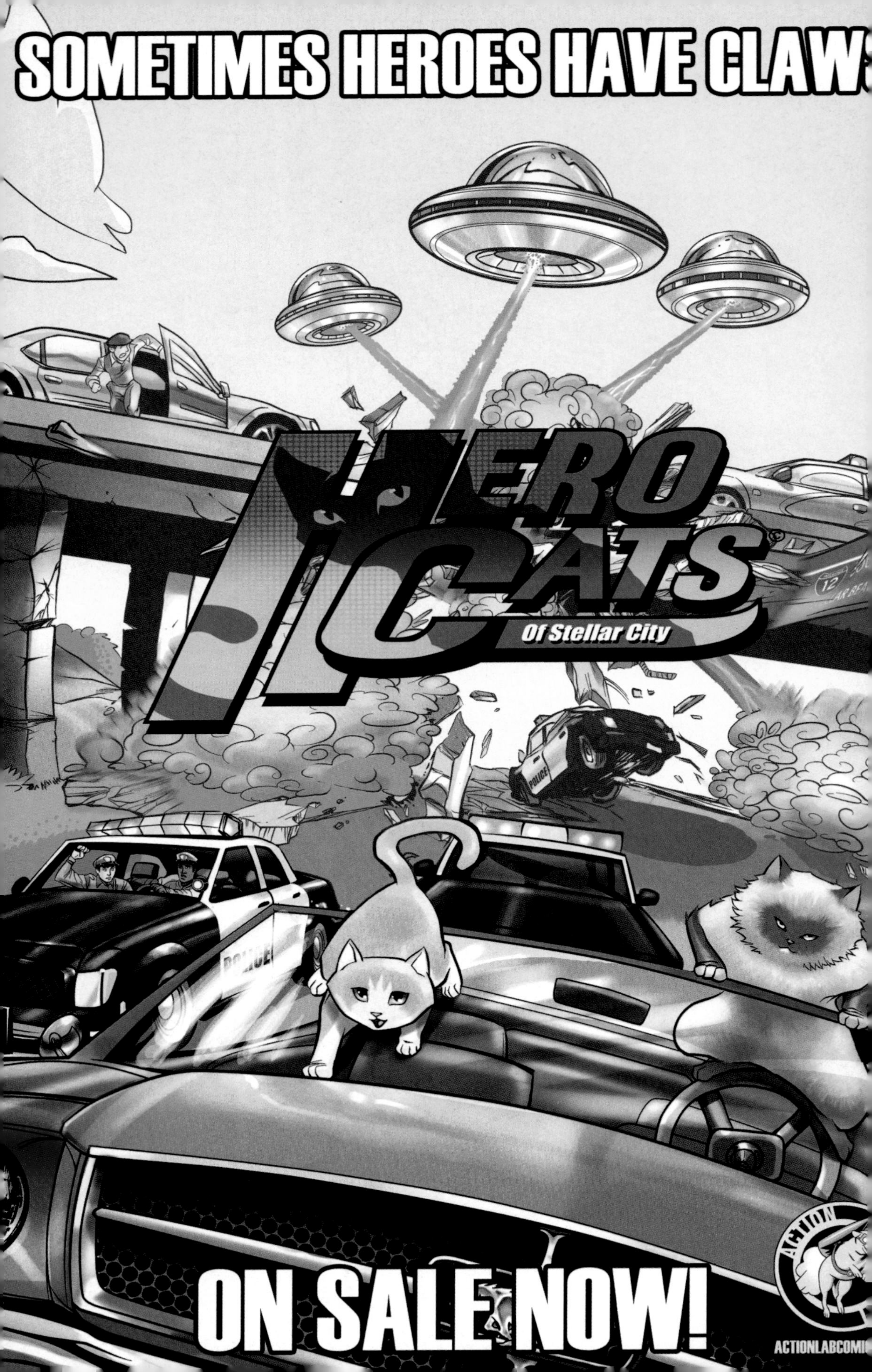
SOMETIMES HEROES HAVE CLAWS
HERO CATS ©
Of Stellar City
POLICE
POLICE
ON SALE NOW!
ACTION
ACTIONLABCOMIC

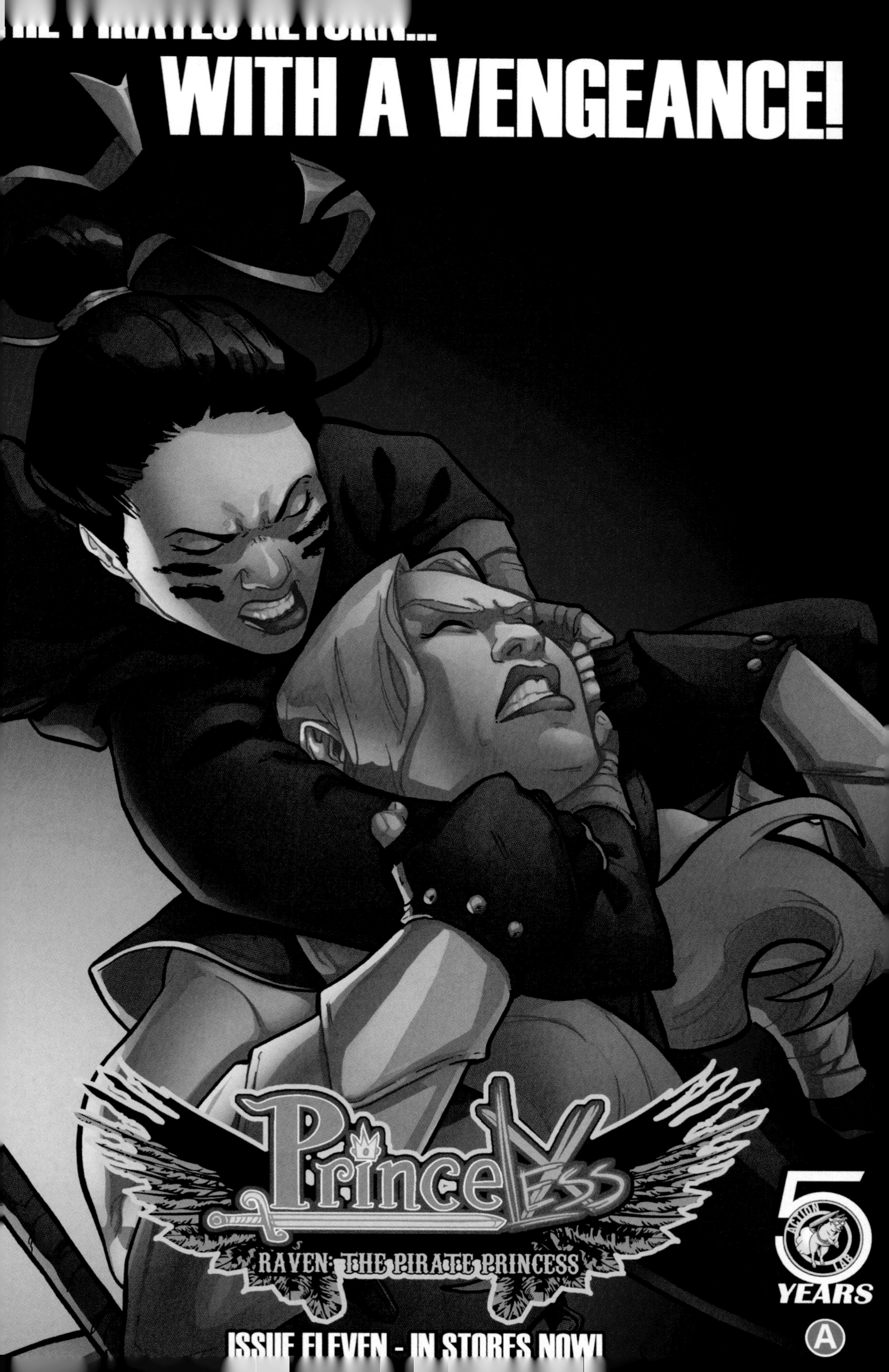
WITH A VENGEANCE!
Princeless
RAVEN: THE PIRATE PRINCESS
5 YEARS
ISSUE ELEVEN - IN STORES NOW!

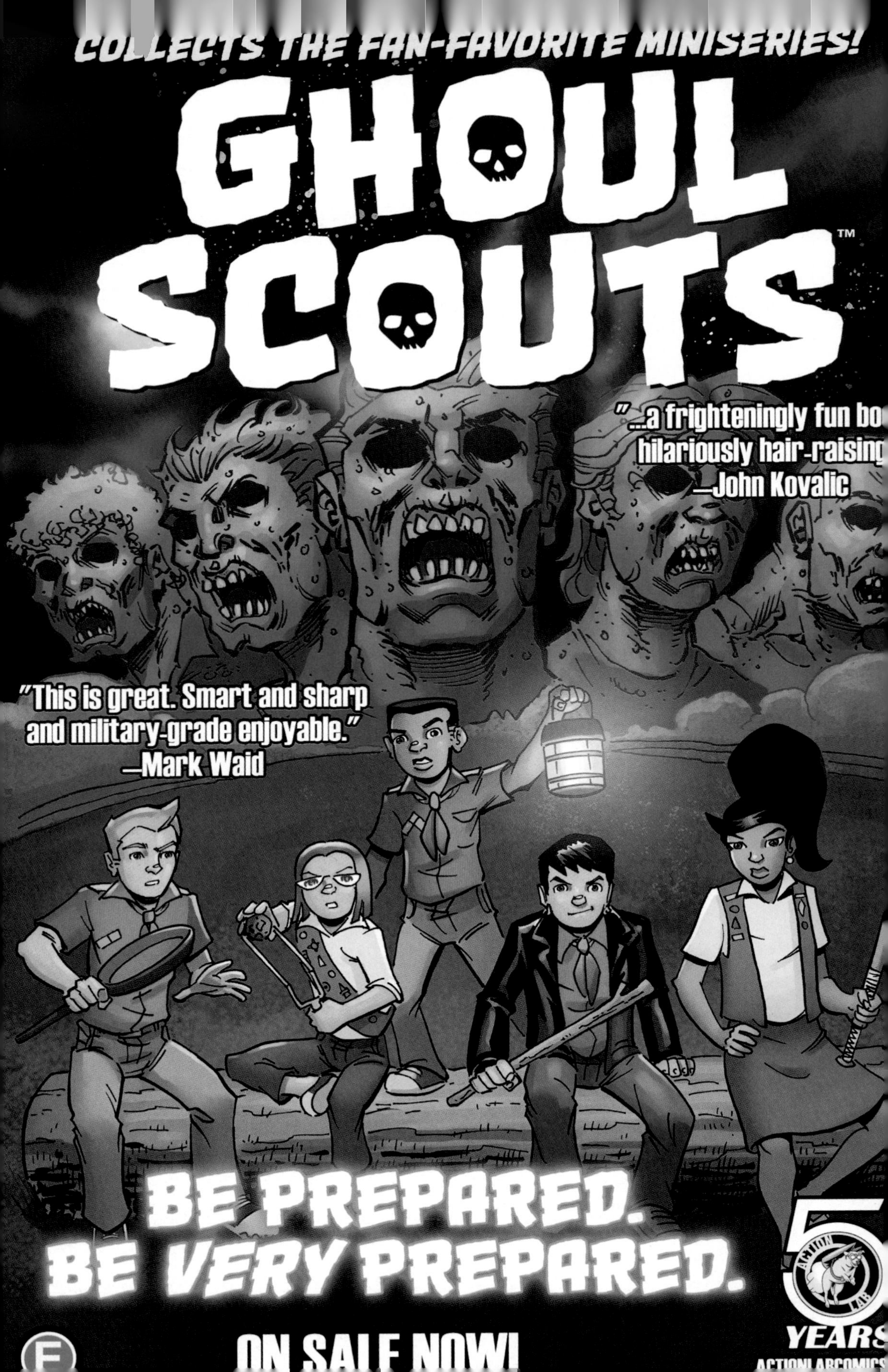
COLLECTS THE FAN-FAVORITE MINISERIES!
GHOUL SCOUTS™
"...a frighteningly fun bo
hilariously hair-raising
—John Kovalic
"This is great. Smart and sharp and military-grade enjoyable."
—Mark Waid
BE PREPARED.
BE VERY PREPARED.
ON SALE NOW!
5 YEARS
ACTION LAB

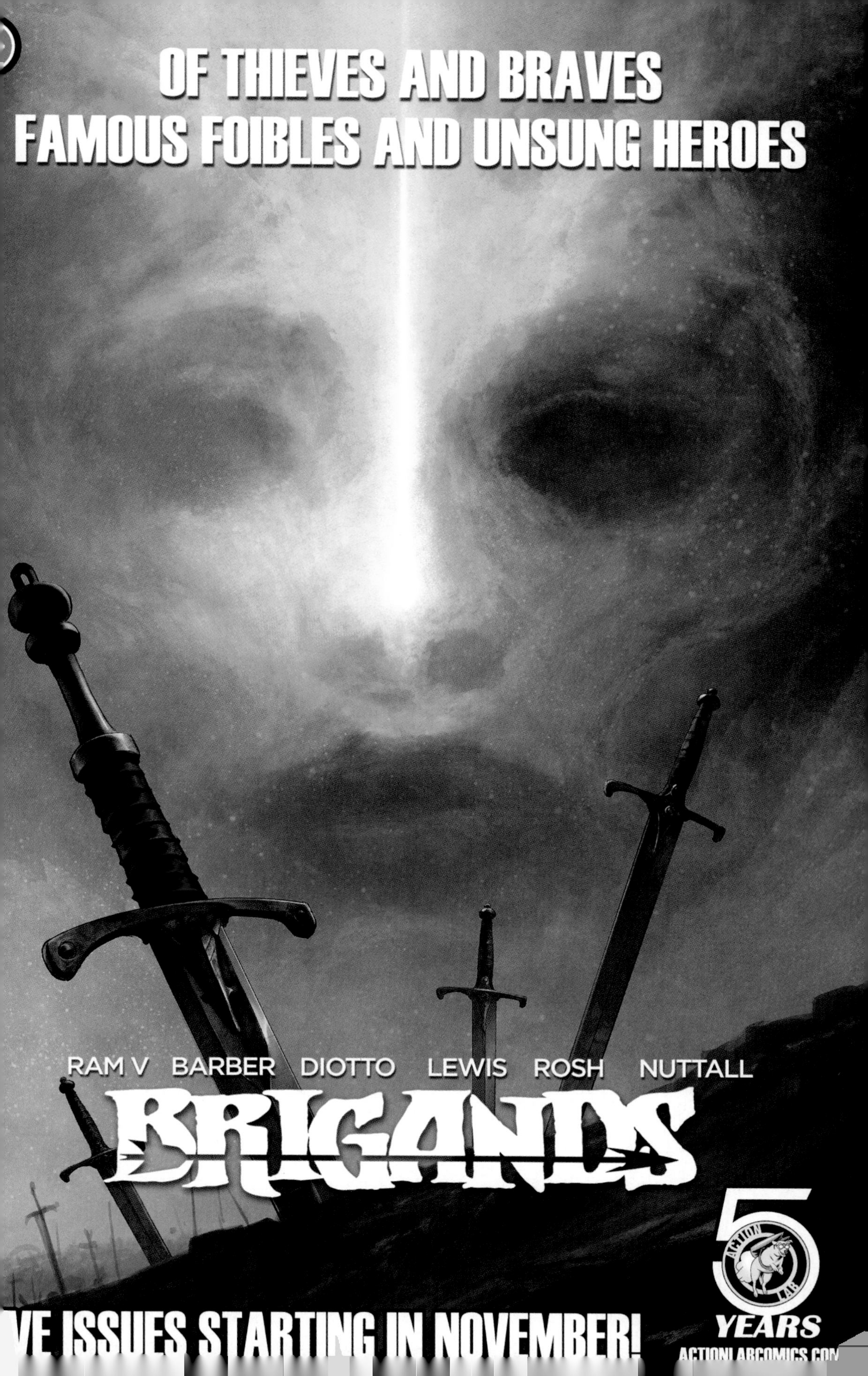

OF THIEVES AND BRAVES
FAMOUS FOIBLES AND UNSUNG HEROES
RAM V BARBER DIOTTO LEWIS ROSH NUTTALL
BRIGANDS
VE ISSUES STARTING IN NOVEMBER!
5 YEARS
ACTION LAB

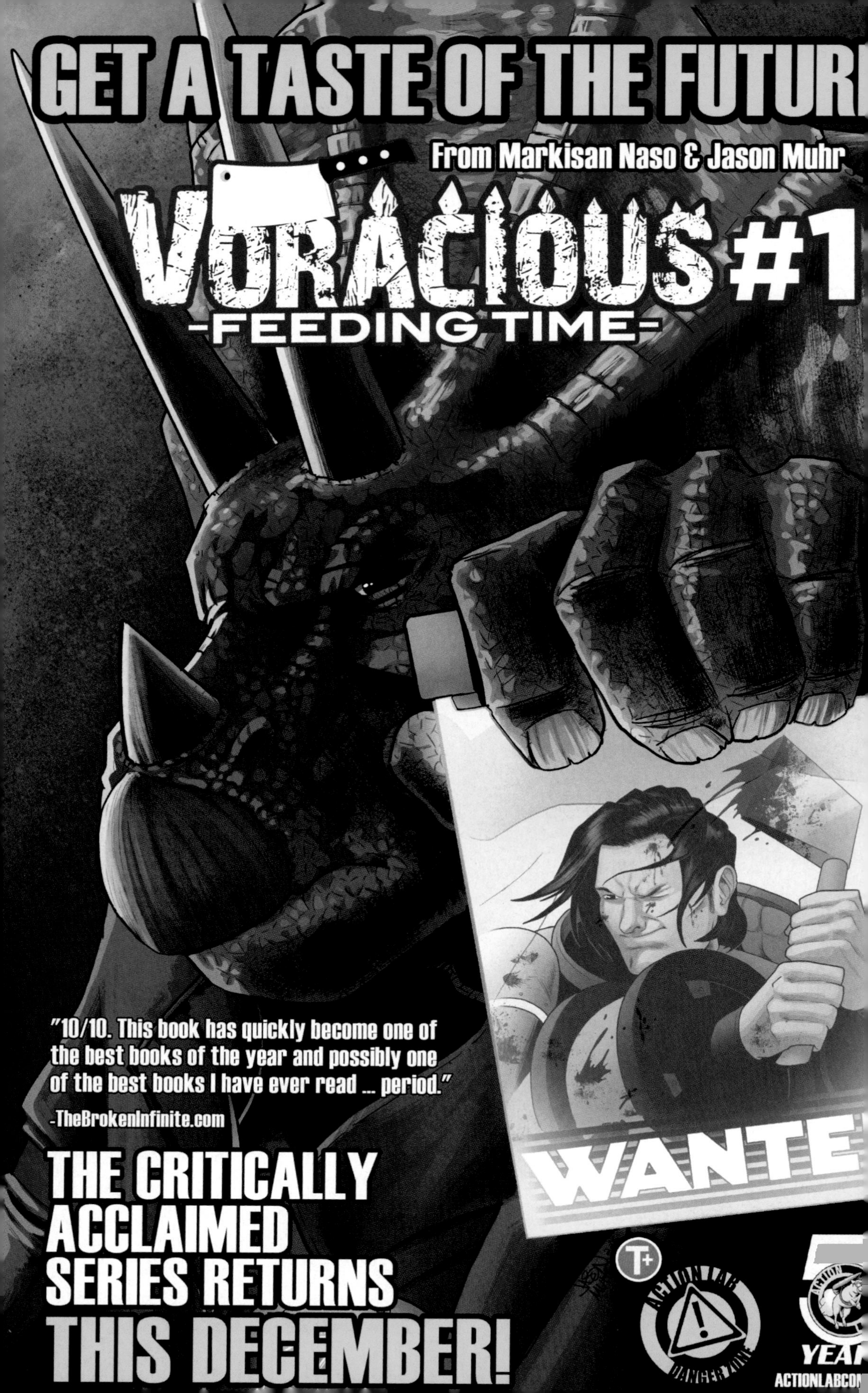
GET A TASTE OF THE FUTURE
From Markisan Naso & Jason Muhr
VORACIOUS #1
-FEEDING TIME-
"10/10. This book has quickly become one of the best books of the year and possibly one of the best books I have ever read ... period."
-TheBrokenInfinite.com
THE CRITICALLY ACCLAIMED SERIES RETURNS THIS DECEMBER!
WANTE
T+
ACTION LAB DANGER ZONE
YEAR
ACTIONLABCOM

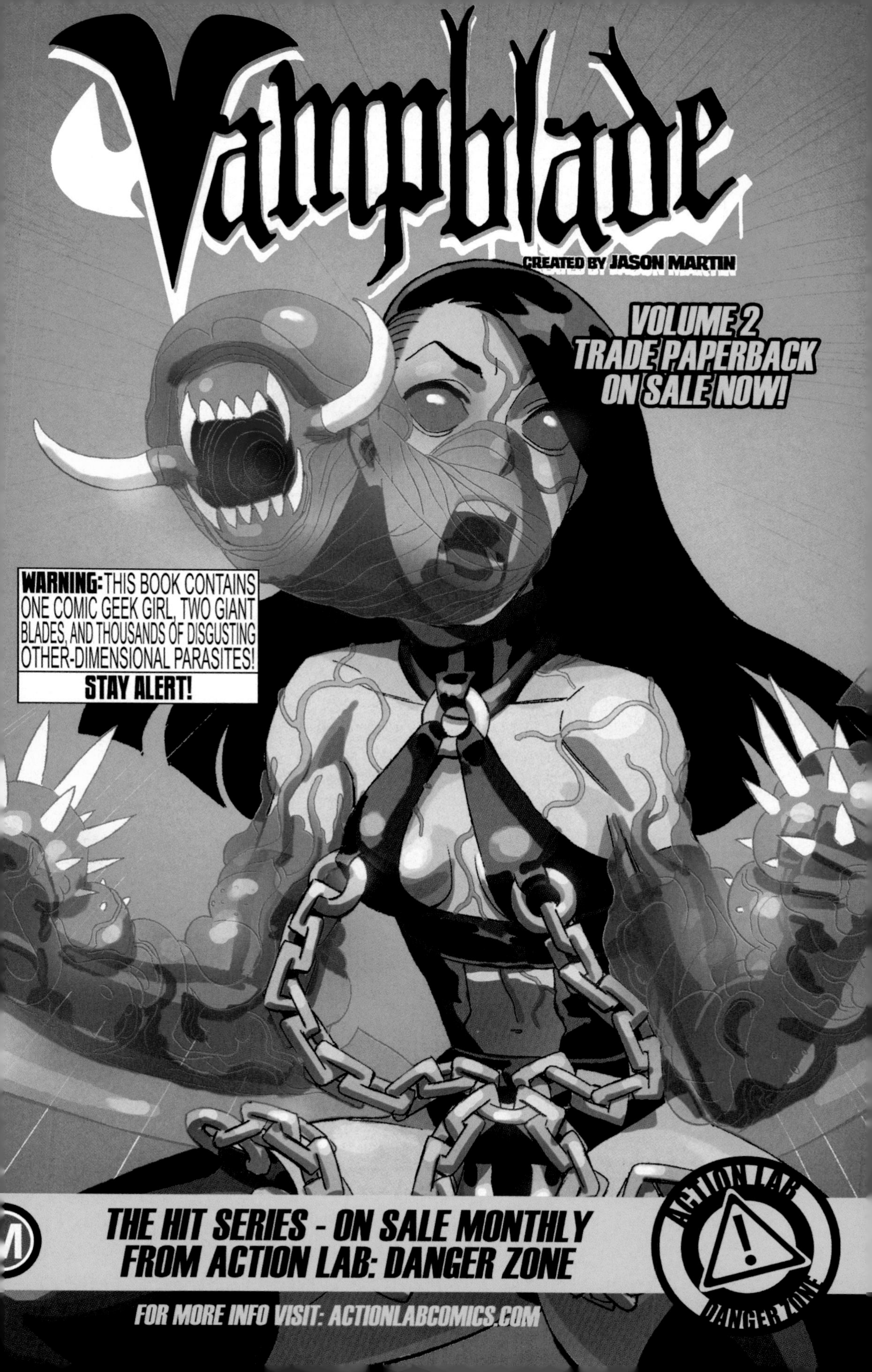
Vampblade
CREATED BY JASON MARTIN
VOLUME 2 TRADE PAPERBACK ON SALE NOW!
WARNING: THIS BOOK CONTAINS ONE COMIC GEEK GIRL, TWO GIANT BLADES, AND THOUSANDS OF DISGUSTING OTHER-DIMENSIONAL PARASITES!
STAY ALERT!
THE HIT SERIES - ON SALE MONTHLY FROM ACTION LAB: DANGER ZONE
FOR MORE INFO VISIT: ACTIONLABCOMICS.COM
ACTION LAB DANGER ZONE

READ MORE NOW

Herald - Action Lab
www.actionlabcomics.com
00911
7 00465 77250 3

ACTIONLABCOMICS.COM

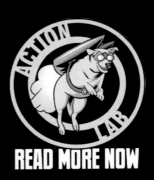